International Social Work

Stefan Borrmann
Michael Klassen
Christian Spatscheck (eds.)

UNIVERSITY OF WALES, NEWPORT
LIBRARY
AND
INFORMATION
SERVICES
CAERLEON

International Social Work

Social Problems, Cultural Issues and Social Work Education

Barbara Budrich Publishers
Opladen & Farmington Hills 2007

A CIP catalogue record for this book is available from
Die Deutsche Bibliothek (The German Library)

© 2007 by Barbara Budrich Publishers, Opladen
www.barbara-budrich.net

ISBN 978-3-86649-087-1

Die Deutsche Bibliothek – CIP-Einheitsaufnahme
Ein Titeldatensatz für die Publikation ist bei Der Deutschen Bibliothek erhältlich.

Verlag Barbara Budrich 🅑 Barbara Budrich Publishers
Stauffenbergstr. 7. D-51379 Leverkusen Opladen, Germany

28347 Ridgebrook, Farmington Hills, MI 48334, USA
www.barbara-budrich.net

Jacket illustration by disegno, Wuppertal, Germany – www.disenjo.de
Printed in Europe on acid-free paper by
paper & tinta, Warsaw

Contents

International Perspectives in Social Work Education 133

Acknowledgement

The idea of the book has been developed in the process of discussions within the *Society for International Cooperation in Social Work* (www.sicsw.org).

We would like to thank the *Hans-Boeckler-Foundation,* Germany, and the *Management Center Innsbruck*, Austria, for their financial support.

Furthermore we would like to thank Kevin Brown – a freelance consultant, trainer and author in social work and education, working in the UK and Austria – for his support.

Stefan Borrmann/Michael Klassen/Christian Spatscheck

Social Work in the International Context

1. Introduction[1]

In July 2001 the International Association of Schools of Social Work (IASSW) and the International Federation of Social Work (IFSW) adopted the following definition of social work.

"The social work profession promotes social change, problem solving in human relationships and the empowerment and liberation of people to enhance well-being. Utilising theories of human behaviour and social systems, social work intervenes at the points where people interact with their environments. Principles of human rights and social justice are fundamental to social work." (IFSW 2001)

While this definition encompasses broad ideological principles that most social work practitioners do not contest, direct social work practice varies from society to society depending on cultural variables such as politics, the economy, culture and religion. Social work practice in countries where a social security system is in place will vary significantly from countries with limited government-funded social security. Also, social work's control and socio-political maintenance functions are more dominant in some contexts than others. Moreover, the notion of what is social work will vary from society to society. For example, the Australian social work context will be different from that in other countries; and particular differences will be apparent in less developed nations' notions of social work practice. These differences do not imply that one is necessarily better than another. Rather, it emphasizes that social work needs to fit into the local context for it to be relevant.

Since social work's essential purpose is to service the needs and requirements of the society in which it is based, it has traditionally been seen as a local, culture-bound activity (Payne, 1991). However, the impact of globalization on all aspects of daily life has challenged most social workers to move beyond local considerations and operate outside and across political, cultural and geographic boundaries (Lyons, 1999). Tensions, ambiguities and contradictions in the international practice of social work present both challenges and a rich abundance to the local-global dialectic, such that social workers must engage with specific, constantly changing historical and political contexts while striving for a degree of universality, scientific accountabil-

---

1   In writing this chapter we would like to take the opportunity to acknowledge Stephanie Johnson, Charles Darwin University, Darwin, Australia for her input to this chapter.

ity, and professional autonomy (Lorenz, 1994). This ambiguity is simultaneously an opportunity and a challenge for social work.

2. Social Problems

The phenomenon of globalization is making the world smaller and easier to access, but is it helpful to the poor? It can be argued that the poor benefit little from globalization and that instead the real winners are big business and the developed nations. Can social work make a difference in a fast-paced global society where "the dollar" is the king, and where economic rationalism and the capitalist market is the religion of the day? And if so, how? It seems that globalization has done little to address poverty, fair trade and equality in our developing nations. As a collective, we as social workers struggle to define what we do and how we do it. Social work's challenge is to hold fast to its legitimate ideological base in social change, empowerment and social justice in an increasingly hostile world of supply and demand.

International cooperation can provide an effective mechanism to prepare social workers to work for the betterment of minorities and marginalized people within the rapidly changing global context. International exposure and experience is an essential response to the social realities of globalization.

The globalized world is not only making it easier to establish international social work cooperation – especially in the field of education – but it also confronts us with the phenomenon of migration, and increasing social problems that are related to that. Thus, even those social workers who do not consider their work as related to the international scene are confronted at home with the outcomes of globalization in negative terms.

The migration of people has challenged the profession to respond to diverse populations and develop relevant responses. It has changed the make-up of social service agency caseloads and affected domestic practice in many countries (Healy, 2001).

Another aspect of international relevance is affecting social work worldwide: ethnic and religious conflicts and natural disasters have produced a worldwide diaspora, so that social workers in many countries are now working with refugees. Migration, either voluntary or involuntary, can lead to problems of adaptation and increased conflict in the community because of accompanying tensions related to economic, political and social integration (Midgley, 1997). Migrants are more likely to be affected by low-paid employment, poor housing, limited education services and restricted health services. Poverty is often the defining life circumstance of the displaced and fundamentally underpins the range of individual and societal problems encountered by the social work profession.

3. Cultural Issues

Even if we agree that social problems are universal, and reflect societies' inabilities to fulfil basic human needs, there are significant cultural differences in the way those social problems are experienced, how societies react to social problems within their cultural context, and what methods of intervention are used by local social workers. The universal is inextricably mediated through culture, thus becoming relativised. The issue of how the dominant culture imposes itself on minority or sub-cultures is addressed in several contributions within this book. From this perspective, international cooperation in the field of the social work education is about mutual understanding and shared learning, rather than about teaching how social problems have to be solved in a specific and universal way, regardless of society and culture.

Working effectively with migrants who are displaced presents clear challenges to the social work profession. It requires not only an understanding of particular cultural and geographic roots but also sensitive and differentiated responses that take into account the range of motivations for migration, the points of origin and destinations of migrants, and their experiences of the migratory process.

4. Social Work Education

As the profession strives to globalize its activities and extend its research agenda to the wider world context, there is a growing interest in international social work education, scholarship and practice (Sammon, Whittaker, Barlow, 2003; Ramanathan, Link, 1999). The general objective of international social work education is to assist students in learning, applying and integrating social work values, knowledge and skills through the provision of international learning experiences offered through international field placements, international exchange programs and international lectures (Rogers, et. al., 1999).

Although movement of people has been a feature of societies since the early hunters and gatherers, it has recently gained prominence on the international agenda because of its increasing scope and resultant impact on world politics (Lyons, 1999). Yet while a commonly referenced hallmark of globalization is the growth of the world economy, international cooperation and exchange has also emerged as a key social component.

While international exchange can be seen as a truly positive phenomenon, within the social work profession it can also be driven by differences between developed countries, countries of the so-called Third World, and those in transition. For example, economic disparity, a dominant force behind the patterns of migration, has also resulted in the movement of social work professionals and academics from less industrialized countries to learn from the West. Thus, it has led to a strong influence of Western social work discipline and practice in countries of the Global South. While social workers in the Global South are very eager to learn from Western countries, their counterparts in the industrialized part of the world may be very eager to teach, but not always so keen to learn (see the chapter in this book by Yasmin Dean).

Many social work schools worldwide offer students the opportunity to complete their field placements in an international setting or to study internationally. Although the research on international social work field placements and education is underdeveloped, what does exist suggests that international study experiences are a powerful learning tool, one that offers students opportunities to confront different views on human behavior, to learn about different systems of social welfare, and to see different ways to tackle social problems (Asahoah, Healy, Mayadas, 1997; Dominelli, 2003; Healy, 2001).

A global survey of members of the International Association of Schools of Social Work (IASSW) carried out in the late 1980s reported that 44% of responding schools had students who completed field placements in other countries, with Europe accounting for nearly half this number. Yet, a closer examination of the data revealed that the placements and study periods abroad were episodic rather than part of a planned curriculum, and that relatively few students were involved (Healy, 1999).

Researchers noted that the historical challenges of international social work field placements and education exchanges have been related to funding shortages, the lack of development of adequate infrastructures, and the inconsistent levels of recognition of the knowledge, skills and values that students develop while they are abroad (Dominelli, 2003; Hokenstad, Khinduka, Midgley, 1992).

* As social work education and field placements move into the global forum, future professional research must crucially address issues such as evaluation equivalencies, the establishment of reliable international partners, the process of student selection, and provision of student support (Coleman, 1996; Clarkson, 1990; Dubois, Ntetu, 2000; Tesoriero, Rajaratnam, 2001).

Summarizing the above, it is important to understand that social work as a discipline and as a profession is about describing, explaining and responding to social problems in society. But are social problems universal? And even if we accept that they are, what cultural differences are there in the way they are experienced and expressed, and in the approaches and methods chosen to address them? Another insight from the discussion above is that, even though the general definition of social work and its role in addressing social problems can be given, there are still considerable cultural differences in the ways social problems are viewed, realized, tackled and (sometimes) solved. That is why a chapter of this book is dedicated to social work and cultural issues. Not only are cultural differences apparent in social work practice, but they are also a critical issue for social work education. Through international social work courses and international field placements, social work education is an important vehicle to teach students about international aspects of their future work and to prepare them for the challenges of the globalized world, not least in terms of enhancing their ability to deal with increasing problems related to international issues. The chapter on social work education therefore makes an important and integral contribution to the development of international social work.

References

Asahoah, Y.; Healy, L. M.; Mayadas, N. (1997). Ending the international-domestic dichotomy: New approaches to a global curriculum for the millennium. *Journal of Social Work Education*, 33, 2, 389-401.

Coleman, R. (1996). Exchanges between British and overseas social work and social work education. In Jackson, Preston-Shoot (eds.) Educating social workers in a changing policy context (pp. 171-189). London: Whiting & Birch.

Clarkson, E. M. R. (1990). Teaching overseas students in Great Britain. *International Social Work*, 33, 353-364.

Dominelli, L. (2003). Internationalizing social work: Introducing issues of relevance. In Dominelli, Bernard (eds.). Broadening horizons: International exchanges in social work (pp. 19-33). London: Ashgate.

Dubois, M.; Ntetu, A. (2000). Learning cultural adaptation through international social work training. *Canadian Social Work*, 2, 2, 41-52.

Hokenstad, M. C.; Khinduka, S. K.; Midgley, J. (1992). The world of international social work. In Hokenstad, Khinduka, Midgley (eds.), Profiles in international social work (pp. 2-9). Washington, DC: The National Association of Social Workers.

Healy, L. M.; Maxwell, J.; Pine, B.A. (1999). Exchanges that work: Mutuality and sustainability in a Caribbean/USA academic partnership. *Social Development Issues*. 21, 14-21.

Healy, L. M. (2001). International social work: Professional action in an interdependent world. New York: Oxford Press.

IFSW (2001): International Definition of Social Work. www.ifsw.org, retrieved August 26, 2006.

Lyons, K. (1999). International social work: Themes and perspectives. London: Ashgate

Lorenz, W. (1994). Social work in a changing Europe. London: Routledge.

Midgley, J. (1997). Social work in international context: Challenges and opportunities for the 21st century. In Reisch, Gambrill (eds.), Social work in the 21st century (pp.59-67). Thousand Oaks, CA: Pine Forge.

Payne, M. (1991). Modern social work theory: A critical introduction. Baskingstoke: Macmillian.

Ramanathan, C.S.; Link, R. (1999). All our futures: Principles and resources for social work practice in a global era. Pacific Grove, California: Brooks Cole.

Rogers, G. Collins; D.; Barlow, C.; Grinnell, R.W. (1999). The social work practicum: A student guide. Ithaca: Peacock Press.

Sammon, S.; Whittaker, W.; Barlow, C. (2003). Preparing and supporting students for international exchanges. The challenge of linking theory and practice. In Dominelli, Bernard   (eds.). Broadening horizons: International exchanges in social work. (pp. 161-173). London: Ashgate.

Tesoriero, F.; Rajaratnam, A. (2001). Partnerships in education. An Australian school of social work and a South Indian primary health care project. *International Social Work,* 44, 1, 31-41.

International Dimensions of Social Problems and Social Work Approaches

In the context of globalization and the evolving world society, many social problems no longer have just regional and national dimensions, but are derived from diverse factors of transnational origins. In this part of the book, some of these emerging international aspects of social problems will be discussed. The authors present different analyses and describe approaches to meet international challenges through interventions at local, national and international levels.

In the first contribution, Siobhan E. Laird points out that the socio-economic situation in many emergent Eastern European countries shows striking parallels to countries of sub-Saharan Africa, like Ghana. The living conditions in these regions have become very similar, and survival strategies to meet basic needs in exceptional circumstances are part of the daily routine for many households and families. Problems like poverty, malnutrition, poor sanitation, no access to clean water, declining rural areas and rising numbers of street children are widespread phenomena in both of these areas, and have increased the dependence on social and family networks. To reduce social problems, traditional Anglo-American and continental European social work often concentrates predominantly on remedial casework with individuals and nuclear families. Being designed for the socio-cultural context of capitalist industrial societies, it is questionable if these approaches can be directly applied to other regions. For social work in transitional Eastern European countries, Laird instead proposes to focus on strategies that are producing good results in countries of sub-Saharan Africa. In her research, she identifies African social work strategies that effectively support deprived rural communities, impoverished households and street children. By shifting from individual casework models towards community development and group work, they focus on structural causes and communal responses through networking and cooperation. On household levels, they respect multigenerational family networks and acknowledge their collective responsibility for the household income. Street children are regarded as active decision-makers and are supported in becoming sustainable breadwinners for their families. Laird shows that many African approaches are highly adaptable to conditions afflicting emergent Eastern European democracies. By identifying and strengthening social networks and facilitating socio-economic improvement, they meet material needs and ease the daily struggle for access to services, goods and employment. Therefore, these material and collective approaches seem to be more suitable than individualistic concepts of psycho-social casework.

In the second chapter of this book, Michael Preston-Shoot, Catherine N. Dulmus and Karen M. Sowers discuss the state of evidence-based social work in a comparative way. The chapter begins by naming the imperatives driving the evidence-based movement. These imperatives are derived from social work's own ethical commitments, from theories and contested notions of professions and professionalization, and from social policy and legislative developments that increasingly emphasize human rights, accountability, and standards. The chapter then explores the contested nature of evidence and knowledge. Debates here center on who controls and produces knowledge and evidence, whose narratives count, what impact they do or could have, and whether any hierarchy of methodologies is appropriate in social work. It also focuses on the involvement of service users as experts by experience and shows that, particularly at this point, major differences between social work in the UK and the United States can be found. After that, the authors explore the strength of social work research in, and its impact upon, higher education institutions, policy-making, practice, and professional education. The chapter closes by highlighting some major difficulties in the use of evidence in social work practice and provides some hints on how to connect these different spheres with each other.

As the final contribution in this chapter, Manoj Pardasani analyzes the vital role social workers play in reconstruction and redevelopment efforts within communities that are affected by natural disasters. In 2001, an earthquake in the Kutch region in the state of Gujarat, India, left most of the social and economic infrastructure of the region destroyed and disrupted. The relief efforts after the disaster serve as an interesting case study for inter-disciplinary cooperation in activities of redevelopment. Coordinated by Central Relief and Rehabilitation Center, and based on a twofold short term and long term action plan, local, national and international governmental organizations and NGOs worked together with local communities and volunteers to establish an effective and sustainable reconstruction of the affected area. After initially directing relief action to secure basic needs for health, food, safety and accommodations, a long term action plan was implemented that aimed at rebuilding social structures and gaining sustainable redevelopment. Social work has played a vital role in these processes. Through professional expertise in community organization and development and the support of participatory and empowering structures, social work can effectively support the cooperation between local residents from different socio-economical and cultural backgrounds. Beyond that, social work can contribute experience, connecting interdisciplinary teams and organizations in democratic structures that also motivate volunteers to contribute their full potential. The experience of the relief efforts after the

Gujarat earthquake shows the importance of transdisciplinary collaboration and participatory coordination. Social workers can effectively support these aims by bringing in their competence in community education, service coordination, processes of participatory decision making and empowerment. The social work profession provides vital contributions towards the realization of transdisciplinary collaboration in redevelopment. In the future, these contributions should be made available for further relief efforts after other natural or man-made disasters.

Siobhan E. Laird

The Application of African Practice Models to the Social Problems of Emergent Democracies

1. The Problem with Western Social Work Methods

Anglo-American remedial casework and the approaches of social pedagogy on continental Europe, dominate the conceptualization and activities of social work internationally (Cannan, et al., 1992; Van Wormer, 1997). Both of these methods focus on the psycho-social aspects of vulnerability and disadvantage at the expense of socio-economic factors. The remedial casework model in particular, concentrates on practice with the individual and nuclear family to the detriment of work with wider kinship networks and the community. These characteristics are directly attributable to the fact that professional social work emerged from the capitalist industrial societies of the nineteenth and twentieth centuries. It therefore remains arguable as to whether its methodologies have a practical application outside of a Western milieu.

Midgley (1981) in his seminal work entitled *Professional Imperialism* identified the tendency of Western social work paradigms to be uncritically replicated in countries with widely divergent cultures and socio-economic environments. Increasingly educators and practitioners from Western European nations have been invited to transfer their knowledge and skills to the training of professionals in former Eastern Block countries. A number of authorities have questioned the relevance of Western practice models for Eastern Europe and the paternalistic manner in which they are transferred (Cemlyn, 1995; Dickens, Groza, 2004). There are many aspects of life in the Russian Federation and other emergent democracies such as Ukraine, Romania and Albania which make social organization and welfare provision fundamentally different from that pertaining in Western Europe. It is necessary to explore these aspects in order to appreciate the extent of the mismatch between Western social work paradigms and reality on the ground in many emergent democracies.

Communism in Eastern Europe and the Soviet Union combined ostensibly full employment (though of an under-employed workforce) with a low wage economy, social housing, free health treatment, universal education and a social security system to cater for sickness and old age. The disintegration of the interdependent trading system between communist states caused by the break-up of the Soviet Union alongside the rapid transition from command economies to free market economies resulted in mass unemployment and high inflation. Many households were thrown into crisis as: industries collapsed or were privatized; the real value of their savings, wages and cash benefits plummeted; salary payments became irregular; and price controls were removed (Pickup, White, 2003: 421; Wallace, Latcheva, 2006: 84). Welfare provision deteriorated over the same period as in some countries, such as Russia, gross domestic product (GDP) shrank by as much as half during the 1990s (Goskomstat, 2000). A large number of countries in the post-communist era are left with greatly impaired health, education and welfare systems which retain their infrastructure without effectively delivering provision or else obstruct access through the introduction of formal and informal charges (Milanovic, 1998; Balabanova, et al., 2004; Micklewright, 1999; Sandu, 2005). The divergence between East and West is even greater when aspects of social organization are considered alongside differences in economic conditions and welfare regimes.

Social organization in former Eastern Block countries reflects both existing norms and adaptation to the dislocations caused by transition to a free market. In Russia as wages in the state sector became irregular, there was a shift into the informal economy with people working at several casual jobs simultaneously. Rural areas have witnessed an increase in subsistence farming. The rapid fall in the value of pensions meant that many people instead of retiring continue to work into old age, often in the informal sector. The sudden and astronomical rise in housing costs resulted in households becoming multigenerational as pensioners attempt to offset living expenses and newly married couples cannot afford their own accommodation. Emigration has also led to family fragmentation (Gustafsson, Nivorozhkina, 2004: 751-753; Lokshin, Yemtsov, 2001).

Survival strategies normally deployed by households to meet basic needs in exceptional circumstances have become routine in the Russian Federation (Shevchenko, 2002: 844). This has transformed families into productive units requiring close cooperation in domestic and economic activities in order to sustain a viable livelihood strategy. Networks of friends and kin have also become vital as personal connections and trust have replaced the contractual relations of the formal economy (Pickup, White, 2003). While many of these adaptations pre-date the transitional period, such strategies have become more integral to household survival both in rural and urban areas (Bühler, 2004: 264-265). Families and individuals in many other post-communist societies have made similar changes to work and living patterns (Wallace, Latcheva, 2006; Michael, Florica, 1998; UNICEF, 2000a). The differences between social and economic conditions in Western Europe and numerous former communist states are plainly considerable. However, there are other regions of the world, such as sub-Saharan Africa, which bear a striking resemblance to the situation inside many emergent democracies.

2. A Comparison of Sub-Saharan Africa with Emergent Democracies

The widespread poverty and social dislocation of communities in Africa are more extreme than those experienced by people in former Eastern Block countries, yet conditions in both regions bear some similarities. Many emergent democracies in Eastern Europe and the former Soviet Union have a Human Development Index (HDI) rank, which while positioning them above African nations such as Ghana, Namibia and Botswana, places them in the same broad category of countries with Medium Human Development (UNDP, 2004: Table 1). In the Russian Federation 53 percent of the population live on less than $4 a day. In Romania and Ukraine around one quarter of the population survive on this amount (ibid., Table 4). This compares with Namibia and Botswana where half the population survives on just $2 or less a day. In Ghana the situation is worse with almost four fifths of people living on less than $2 a day (ibid., Table 3). Plainly, extreme deprivation affects the countries of both regions.

There are other parallels. For example just over half the population of Romania has access to sustainable improved sanitation and water sources. This contrasts to Ghana where almost three quarters of the population had such access (ibid., Table 7). In Albania child malnutrition is estimated at 14 percent of children, which compares to a similar figure in Botswana and the admittedly higher figure of 25 percent in Ghana (World Bank, 2004: Table 2). The growing numbers of street children in Eastern European capitals though not yet comparable to the high numbers in African cities are certainly increasing. For example in Accra, the capital of Ghana, the number of street children is estimated to be upwards of 15,000 (CAS, UNICEF, 1999: 1). For Bucharest figures range from 400 to 600, while for Romania as a whole they vary between 1,500 and 3,500 children (ASIS, CSC, 2004: 15). In Tirana there are reckoned to be 800 street children. (NCWF, 2001: 5) Approximately half the population of Romania and Albania live in rural areas, which is similar to the proportions for Botswana and Ghana (UNDP, 2004: Table 5). In short there are many socio-economic similarities between a number of emergent democracies and countries of sub-Saharan Africa.

Confronted with the social problems indicated by these statistics neither government nor civil society in many Eastern European countries or the successor states of the Soviet Union have been able to adequately respond. This is due principally to the adverse impact of the transition from planned to market economies which impoverished populations while simultaneously damaging welfare infrastructures (Deacon, et al. 1992; Milanovic, 1998; Stiglitz, 2002). The abrupt social upheaval caused by rampant inflation and high unemployment in conjunction with the loss of automatic access to: social security; health care; low cost housing; and a range of state services have also made it difficult for communities to successfully adapt. These are not very different circumstances from those pertaining in a number of sub-Saharan countries. Highly indebted African governments presiding over impecunious public sectors are unable to provide comprehensive services to meet people's health and social care needs (UNDP, 2004: Tables 13 and 18).

3. Social Work in Sub-Saharan Africa

The advanced industrialized nations are not the only source of social work methodology and practice. In developing regions of the world, such as sub-Saharan Africa, new methods are being elaborated. Professionals in both the state sector and non-governmental agencies are fashioning innovative approaches to social problems and welfare provision. Their great advantage over dominant Western models of social work is that they retain a focus on structural causes of deprivation and psycho-social stress alongside an emphasis on communal rather than individualized responses.

Approaches by social workers and allied professionals in Ghana are similar to those used elsewhere in sub-Saharan Africa (Government of South Africa, 1997). To address impoverishment, exacerbated by limited access to public utilities and minimal welfare provision, practitioners in Ghana have developed a number of approaches.

Since social work practice in Africa remains largely unrecorded in the literature, these interventions are described through direct quotation. These are excerpted from semi-structured interviews conducted with one hundred fieldworkers from the public and voluntary sectors during 2002 in Ghana. The interviews were in English (the official language) and lasted around an hour and a half; each was conducted and transcribed by the author. The transcripts were given back to the participants for amendment and the originals destroyed. The revised transcripts were analyzed using grounded theory based on Strauss and Corbin (1998) and facilitated by Nud*ist, a qualitative software package which enables the rapid and systematic coding of text.

3.1 Practice with Deprived Rural Communities

In Ghana's capital 20 percent of households do not have electricity, 6 percent lack access to a safe water source and 9 percent are without sanitation. The figures are much higher for rural areas, for instance in Upper West Region, comparable figures are 90 percent, 27 percent and 75 percent respectively (GSS, 1993). Plainly, rural communities are grossly disadvantaged relative to urban populations with most households lacking access to basic utilities. This is reflected in the finding that 86 percent of absolute poverty in Ghana is concentrated in rural districts (GSS, 2000a: Table 2). Rural households are confronted by further disadvantage as they have less access to health and educational provision than their urban counterparts. This is for a number of reasons. Firstly, medical and educational facilities are concentrated in cities and towns. Secondly, rural clinics and schools have received much less funding than those in urban locations (Demery, et al., 1995; GoG, UNICEF, 2002: 95). Thirdly, the World Bank and the International Monetary Fund (IMF) required indebted countries to introduce charges for public sector health care and education as a condition of lending during the 1980s. The cost of medical treatment or putting a child through school is now beyond the means of many rural households (GSS, 2000: 28; GoG, UNICEF, 2002: 51; GSSa, 2000, Fig.18 and 20; GoG, 2003: 23). The disparities between the utilities and services available to rural households relative to urban ones is reflected in the much higher incidence of child malnutrition, infant and maternal mortality and illiteracy in the countryside (GSS, 1999; GoG, UNICEF, 2002: 64-66).

Historically, rural societies in developing countries have coped with lack of basic utilities and impoverishment through communal activity. Scott (1976) explored what he termed 'the moral economy of the peasant'. He argued that the necessity of distributing risks across households in subsistence communities in order to ensure that everyone could meet their survival needs was codified in strict social norms of mutual obligation. In circumstances of extreme poverty, where people have few assets, social capital is a critical safety net for meeting basic needs in adverse circumstances. These rights to assistance constitute a form of social insurance, but also a liability, as aid rendered, creates reciprocal obligations. Additionally, in Ghana the institution of chieftaincy has generally meant leadership and cohesion of village communities (Nukunya, 1992: 67-73).

Social workers and community development professionals alike use the social organization of communities to gain access to them. Interaction with traditional authorities, such as the chief, who are known and generally trusted by their communities, pivots around initial entry to the locality and the organization of mass meeting for fieldworkers to address:

"You can only get them through the leaders that they know, the opinion leaders, the chiefs, the assemblymen, these are the people in the community they know, they do not know you. So when these people, the opinion leaders call them they will listen to them and they will come. When the people have gathered you then tell them your mission" (DD120-124).

Moreover, practitioners sometimes rely on traditional authorities to endorse and sustain aspects of agency activity. One development worker conducting activity to improve environmental sanitation in a village cites an instance of the chief making a ruling that livestock are to be penned up and any animals found wandering are to be confiscated until such times as the owner pays a fine for its return (CF276-282).

Another approach is to undertake work with the community through a network of groups. As one social worker indicates:

"... the churches too, they have these women's groups, youth groups and men's fellowships. So the groups are already in the communities. So we take the chance to do group work with them, educating them on some of the rights of children" (EP49-52).

A fieldworker from an NGO in an urban area exemplifies this approach recounting:

"... we started from the churches, it has a contact person and through the contact person you can find groups in the church. We know there are some registered groups with the metropolitan assembly so we get their names and we trace them. We know that in the market we have various groups so we just go about asking" (KB197-201).

In this case, the sheer variety of groups identified within different settings enables the agency to reach a very wide variety of potential beneficiaries. A professional at another agency adds:

"... some are welfare clubs, some are youth clubs, then there are other fun making ones, but we are changing their mind not to just making merry, but to development" (AC123-125).

Here existing community-based organizations founded for one purpose, such as mutual assistance or leisure, are co-opted by fieldworkers to serve another in terms of agency activity.

Beneficiaries participating in groups which are used to transfer skills on nutrition, sanitation and small scale business enterprises are according to one fieldworker not necessarily the most disadvantaged:

"... some are educated, some are also illiterates, some are school drop-outs, some are older women who have not been to school, others have been but they have not completed. We have a variety" (DB165-167).

Another relates that "the type of people we work with, they are without education, formal education. About five percent of them are educated, we have nurses, teachers among them. I can say there are about five percent that are gainfully employed. The majority, the rest of the people are illiterates and they are doing petty trading, selling fish, making meat pies and pastries to sell" (DD163-168).

Community workers see clear advantages in this mix as all groups need people who are literate and numerate so that they can assist to keep accounts for any commercial enterprise run by the group. Concentrating only on the poorest and neglecting the potential contribution of less disadvantaged members of the community by excluding them from intervention would plainly undermine successful activity.

In circumstances where government agencies and small NGOs lack resources, communities are required to make a contribution to the establishment and sustaining of agency intervention. For example, one NGO assisting in the construction of schools, latrines and wells, requires members of the community to volunteer to sit on committees which then oversee and manage these projects (CA741-748; CD42-62; CF100-111). The same organization which provides latrines obliges community members to supply the sand and stone necessary for the structure and to use their own labor to dig the pit (CE200-205). Community members are also responsible for maintaining amenities provided to their locality, such as a borehole for water accessed by a hand-pump (CA741-748). Taking this a step further in terms of community empowerment, some volunteers from the locality are trained by the agency to engage with their own communities to identify local problems, their causes and solutions. Once ascertained, these problems are prioritized at mass meetings and integrated into a Community Development Outline which is presented to the NGO. At this stage the community negotiates with the agency for the assistance it requires to resolve the problems identified in the Outline document.

In the face of mounting poverty and social exclusion people in post-communist societies have increasingly relied on their social networks which combines kin, friends, neighbors, work colleagues and personal contacts to obtain assistance or access to goods and services (Goodwin, et al., 2000; Lokshin, Yemtsov, 2001). Social capital in this sense enables people to utilize informal networks, held together by mutual trust and obligation, to gain their objectives. These social networks have long been a feature of communist societies as they substituted for the inefficiencies of the planned economy, the unresponsiveness of state bureaucracy and the weak rule of law (Sätre, Åhlander, 2000: 448-449; Stoer, Rodrigues, 2005: 194). This reliance is so pervasive that a survey in Russia found up to 90 percent depend on social networks to get things done rather than public institutions or civil society organizations (Rose, 1998: 7). Commonly referred to in Russia as *blat* exchanges, these depend on a system of 'functional friendships' which permit the trade in favors governed by strict social norms of reciprocity. Such networks attract considerable loyalty and are built on bonds of mutual dependence.

Cooperatives, which under communism were usually an expression of compulsory collectivism, in the post-communist era are often voluntary associations having contractual relations with the state sector. For instance a consumer cooperative in Pakov near the Russian-Estonian border supplies food products and services to the rural population alongside skills training for food production and social assistance to poor people in the form of vouchers and credit. The same cooperative has also expanded into areas of public health. In return for these services local government grants tax reductions to the cooperative (Sätre, Åhlander, 2000: 451). Informal organizations composed of women to disseminate information and exchange views on issues of common concern have also been documented in Russia. Many of these have expanded into job-clubs, financial advice, support groups, and training for small-business set up (Sätre, Åhlander, 2000: 453-455).

3.2 Practice with Impoverished Households

Multigenerational extended family households predominate among Ghanaians with approximately 70 percent of the population adopting this living arrangement (GSS, 2000a: Table 6.1). Though it is equally true that the migration of young people from villages to towns in search of better opportunities is eroding the mutual obligations upon which extensive interdependent kin relations depend (Nukunya, 1992: 155). The household in Ghana is effectively a productive and reproductive entity, which constitutes both the locus of socialization and economic activity (Nukunya, 1992; Turner, 1996). The extended family acts as a complementary portfolio of domestic and commercial endeavors, which sustain a variety of small-scale income-generating activities. Domestic and economic complementarity is based around the roles of household members, which are often ascribed according to age and gender. For example girls are expected to collect fuel-wood and water alongside assisting their female relatives with food preparation and child care. Conversely, boys are likely to be engaged in more economically lucrative activities alongside their male relatives. Age related roles are evident around female trading activities with older women in the family engaging in doorstep trading, thus providing supervision of small children while their daughters and granddaughters are freed to conduct business outside of the home. Similarly, young children may provide ancillary services to older household members such as transporting produce in order to facilitate the trading activities of their mothers and grandmothers (Koomson, et al., 1996).

The collapse of the manufacturing sector during the 1980s considerably worsened the availability of job opportunities in Ghana. Only 14 percent of the population are in waged employment while 70 percent are in self-employment, predominantly within the informal sector, which is characterized by unskilled, casual and poorly paid work. A further 17 percent are unpaid family workers, but twice as many women fall into this category as men (GSS, 2000b: Table 4.4). Exacerbating problems of labor market participation is the finding that underemployment varies as between 64 percent up to as high as 80 percent in some parts of the country (ISSER, 1995). With such a small segment of the workforce engaged in full-time waged employment social protection through a contributory insurance scheme is minimal. In circumstances of dire poverty and few real employment opportunities child labor is pervasive. The difficulties of accessing education converge with the vital contribution of children's domestic and economic activity towards household livelihood. The pernicious effect of this is that large numbers of children dropout of school in order to pursue small scale income-generating ventures. For instance boys will help their fathers to fish or girls assist their mothers with petty trading in the local town. Children's participation in farming activities is almost universal in rural areas (GoG, UNICEF, 2002: 94; GSS, 2000b: Table 4.2). The Government of Ghana (GoG) and UNICEF (2002: 126) found positive correlations between child labor and school attendance. It is widely recognized that child labor is a function of poverty (Bequele, Boyden, 1995).

The inter-related aspects of economic activity undertaken by different family members mean that agency intervention tends to be based on an analysis of the outputs and income flows of the whole household rather than that of an individual. One NGO worker outlines the questions which are central to their assessments:

"...what are the livelihood activities each person in the house is engaged in. After you know what activity each person is engaged in then you look at what the person puts into that activity and then what also comes from that activity to the house" (ID67-71).

This kind of approach involves identifying the contribution of children and extended kin networks to household livelihood. It is the recognition of the inextricable linkage between poverty, child labor and schooling which informs subsequent agency intervention.

Micro-credit and/or training for savings schemes are commonly given by NGOs, often in collaboration with social workers who identify potential beneficiaries. One program, known as 'Enhanced Savings and Credit Association for Poverty Eradication' and referred to by the acronym ESCAPE, comprises group sessions during which beneficiaries are taught how to save, open a bank account, disburse loans and charge interest using their own financial resources (AF35-41; AF51-63). The sole purpose of contact by the professional is to transfer to group members the skills necessary for them to be able to manage the ESCAPE program on their own and then to end agency contact. Although this program is not specifically targeting parents, other agencies see a direct connection between providing micro-credit facilities and the welfare of children:

"... if we are giving the mothers or fathers credit we are hoping that when that money is given to the mother, we are even hoping that she will take that money to pay the school fees or buy food or buy shelter for the child" (CG573-6).

The rationale for providing loans is that "most of our clients are not in a position to have building structures, properties or other physical assets that can be used to contract for the loan. So we put them into groups, each member becomes liable for the loan that the other gets. So if another group member refuses to pay the other members in the group are held responsible" (KB74-8).

Poverty and the lack of assets to provide security mean that financial institutions often will not lend to poor people. In the absence of individual assets NGOs lend to groups where these constitute social collateral for the loan that is being given by the agency.

While conditions on the African continent are undoubtedly more acute than those pertaining in most post-communist societies there are strong similarities. Many former communist states have witnessed a steep decline in enrolments for pre-school and upper-secondary education alongside a slashing of the education budget which has resulted in: cut backs in the provision of free or subsidized school meals; the deterioration of building structures; a shortage of text books; and teachers going unpaid for months at a time. This has coincided with a period when households have experienced a large drop in household income and spending power. Consequently, parents are poorly positioned to replace the nutritional deficit created by the reduction in school meals or the need to materially contribute to children's education through the purchase to text books.

The introduction of formal fees and informal tuition charges has also increased the cost of education (Micklewright, 1999; Korintus, et al., 2000; INSTAT, 2003). Pre-school and upper-secondary attendance is linked to household income, with the children of wealthier parents much more likely to attend pre-school or stay on in education after 16 years than those of poorer parents (UNICEF, 1998: Fig. 3.11). Similarly, evidence from Romania demonstrates a positive correlation between household consumption (a proxy for wealth) and enrolment rates in primary, secondary and tertiary education. Research has also revealed a strong association between household income, school enrolment and child labor (ibid.: 367). This is particularly the case in Romania (Korintus, et al., 2000: 34-35). In Albania 45 percent of children living in rural areas and 7 percent in urban ones are estimated to be engaged in paid or unpaid labor either within their own home or outside of it (UNICEF, 2000b: 33).

In the face of dramatic drops in household income many individuals in post-communist societies have taken on second and third jobs predominantly in the informal sector. For large numbers of people household consumption is partly dependent on the cultivation of their own plot of land in peri-urban and rural locations (Bühler, 2004: 261; Stoer, Rodrigues, 2005: 193). In Russia around half of urban households depend on growing some of their own food for household consumption, while for many others the sale of agricultural produce can contribute up to one third of household income (Bühler, 2004: 266). Farming activity is usually undertaken by all members of the household regardless of age or gender and including children (Pickup, White, 2003: 425).

3.3 Practice with Street Children

Perhaps the starkest demonstration of the connection between poverty and child labor is the phenomena of street children estimated to number 15,000 in Accra (CAS, UNICEF, 1999). UNICEF and 'Save the Children' (SCF) have differentiated between two groups: *Children on the street* are those who retain family contact and return home to sleep, but whose daily life and sphere of activity is conducted in the street; *children of the street* have little if any family contact and instead pursue an independent mode of life on the streets, sleeping rough in lorry parks and open market areas (SCF, 1994). The majority of *children of the street* are migrants from rural districts attempted to escape the bludgeoning poverty of the countryside by seeking opportunity in the cities and towns of Ghana (CAS, UNICEF, 1999).

A study of street children in Accra by Van Ham, et al. (1991) revealed that around 75 percent of them are *children on the street* who remain members of a family unit. Indeed, of those categorized as street children 87,3 percent reported that they had received financial assistance from a relative to support their economic activities while 80 percent stated that they were presently engaged in some form of work. Out of all the children surveyed 29 percent were attending school, 35 percent had dropped out of school and 23 percent had never attended school.

Another disturbing aspect of the street children phenomena in Ghana is the age profile of those living with limited parental supervision or family contact. Van Ham, et al. (1991) found that of those living on the streets in Accra 12 percent were aged 7-11 years, while 51 percent were aged 13-15 years. The extreme vulnerability of street children due to their youth and the absence of effective family support means that they undertake the most poorly paid and demanding forms of casual work while being exposed to abuse and sexual exploitation. Girls commonly engaged in petty trading and sometimes in prostitution while the majority of street boys work as porters or as shoe shines (MESW, 1995).

The intervention strategies adopted toward *children on the street* and *children of the street* are different. For *children on the street* agencies engaged parents in micro-credit schemes and skills transfer for small enterprise development in an effort to reduce the need for them to depend on children to earn an income. Hence interventions are similar to those adopted for households as already discussed. As regards *children of the street* agencies use a wide variety of approaches most of which acknowledge the independence and early maturity street children had attained. These interventions tended to treat street children as autonomous and capable of making their own decisions in the absence of parental guidance.

As in community oriented interventions those addressing the problems of street children endeavor to engage with informal groups. The Ghana Youth

Protest Association, a grouping of street youth, is used by social workers to assist in the identification of kayayee (female head porters) and their leaders who are the target of activity in Accra (EJ199-217). The involvement of this association also functions to reassure prospective beneficiaries that they can have confidence in the fieldworkers who are not known in their own right. An outreach social worker at an NGO engages the support or at least acquiescence of informal gang leaders who control particular vicinities. This protects social workers who are vulnerable to physical assault as unfamiliar persons in the locality. It also serves to bolster rapport with street children who receive assurances from someone they relate to, the gang leader, about someone they do not know, the worker (FF220-231).

Providing facilities for street children can be extremely problematic given that they literally roam the streets. Responding to the needs of street children a fieldworker from the NGO recounts:

"When we talk to them about the refuge they do complain about the distance and the money needed to take a vehicle. So we discussed it and we decided to put up a mini refuge" (FK148-50).

There are three mini refuges located around the city which act as a resource for street children and an opportunity for staff to encourage them to join the vocational courses being managed by the NGO. Social workers specifically target street children by going to the areas where they are known to congregate. One working with an NGO explains:

"... these children are from the streets. As I mentioned social workers from the agency, they go to identify them, sort of befriend them and introduce the agency to them" (FH101-3).

From their experience on the streets professionals from this NGO realize that street children gather at certain places, termed 'meeting points'. As one fieldworker points out:

"... apart from meeting at the meeting point I also go round to locate new areas or new meeting points" (FN30-31).

In other words agency workers are constantly endeavoring to target new street children by discovering those localities in which they may be found in greatest concentration. For those children reluctant to engage directly with the agency and who remain on the streets, social workers deliver 'street corner education' in sessions on the street, in lorry parks or markets places (ie. where street children congregate) on subjects such as HIV/AIDS prevention, personal hygiene and drug abuse (FB592-602; FF250-258).

Having identified and engaged street children the NGO also provides vocational training. Beneficiaries are encouraged to attend demonstration workshops in carpentry, pottery, weaving, hairdressing etc. in anticipation that they will decide on what kind of apprenticeship to pursue. This period is also used by social workers to assess whether the street child has the aptitude and determination to complete a three year training course paid for by the agency (FE68-87; FH159-71). In addition the agency will also pay for the beneficiary's accommodation and provide an allowance for daily expenses. Many agencies involved in vocational training also offer literacy courses to beneficiaries.

To some extent this is because "there are some who cannot even read basic instructions, especially those who are into hairdressing, they do not even know simple, simple instructions on certain chemicals, like shampoos" (FG178-80).

In other words, functional literacy is a condition of successfully completing vocational training, obtaining work thereafter or managing income-generating ventures. These initiatives are inter-sectoral and recognize the interdependence of different agency activities in resolving beneficiaries' problems. In fact the same agency provides a range of mutually reinforcing interventions which include: free washing facilities; medical treatment; vocational and educational sponsorship; instruction on literacy, numeracy, disease prevention and managing money.

According to the 'Asociatia Sprijinirea Integrarii Sociale' (ASIS) of Rumania and the Consortium for Street Children (CSC) (2004: 16) approximately 60 percent of street children in Bucharest return home to their family after working on the streets. Another 20 percent organize their lives without reference or contact with their families. A further 7 percent live on the streets together with their families and may be second generation street children. The activities of street children are wide ranging and include: begging; car washing; selling merchandise; carrying loads and sex work. Those falling into the age group 12-14 years comprise 30 percent of street children. These children evidenced high rates of school drop-out and consequently low levels of education. Household poverty, abandonment or physical abuse by parents, were pervasive factors in their streetism (ibid.). Informal social structures have also been recorded among street children with older more established street children adopting leadership roles. This is supplemented by children banding together in groups for mutual support and protection on the street (ibid.: 19-20).

4. Conclusion

In Ghana, as in other African nations, attention has shifted way from the predominant remedial casework model towards community development and group work. There has also been a move away from a psycho-social emphasis during intervention to one which focuses on addressing material deprivation at community and household level through skills transfer and small loan provision. Community mobilization in both rural and urban areas is a widely employed strategy. Group work is undertaken utilizing existing social networks or organizing these within communities where none exist. Often these groups are used as the setting for a sequence of interventions ranging from education on nutrition to skills transfer for employment or small-enterprise development and microfinance schemes. Where households have broken down as in the case of street children informal social networks are still identified and used to facilitate socio-economic intervention.

The imperatives for most communities and households in the emergent democracies of Eastern Europe and the successor states of the Soviet Union revolve around access to goods, services and employment. Of course psycho-social problems do exist, indeed these are often attributable to the stress caused by conditions of deprivation. Yet, the pressing needs of people are essentially material and require a social work response which directly addresses them. While acknowledging the differences in social organization and economic conditions many of the approaches used by professionals in Ghana are clearly relevant and adaptable to conditions in emergent democracies. The recognition that lack of access to utilities affects communities as a whole and not individual households forces intervention into the domain of community development and away from one-on-one casework.

The lack of trust in formal state structures and the dependence on social networks are important aspects of post-communist societies which need to be realized and incorporated into social work intervention. The re-structuring of the household as an economic unit sustained by multiple livelihoods also require approaches which are essentially economic in nature. This is particularly necessary once it is appreciated that children's welfare is imperiled by their share of the domestic and economic labour of the household. At the same time such children cannot simply be treated separately as their labor is an integral aspect of meeting the household's survival needs. For those households fragmented by the poverty created during transition and where this has resulted in migration, their needs remain essentially material. Unlike the predominant tendency in Western European nations for social workers to treat children as dependents, in many transitional societies children are often decision-makers and breadwinners for their families. When it is clear that family relationships have broken down to the extent that they are self-caring as is the case for *children of the street* notions of family reconciliation must come second to assisting children to re-engage with schooling or obtain vocational skills for employment. In short the interventions used by social workers and community development professionals in sub-Saharan Africa are more pertinent to the living conditions and needs of people in many emergent democracies than are the approaches utilized by social workers in Western Europe.

References

ASIS, CSC = Asociatia Sprijinirea Integrarii Sociale, Consortium for Street Children (2004). Street Children and Juvenile Justice in Romania. London: Asociatia Sprijinirea Integrarii Sociale, The Consortium for Street Children.

Balabanova, D.; McKee, M.; Pomerleau J.; Rose R.; Haerpfer, C. (2004). Health service utilization in the former Soviet Union: Evidence from Eight Countries. *Health Service Research,* 36, 6, 1927-1949.

Bequele, A.; Boyden, J. (eds.)(1995). Combating Child Labour. Geneva: International Labour Office.

Bühler, C. (2004). Additional work, family agriculture, and the birth of a first or a second child in Russia at the beginning of the 1990s. *Population Research and Policy Review,* 23, 259-289.

Cannan, C.; Berry, L; Lyons, K. (1992). Social Work and Europe. London: Macmillan.

CAS, UNICEF = Catholic Action for Street Children, UNICEF (1999). The Exodus. Accra: Catholic Action for Street Children, UNICEF.

Cemlyn, S. (1995). Social work in Russia and the UK: what are we exchanging? *Social Work Education,* 14, 1, 77-92.

Deacon, B.; Castle-Kanerova, M.; Manning, N.;Millard, F.; Orosz, E.; Szalia, J.; Vidinova, A. (1992). The New Eastern Europe: Social Policy Past, Present and Future. London: Sage.

Demery, L.; Chao, S.; Bernier, R.; Mehra, K. (1995). The Incidence of Social Spending in Ghana. PSP Discussion Paper Series, 82, Washington: World Bank.

Dickens, J.; Groza, V. (2004). Empowerment in difficulty: A critical appraisal of international intervention in child welfare in Romania. *International Social Work,* 47, 4, 469-487.

GoG = Government of Ghana (2003). An Agenda for Growth and Prosperity: Ghana Poverty Reduction Strategy 2003-2005, Vol. 1, Accra: Government of Ghana.

GoG, UNICEF = Government of Ghana, UNICEF (2002). Situation Analysis of Children and Women in Ghana 2000. Accra: Government of Ghana,UNICEF.

Goodwin, R.; Nizharadze, G.; Nguyen, Luu L.A.; Kosa, E.; Emelyanova, T. (2001). Social support in a changing Europe: an analysis of three post-communist nations. *European Journal of Social Psychology,* 31, 379-393.

Goskomstat (2000). Rossiiskii Statisticheskii Ezhegodnik (Russian Statistical Yearbook). Moscow: Goskomstat.

Gustafsson, B.; Nivorozhkina, L. (2004). Changes in Russian poverty during transition as assessed from microdata from the city of Taganrog. *Economics of Transition,* 12, 4, 747-776.

GSS = Ghana Statistical Service (1993). Ghana Demographic and Health Survey 1993. Accra: Ghana Statistical Service.

GSS (1999). Ghana Demographic and Health Survey 1998. Accra: Ghana Statistical Service.

GSS (2000a). Poverty Trends in Ghana in the 1990s. Accra: Ghana Statistical Service.

GSS (2000b). Ghana Living Standards Survey. Report of the Fourth Round GLSS 4 Apr. 1998 – Mar. 1999. Accra: Ghana Statistical Service.

Government of South Africa (1997). White Paper for Social Welfare. Pretoria: Government of South Africa.

INSTAT (2003). Youth and Transition: Issues Confronting Albania's Key Resource. Tirana: National Institute of Statistics.

ISSER = Institute of Statistical, Social and Economic Research (1995). The State of the Ghanaian Economy in 1994. University of Ghana, Legon: Institute of Statistical, Social and Economic Research.

Koomson, J.; Williams, N.; Apt, N. A.; Grieco, M. (1996). Protected by their past, working for their future: doorstep trading and elderly women. In Grieco, Apt, Turner (eds.). At Christmas and on Rainy Days: Transport, Travel and the Female Traders of Accra (pp. 187-212). Aldershot: Avebury.

Korintus, M.; Pro Excellentia Foundation; National Institute for Family and Social Policy (Hungary) (2000). Early Childhood in Central and Eastern Europe: Issues and Challenges. Paris: UNESCO Early Childhood and Family Education Unit.

Lokshin, M.M.; Yemtsov, R. (2001). Household Strategies for Coping with Poverty and Social Exclusion in Post-crisis Russia. Policy Research Working Papers 2556. Washington, DC: The World Bank.

MESW = Ministry of Employment and Social Welfare (1995). Draft Policy on Street Children. Accra: Ministry of Employment and Social Welfare.

Michael, S.; Florica, B. (1998). Opportunities, constraints and pluriactivity in rural Romania during the transition period; preliminary observations *GeoJournal*, 44, 4, 783-796.

Micklewright, J. (1999). Education, inequality and transition. *Economics of Transition*, 7, 2, 343-376.

Midgley, J. (1981). Professional Imperialism: Social Work in the Third World. London: Heinemann.

Milanovic, B. (1998). Income, Inequality, and Poverty during the Transition from Planned to Market Economy. Washington, DC: World Bank.

NCWF = National Committee on Women and Children (2001). National Strategy for Children. Tirana: National Committee on Women and Children.

Nukunya, G.K. (1992). Tradition and Change in Ghana. Accra: Ghana Universities Press.

Pickup, F.; White, A. (2003). Livelihoods in post-communist Russia. *Work, Employment and Society,* 17, 3, 419-434.

Rose, R. (1998). Getting things done in an anti-modern society: social capital networks in Russia. Social Capital Initiative Working Paper No. 6, Washington, DC: The World Bank.

SCF = Save the Children (1994). Street and Working Children: A Guide to Planning. London: Save the Children.

Sandu, A. (2005). Poverty, women and child health in rural Romania: uninformed choice or lack of services. *Journal of Comparative Policy Analysis,* 7, 1, 5-28.

Scott, J.C. (1976). The Moral Economy of the Peasant. Newhaven: Yale University Press.

Shevchenko, O. (2002). "Between the holes": emerging identities and hybrid patterns of consumption in Post-socialist Russia. *Europe-Asia Studies,* 54, 6, 841-866.

Stiglitz, J. (2002). Globalisation and its Discontents. London: Penguin.

Stoer, S. R., Rodrigues, F. (2005). Perceptions of health and well-being in transition societies: some results of a qualitative study carried out in the Ukraine. *European Journal of Social Work,* 8, 2, 181-200.

Strauss, A.; Corbin, J. (1998). Basics of Qualitative Research. Thousand Oaks, CA: Sage.

Turner, J. (1996). Female domestic responsibilities and household survival: travel strategies in a developing economy. In Grieco, Apt, Turner (eds.). At Christmas and on Rainy Days: Transport, Travel and the Female Traders of Accra (pp.129-152). Aldershot: Avebury.

UNDP (1997) *Ghana Human Development Report 1997* Accra: United Nations Development Programme

UNDP = United Nations Development Programme (2004). Human Development Report: Cultural Liberty in Today's Diverse World. New York: United Nations Development Programme.

UNICEF (1998). Education for All? The MONEE project. Regional Monitoring Report No. 5, Florence: UNICEF, International Child Development Centre.

UNICEF (2000a). Assessment of Social & Economic Conditions of Districts in Albania. Tirana: UNICEF.

UNICEF (2000b). Multiple Indicator Cluster Survey Report Albania. Tirana: UNICEF.

Van Ham, N.A.; Blavo, E.Q.; Opoko, S.K. (1991). Street Children in Accra: A Survey Report. Department of Sociology, University of Ghana Legon.

Van Wormer, K. (1997). Social Welfare: A World View. Chicago: Nelson Hall.

Wallace, C.; Latcheva, R. (2006). Economic transformation outside the law: corruption, trust in public institutions and the informal economy in transition countries of Central and Eastern Europe. *Europe-Asia Studies,* 58, 1, 81-102.

World Bank (2004). World Development Report. Washington, DC: World Bank.

Michael Preston-Shoot, Catherine N. Dulmus, Karen M. Sowers

Evidence-Based Social Work: Challenges for Policy, Practice and Professional Education

1. Introduction

National governments concerned with providing effective intervention strategies to promote health and social well-being are now, more than ever before, looking to document effective policies, strategies and interventions for replication. The social work knowledge base now contains a growing array of evidence-based interventions for social workers to utilize when working with service users. Indeed, in both the United States (Bellamy, et al., 2006) and the United Kingdom evidence-based social work has become institutionalized through a variety of agencies and organizations. In England, these include the Social Care Institute for Excellence and EPPI; in the United States, federal guidelines of evidence-based practices are readily available on national web-sites of the National Institute of Mental Health, the National Institute of Drug Abuse, the Office of Juvenile Justice and Delinquency Prevention. However, despite the growing body of research to guide policy and practice decisions, the movement towards evidence-based social work continues to face challenges in both policy and practice and in the social work curriculum. Thus, what is the state of evidence-based social work and how might social work researchers, practitioners and educators play a pivotal role in responding to the needs presented to social welfare organizations?

This chapter reviews the state of evidence-based social work and the relationship between evidence and policy-making, welfare service delivery and social work training. It considers the imperatives driving the movement, the contested nature of evidence and knowledge, the strength of social work research and the involvement of experts by experience – those people who rely on social work services. The chapter will consider how social work academics, policy-makers, managers and practitioners do and might use research evidence and knowledge to respond to the challenges involved in delivering professional education, policies and regulations, and practice environments fit for contemporary social services. It will draw particularly on experiences from the United Kingdom and the United States.

2. Imperatives Driving Evidence-Based Movements

Several imperatives are driving the evidence-based movement. Some of these drivers emanate from within social work itself whilst others are imposed from without. Arguments rage over the degree to which the imperatives are supportive or constraining of social work. They rage too around the politics of knowledge and around social relations (Frost, 2002; Clegg, 2005), how problems are defined and how evidence comes to be used and to govern practice.

2.1 Regulation

The Council on Social Work Education, which is the accrediting body in the United States for social work programs, has included evidence-based practice as a required standard for accreditation for undergraduate and graduate social work education programs. In addition, the National Association of Social Workers (NASW), which is the largest professional social work organization in the United States, includes the use of evidence-based practice in its practice guidelines and Code of Ethics for social workers. Furthermore, some states are now requiring mental health providers to utilize evidence-based practice in their service provision, and some private third party insurers will only reimburse for services to clients which are evidence-based.

In England, national occupational standards include within a definition of professional competence the ability to provide evidence for judgements and to monitor effectiveness in meeting need (TOPSS, 2002). The benchmark statement for the content of social work degrees (QAA, 2000) includes using research concepts and tools to guide action and to evaluate practice outcomes. The modernization agenda, set by the New Labour government for social work and social care (DH, 1998), requires that services should be evidence-based, envisaging that this will combine with other measures to afford service users protection from abusive practice and to guarantee provision of consistent quality. However, the code of conduct (GSCC, 2002), to which all social workers who must be registered to practice subscribe, is rather more equivocal in its references to research than its counterpart in the United States. The code of conduct does not refer to the use of research or evidence, only to the responsibility of practitioners and employers to maintain knowledge and skills for practice.

If a difference can be detected, it is in the degree to which the professional community, and those who regulate it, explicitly locates centre stage the use of research-based evidence.

2.2 Ethics

Pollio (2002) argues that the failure to incorporate evidence into practice amounts to an ethical violation. Macgowan (2006), in the context of group-work practice, also emphasizes the values and ethics underpinning social work. Sheldon and Chilvers (2002) similarly comment on a practitioner's ethical obligation to service users, namely to keep up-to-date with research that will facilitate an understanding of individual and social problems, and of interventions to tackle them. The appearance of the use of evidence and research in codes of conduct and ethics in the United States and the United Kingdom attests to this driver. Thus, in the United States the code of ethics calls on social workers to draw on practice-related research findings to inform service delivery (Gambrill, 2001). In the United Kingdom, members of the British Association of Social Workers must uphold its code of ethics (2003) which requires, inter alia, the use of professional knowledge and experience, and engagement in facilitating and developing evaluation and research, to contribute to the development of policy and to the upholding of human rights.

If a difference can be detected, it is in how narrowly or broadly evidence is defined. What is common, however, is the recognition that the availability of knowledge from evidence, research and/or practice will not necessarily ensure ethically informed and morally active practitioners and managers.

2.3 Anti-Oppressive Practice

Social work's mission combines individual change and social justice (IASSW, 2001). For many social workers the right of service users to the most effective services is a clear issue of social justice. There is a burgeoning consensus among social work educators in the United States, for example, that the central mission of social work is the promotion of social justice based on an altruistic belief in human dignity (Brill, 2001; NASW, 2003; Pelton, 2001; Steiner, et al., 1984), which distinguishes the social work profession from other professions and disciplines such as psychology and sociology. The tenets of the social work profession are derived from an emphasis on social and economic justice, the right of equal access to resources, and the right to high quality services and opportunities while eliminating oppression and discrimination in all disadvantaged populations (NASW, 1996, 2003).

Social work researchers express a growing commitment to contributing to social justice through their research (Longress, Scanlon, 2001). The scope and character of social work research includes a concern with social inclusion and social justice, and a focus on social change, with the ability to address major social and economic challenges, such as how to respond to demographic changes, to promote choice but also equity and quality in services provision, and how to manage damaging social phenomena whilst also respecting individual autonomy and human rights (JUC/SWEC, 2006). However, if a difference can be detected in how researchers in the United States and in the United Kingdom, it falls in the degree to which they advocate the use of evidence-based practice as a means to achieve equality for clients in need of services.

Longress and Scanlon (2001) in one study found that social work researchers defined social justice as the responsibility to provide access, resources and opportunities to service users. Gambrill (2001) sees the roots of evidence-based practice partly in the alarming variations in services offered to individuals experiencing the same problems. However, Humphreys and colleagues (2003) are skeptical of the capacity of evidence-based practice, narrowly defined, to challenge inequality and injustice, and to advance an anti-oppressive agenda, arguing that quantitative research is likely to keep the subjects of the research disempowered and marginalized. The criticism is that the positivist tradition does not engage with people's experiences, understanding, identity and explanatory ideas but effectively separates research practice from what and who is being researched. The criticisms are that evidence-based practice:

- Neglects an empowerment agenda since it marginalizes the views and potential contribution of service users and practitioners.
- Maintains the power of research purchasers and researchers in defining agendas, research questions, data collection methodologies and scope of dissemination.

2.4 Accountability

Support for the empirical practice movement partly arose from the growing emphasis on more accountability for social workers and service providers (Blythe, 1992; Reid, 1994). Thus, in the United Kingdom, concerns about the ineffectiveness of practice and the gap between research and practice (Randall, 2002), have led to an emphasis on value for money and on outcomes (Humphreys, et. al, 2003). This driver emanates in part from a distrust of professionals, from a challenge to professionalism based on trust relations and self-regulation (Nutley, 2002). The use of the best available evidence, sifted through external review (Clegg, 2005), provides a transparent rationale for decision-making. Evidence-based practice is seen as protecting service users from interventions that have been shown to be ineffective whilst also saving resources by not wasting time and money on interventions that do not help them. Service users also deserve access to services that are tailored to their unique needs. Evidence-based practice allows for the tailoring of evidence-based interventions to the individualist characteristics of the service user, such as race, culture, and sexuality. In addition, social workers should provide service users with options based on research and present such evidence so that service users may choose their preferred options. Social workers at all levels are obligated to know how to use the available research to provide evidence-based services to all service users.

2.5 Professionalism

Critics of evidence-based practice argue that, especially if narrowly defined, it can undermine professional judgement and discretion in social work (Webb, 2001). Webb (2002) ventures that the preoccupation with evidence-based practice is an attempt to manufacture trust and to legitimate the exercise of professional authority. In addition, Smith (2002) suggests that the demand that practice should be based on evidence reveals an oversimplified and over certain view of what evidence does or might consist of, and of how it should be interpreted and used. However, others argue that evidence-based practice is the best approach to providing promising practice options to service users. Thus, Newman and McNeish (2002) suggest that evidence-based practice, prioritizing interventions that are derived from sound evidence, has an empowering potential for service users and practitioners.

In the United States the social work profession is developing awareness of the necessity for all professions to have measurable practice goals (Brill, 2001). In light of this, a goal directed move toward evidence-based practice furthers the credibility of the social work profession (Cournoyer, Powers, 2002; Howard, et al., 2003; Rosen, et al., 2003), illuminates knowledge gaps (Howard, et al., 2003), and generates evidence that could stand up in court cases and be used to justify funding for services (Brill, 2001). In addition, the emphasis of evidence-based practice in baccalaureate education provides entry-level social workers with the knowledge necessary for practice at the highest levels of competence. Social workers who provide access to such services are essentially acting as agents of social justice.

The challenge with which researchers, whether advocates of evidence-based practice or a more broadly defined knowledge-informed practice, must engage is the complexity of the practice environment. That complexity includes a number of features, namely:

- Skepticism that political and managerial commitment does not exist to alter policy or practice in line with evaluation findings (Humphreys, et al., 2003);
- Concerns that strategies to maximize quality of services evaluate only what is easily measurable;
- Criticism of exclusive focus on outcomes because this may lead to a

neglect of process and indeed assume that outcomes can be defined when what is competent and effective practice is contested between practitioners, managers and service users (Preston-Shoot, 2004).

3. Contested Nature of Evidence and Knowledge

One of the difficult issues for practitioners, managers and social workers in training is the variety of definitions, or rather the divergent parameters used to attempt to categorize evidence-based practice. Indeed, Clegg (2005) makes reference to paradigm wars surrounding the concept, which ignore many realities of practice.

Evidence-based practice has been defined simply as "treatment based on the best available science" (McNeece, Thyer, 2004). Others authors (Cournoyer, Powers, 2002; Dawes, et al., 1999; Howard et al., 2003; Sackett, et al., 1997; Thyer, Wodarski, 1998) have identified that evidence-based practice standards generate the best possible intervention protocols and guide the process of using research in direct practice. Sackett and colleagues (1997: 2) indicate that "evidence-based practice is the conscientious, explicit and judicious use of current best evidence in making decisions about the care of individuals". Cournoyer and Powers (2002: 799) describe evidence-based practice as being "grounded in prior findings that demonstrate empirically that certain actions performed with a particular type of client or client system are likely to produce predictable, beneficial and effective results". In addition, evidence-based practice is grounded in a commitment to ongoing assessment to measure intervention effectiveness (Cournoyer, Powers, 2002). Thus, evidence-based interventions with clients and client systems have scientific merit and should be considered first when choosing interventions (Thyer, Wodarski, 1998).

Thus, the evidence-based practice movement in the United States has been characterized by the recognition of a need to create knowledge and increase the use of research methods to identify interventions that are shown to be effective (Reid, 1994). However, this social work knowledge base, with its array of evidence-based interventions for social workers to utilize when working with service users, accessible in empirically oriented books and evidence-based practice websites (McNeece, Thyer, 2004), has been criticized for being conceptually narrow and theoretically limited (Grey, McDonald, 2006). Humphreys and colleagues (2003) and Frost (2002) see the evidence-based agenda as an oversimplification of some of the problems and complexities of social work practice, driven by a mistrust of the profession, and argue against what they see as a narrow and deterministic positivist approach to what constitutes knowledge. As one example of the oversimplification, both Schneewind (1996) and Parton (2000) point to the assumption explicit in evidence-based approaches that practice aims to accomplish measurable change based on clear objectives within defined timescales, effectively seeing practice as one-dimensional and playing down the unique features of each situation encountered by practitioners. It is this complexity of the practice environment, that contains conflicting imperatives and dilemmas, such as rights versus risks or care versus control, which leads Grey and McDonald (2006) to argue for ethical reasoning skills and Braye and Preston-Shoot (1997) for the use of decision-making frameworks. Both Macgowan (2006) in respect of groupwork, and Frost (2002) suggest that available evidence should be moderated by the circumstances and preferences of service users. Perhaps it is this uniqueness that leads adherents of the concept of evidence-based practice as rooted in using the best scientific knowledge that is available to guide practice interventions, to also require social workers to provide service users with information related to the effectiveness of available interventions while allowing service users to make final intervention and service decisions for themselves (McNeece, Thyer, 2004; Thyer, 2003).

It has been questioned whether the array of evidence-based interventions is as large as assumed (JUC/SWEC, 2006). Certainly in the United Kingdom it has been suggested that the knowledge base to underpin existing services, to support their improvement and to determine their cost-effectiveness is currently inadequate. Indeed, taking groupwork as the example, evaluative research on outcomes of practice and on groupwork's conceptual base is scarce, making it difficult to advance groupwork as the method of choice or to distinguish between the merits of different approaches (Preston-Shoot, 2004).

Nonetheless, this scientific approach to evidence-based practice is contrasted with other methods of evaluation and intervention on which social workers in the United States and the United Kingdom rely for their work with service users, such as the advice of their colleagues and supervisors, personal experiences, theory, practice wisdom and authoritative intervention texts (Howard, et al., 2003; Reilly, et al., 1995). Somewhat disparagingly, these non-scientific approaches to intervention are sometimes viewed as allowing the social work profession to be infused with popular therapeutic methods, which may or may not have been evaluated for effectiveness (Reamer, 1995). This contrasts quite markedly with a position that, when considering evidence of effectiveness, truth is contested, complex and ambiguous, and that evidence alone will not necessarily change behavior (Randall, 2002), in part because decisions are affected by factors and complexities other than evidence (Webb, 2002) and because the relationship between outcomes, context and theory or intervention programs is not straightforward (Smith, 2002). Once again, the debate focuses around the types of knowledge required in order to engage with the complexity of practice.

Thus, Humphreys and colleagues (2003), arguing for knowledge-based practice, refer positively to how the triangulation of research, practitioner wisdom and service user perspectives can inform practice. In groupwork, Macgowan (2006) argues for a broader conceptualization that includes practice evaluation and expert opinion alongside qualitative and quantitative research. In similar vein, in order to understand what works in social work, Pawson and colleagues (2003) argue for the need to pull together different ways of knowing, drawing on people's direct experience alongside empirical and theory-building research. Several other authors argue similarly for broader forms of evidence, such as can be drawn from systematic reviews and analysis that synthesizes data from qualitative, quantitative and non-research sources (Campbell, et al., 2003; Grey, McDonald, 2006; Wallace, et al., 2004). Indeed, Newman and McNeish (2002) warn against the adoption of authoritarian positions on all sides of the debate.

However, what is competent and effective practice is a contested concept. Between service users, practitioners and managers there are different views on how effectiveness is understood and on the outcomes sought from intervention. For example, there is some evidence that practitioners and service users emphasize process and interpersonal skills, and knowledge from research and methods of intervention, whilst managers elevate procedural skills and knowledge of law (Preston-Shoot, 2004). Similarly, Smith (2002) notes that knowing what counts as evidence, what it is evidence of, and how it should be used is more complicated than some adherents of evidence-base practice, politicians and service managers would like to believe. Thus, Clegg (2005) argues for research that provides insight into the worlds of people's experiences. In groupwork, Macgowan (2006) suggests that research on group processes and the external environment is important, whilst Smith (2002) urges researchers to focus on processes as well as outcomes, suggesting that knowledge of the latter is of little use unless what produced them is also understood.

A challenge, therefore, is the degree to which researchers, managers, practitioners and social work educators can embrace diverse forms of evidence, interrogate and synthesize them.

4. Experts by Experience

Discussion about the involvement of service users and carers, as experts by experience, in the generation, analysis and dissemination of evidence, is much more prominent in United Kingdom than in United States literature. In the latter there is, for example, acknowledgement that service user involvement can help in determining what is appropriate and relevant evidence

(Macgowan, 2006). However, in the United Kingdom, inclusion and involvement of experts by experience, to ensure that their perspectives shape service design, planning, development and evaluation, is mandated by central government policy (DH, 1998). Accordingly research organizations, such as the Social Care Institute for Excellence, and regulatory and inspection organizations, such as the General Social Care Council and the Commission for Social Care Inspection, involve experts by experience in their governance and their work.

The argument for inclusion rests not only in social policy but also in the belief that professional power can exclude, patronize and inhibit both the development of new knowledge and understanding and the pursuit of social justice, equal opportunities and partnership (Randall, 2002; Tew, et al., 2004). Phrased positively, the benefits of service user and carer involvement in research to inform policy and service development rest in the challenges, new dimensions or insights and transformatory perspectives such inclusion opens up (Braye, Preston-Shoot, 2005; Tew, et al., 2004), in the added sensitivity that their direct experience brings (Fisher, et al., 2006).

However, if the rationale for inclusion rests on claims about the testing of findings and the scrutiny of research assumptions, and therefore for the greater credibility of research outcomes, there remain barriers to the involvement of experts by experience. Braye and Preston-Shoot (2005) refer to the difficulty of shifting hierarchical relationships (who is seen as expert, what knowledge is privileged (Clegg, 2005), assumptions about people's capabilities, and imposed identities. They refer to the tight time frames within which research commissions are often set, to the danger of skepticism that arises from exploitative research practice, to an outcome driven focus and neglect of processes within projects, and to the imbalance of power between researchers and experts by experience that emanates from the number of opportunities to engage in research projects and to use the findings.

As Fisher and colleagues acknowledge (2006), the nature of involvement, at least in systematic reviews, is still to be worked through. They suggest that experts by experience have important contributions to make in decisions about inclusion criteria, quality of published work, and analytic themes but less obviously in data extraction and synthesis or the technical processes of review.

Indeed, the involvement of experts by experience in systematic reviews has been variable (Braye, Preston-Shoot, 2005), as in other forms of research. There are also different models of involvement (Tew, et al., 2004) where it is possible to distinguish between a participatory approach, which seeks to model different relationships between researchers and service users, and an emancipatory approach, the objective of which is a more fundamental power shift. From an anti-oppressive perspective the challenge is to hand over as much control as possible to experts by experience for the framework of any project, for decision-making about research questions and data collection and analysis, and for use of the findings. This may not be easy in a policy context where the language of demand, customer, citizenship, and inclusion is being used by policy-makers to undermine professional claims to knowledge and authority rather than to liberate the voices of service users and carers. However, social work can occupy the space, which has been opened up by the policy language of service user involvement and inclusion, and push its boundaries.

However, within research projects as well as more generally, expert by experience involvement needs to be embedded. This requires (Braye, Preston-Shoot, 2005) leadership and a commitment to social justice. Time and other resources are necessary for preparation, networking and practicalities, together with an acceptance that there are different ways through which service users and carers can be involved and participate. Groupwork skills to facilitate partnership working will also need to be evident.

5. The Status and Strength of Social Work Research

Social work educators have a responsibility to educate students about evidence-based or, using the broader definition of knowledge (Pawson, et al., 2003), research-informed methods and should equip students with the skills necessary to access relevant research in their area of practice. Social work educators bear the burden of helping students understand the importance of using research-based methods to inform their practice. Social work educators must tie the issue of evidence-based practice to the issue of social justice for all clients.

In the United States masters and doctoral level social work programs seem to be incorporating evidence-based concepts. For example, the prominent George Warren Brown School of Social Work at Washington University in St. Louis has instituted the teaching of evidence-based interventions as the basis for their MSW programs (Howard, et al., 2003). Baccalaureate programs, however, may be lagging behind in teaching evidence-based practice skills to students.

All social work students must be graduated with critical thinking skills that allow them to identify, evaluate and select interventions with demonstrated effectiveness (Zayas, et al., 2003). Evidence-based skills can be infused into the curriculum in a number of ways. One way is to incorporate evidence-based practice skills into course lecture and discussions. Another method is to require students to read and critically analyze relevant articles related to evidence-based practice interventions and research. Finally, students can learn about evidence-based practice through their field practicum experiences. The majority of assignments in all courses should be tied to evidence based practice in a variety of ways.

Students should be taught the value of evidence-based practice, and how to choose appropriate interventions and target them to client's specific needs in both direct practice efforts and policy advocacy (Howard, et al., 2003). Students should also be taught how to adapt evidence-based practice interventions into their area of practice and how to use evidence based approaches to define practice questions. Although many students are resistant to the importance of conducting their own research, the notion of practitioner evaluations of practice must be framed by educators as a social justice obligation to improving services to clients. The importance of social worker self-evaluation over the course of one's career is also an important area that needs to be emphasized in the classroom. Finally, students need to be aware of the evidence-based practice literature resources and how to critique and utilize the conclusions generated by such (Howard, et al., 2003).

The picture in the United Kingdom, with the introduction of the three-year social work degree, is unclear. The academic benchmark for social work degree programs (QAA, 2000) requires that graduates are able to make appropriate use of research when evaluating practice outcomes, can identify and apply research-based concepts that contribute to social work's knowledge base, are able to critically reflect on evidence, and can evaluate outcomes. The national occupational standards in England (TOPSS, 2002) define competence as including the use of principles of best practice and a continuously evaluative approach to practice that draws from current and emerging research. Qualifying social workers must be able to understand, analyze, evaluate and apply approaches to evidence and knowledge-based practice, to research, analyze and review knowledge-based practice, and to monitor and evaluate the effectiveness of a programs of work. Whether the social work degree, which as the qualification for social work practice can be delivered at undergraduate and postgraduate levels, is preparing social workers in training to meet these standards, will only be known once the first graduates emerge into practice from September 2006 onwards. It has been suggested (JUC/SWEC, 2006), however, that there remains too little teaching on research methods on qualifying programs, too little opportunity to develop students' understanding and practice of research methods and ethics in a social work setting, with a corresponding impact on research capacity and capability. It inhibits identification and critical use of research findings in the workplace and impacts on the ability of universities to recruit research-informed practitioners into teaching.

What is clear already, however, is the scarcity of evaluative research on outcomes in social work education and the problematic nature of its current evidence base (Carpenter, 2005). In terms of social work practice, at least in some fields studies do not build on each other, which suggests that researchers could improve their work by conducting systematic literature reviews before embarking on their own research projects (Fisher, et al., 2006). Similarly, whilst the research base might be strong in some fields, such as outcomes for children in the care of public authorities or for older people requiring assistance to remain living in the community, in other fields the evidence base is less secure, such as in groupwork (Preston-Shoot, 2004). In a United States context, Federal guidelines of evidence-based practices are readily available on national web-sites of the National Institute of Mental Health, the National Institute of Drug Abuse, the Office of Juvenile Justice and Delinquency Prevention. Unfortunately, there continues to be a paucity of information available relevant to evidence-based macro-level social work.

Social work research can be distinctive and forceful when it is consistent with social work purposes, that is when it enhances social work theory and knowledge, offers evidence to inform decision-making, and promotes social justice and change (Shaw, forthcoming). Moreover, there are models available for developing research-focused practitioners and organizations (Whitaker, Archer, 1994). Social work education can respond by including in curricula how to select best evidence, how to evaluate practice and how to adapt evidence for practice (Macgowan, 2006). It needs to reinforce research – practice comparability, for instance by highlighting the connections between research and practice surrounding:

- Survey – what do I (need to) know?
- Assessment – where are we now?
- Data collection and analysis – how will I know when I know?
- Recording – how best to capture the essential points and themes?
- Dissemination – with whom will I share this information?

However, the newly developed post-qualifying social work framework in England does not extend as yet to doctoral level and the focus of the M level routes available is on service user groups, such as child care or mental health, without necessarily a distinctive research pathway. There are also concerns about the vitality of social work research in universities (JUC/SWEC, 2006). Although social work has now been recognized as a research discipline by the Economic and Social Research Council, central government spending on social work research is minimal in comparison with what is expended on health care research. There are shortages in the numbers of skilled researchers and in the quality of the skills they possess, especially in basic and advanced quantitative methods, in advanced qualitative methods, and in economic costing. The JUC/SWEC report argues for the need to level up research activity and to develop networks of specialism and excellence.

6. Using Evidence in Practice

It is one thing having a research base; it is entirely another embedding the use of this evidence in policy-making and practice. Writing from a United States context Bellamy and colleagues (2006) argue that the majority of social workers do not appear to draw on research findings to inform their practice. Similarly, Macgowan (2006) found that findings were rarely used in practice and that groupworkers, in his study, were poorly informed. In England Walters and colleagues (2004) found a picture only of pockets of research-aware individuals at different levels within organizations. Sheldon and Chilvers (2002) reached the same conclusion, leading them to state that an essential element of social work is to appraise effectiveness since, otherwise, it is difficult to conceive how practitioners can comment authoritatively about the needs they encounter, the impact of social policies, and about the empowering aspects of practice. The JUC/SWEC report (2006) refers to the generally low value placed on research in social work agencies.

In the United States, McNeece and Thyer (2004) have argued that practitioners engaged in macro-level social work seem much less likely to be concerned with evidence-based practice. In England Walter and colleagues (2004) have suggested that research is less used in the independent care sector. What, then, are the barriers to using research in practice? The following have been noted:

- Inaccessibility, for example of databases of findings (Randall, 2002; Webb, 2002), or lack of visibility and impact (JUC/SWEC, 2006) because of a failure to think through effective dissemination mechanisms or to engage with public debates, for example through use of the media;
- Limited robust evidence of what works in promoting research use. Walter and colleagues (2004) identified three models for developing the use of research in social care but only limited evidence of their effectiveness;
- Lack of organizational support, including the absence of management commitment and resources, training, and the inclusion of research discussions in supervision (Bellamy, et al., 2006; Frost, 2002; Harry, et al., 1997/98; Macgowan, 2006; Randall, 2002; Sheldon, Chilvers, 2002; Webb, 2002);
- Organizational structures militating against continuous learning and application of evidence, and responding to urgent operational priorities (Randall, 2002);
- A perceived training deficit (Bellamy, et al., 2006; JUC/SWEC, 2006; Preston-Shoot, 2004; Sheldon, Chilvers, 2002; Webb, 2002), leading practitioners to doubt their competence to understand, critique and use research findings;

- Volume of research and evaluation materials, with insufficient work done on synthesizing the data and avoiding duplication of research effort (Fisher, et al., 2006; Frost, 2002; Macgowan, 2006; Walter, et al., 2004);
- Linear assumption that assumes ease of transition from research to practice, with insufficient understanding of context and allowance for knowledge produced in practice (Clegg, 2005);
- Research scepticism amongst practitioners (Clegg, 2005) and service users (JUC/SWEC, 2006) who point out that evidence is often used to legitimize a policy rather than to inform it, and/or that research often does not engage with questions raised by experts by experience, practitioners or policy-makers;
- Dissemination under-resourced by research commissioners and researchers, such that insufficient attention is paid to the working environment realities for practitioners and managers, and to communicating the added value that particular findings offer, their compatibility with practice, and the ease with which they might be implemented (Harry, et al., 1997/98; Kolbo, et al., 1997/98);
- Practice not seen as a site of research, partly because of perceived lack of time to engage, reinforced by lack of training and suspicions of researchers and their perceived immunity from being challenged by practice (Bellamy, et al., 2006; Shaw, forthcoming). Practice skills, involving assessment, data collection and analysis, recording and information sharing are not seen as comparable with research skills.

Thus, even where there is a belief in the importance of research for improving practice, what might work in ensuring that research knowledge is used is unclear. Harry and colleagues (1997/98) suggest development days in order to demystify research and evaluation as an exclusive specialism and to promote organizational change. Newman and McNeish (2002) advocate the circulation of reviews of effective interventions and packs of research literature. Bellamy and colleagues (2006) also highlight the use of tool kits and practitioner guidelines, arguing that traditional approaches to dissemination through journal articles and training have been unsuccessful. Several commentators advocate the development of research partnerships and practice research networks (Bellamy, et al., 2006; Macgowan, 2006; Randall, 2002; Webb, 2002; Whitaker, Archer, 1994), such as *Making Research Count* (Humphreys, et al., 2003), through which the comparabilities between research and practice can be reinforced and findings produced in a way that adds to knowledge and understanding, and explores the implications for decision-making and service delivery. Several commentators reinforced the need for strategic commitment from senior managers and the allocation of resources for training and study (Newman, McNeish, 2002; Randall, 2002).

These recommendations and suggestions reflect one or more of the three models identified through a systematic literature review on improving the use of research in social care (Walter, et al., 2004). The research-based practitioner model locates responsibility with the individual practitioner, sees education and training as important in enabling research use, and urges practitioners to change their practice on the basis of research findings. The embedded research model advocates integrating research into policies, procedures, standards and tools, initial responsibility therefore resting with policy-makers and managers. The organizational excellence model sees research utilization as dependent on leadership within and organization of social work organizations, where the culture is learning oriented, underpinned by partnerships with universities and researchers. Whilst the models overlap, research is required into their efficacy.

7. Conclusion

Shaw (forthcoming) argues that social work must retain its distinctiveness by not losing sight of its knowledge of social and political contexts and the uses to which research is put. He advocates knowledge for, and sensitivity to conducting research in emancipatory ways, understanding how inequality shapes research questions and seeking to incorporate the perspectives of all research users. Research use, then, is not just a technical event but is impacted by wider issues of role, purpose, and context. The activity is political since knowledge definition, generation and use brings into sharp focus the interplay and tensions between different parties, with diverse interests, motives and imperatives.

In the United Kingdom, there have been calls for practitioners, managers and policy-makers to be evidence aware and influenced (Nutley, et al., 2002), and to draw on research that is fit for purpose (Boaz, Ashby 2003). Essentially, that means finding the balance in each unique situation between empirical research and multiple methods or different types of knowledge. This links with Grey and McDonald (2006) who call for social workers to be reflective and informed. What this chapter has shown, however, is that how such evidence for practice and for policy is defined is contested and that, even if it can be agreed what knowledge might be useful for policy development and for practice that delivers the aspirations contained in social work's international definition (IASSW, 2001), the capacity of social work researchers to provide it and for social work practitioners to utilize it, remains in doubt.

References

BASW (2003): Code of Ethics for Social Work. Birmingham: British Association of Social Workers.

Bellamy, J.; Bledsoe, S.; Traube, D. (2006): The current state of evidence-based practice in social work: a review of the literature and qualitative analysis of expert interviews, *Journal of Evidence-Based Practice*, 3, 1, 23-48.

Blythe, B. (1992): Evolution and future development of clinical research utilization in agency settings. In Grasso, Epstein (eds.): Research Utilization in the Social Services: Innovations in Practice and Administration (pp. 281-300). New York: Haworth Press.

Boaz, A.; Ashby, D. (2003): Fit for Purpose? Assessing Research Quality for Evidence Based Policy and Practice. Working Paper 11. London: ESRC UK Centre for Evidence Based Policy and Practice.

Braye, S.; Preston-Shoot, M. (1997): Practicing Social Work Law (2nd ed). London: Macmillan.

Braye, S.; Preston-Shoot, M. (2005): Emerging from out of the shadows? Service user and carer involvement in systematic reviews, *Evidence and Policy*, 1, 2, 173-193.

Brill, C. (2001): Looking at the social work profession through the eye of the NASW code of ethics, *Research on Social Work Practice*, 11, 223-234.

Campbell, R.; Pound, P.; Pope, C.; Britten, N.; Morgan, M.; Donovan, J. (2003): Evaluating meta-ethnography: a synthesis of qualitative research on lay experiences of diabetes and diabetes care, *Social Science and Medicine*, 56, 4, 671-684.

Carpenter, J. (2005): Evaluating Outcomes in Social Work Education. London and Dundee: Social Care Institute for Excellence and Scottish Institute for Excellence in Social Work Education.

Clegg, S. (2005): Evidence-based practice in educational research: a critical realist critique of systematic review, *British Journal of Sociology of Education*, 26, 3, 415-428.

Cournoyer, B.; Powers, G. (2002): Evidence-based social work: the quiet revolution continues. In Roberts, Green (eds.): Social Work Desk Reference (pp. 798-807). New York: Oxford.

Dawes, M.; Davies, P.; Gray, A.; Mant, J.; Seers, K.; Snowball, R. (1999): Evidence-Based Practice: A Primer for Health Care Professionals, Edinburgh, UK: Churchill Livingstone.

DH = Department of Health (1998): Modernising Social Services. London: The Stationery Office.

Fisher, M.; Qureshi, H.; Hardyman, W.; Homewood, J. (2006): Using Qualitative Research in Systematic Reviews: Older People's Views of Hospital Discharge. London: Social Care Institute for Excellence.

Frost, N. (2002): A problematic relationship? Evidence and practice in the workplace, *Social Work and Social Sciences Review*, 10, 1, 38-50.

Gambrill, E. (2001): Evaluating the quality of social work education: Options galore. *Journal of Social Work Education*, 37, 418-430.

Grey, M.; McDonald, C. (2006): Pursuing good practice? The limits of evidence-based practice, *Journal of Social Work*, 6, 1, 7-20.

GSCC = The General Social Care Council (2002) Codes of Practice for Social Care Workers and Employers. London: General Social Care Council.

Harry, R.; Hegarty, P.; Lisles, C.; Thurston, R.; Vanstone, M. (1997/98): Research into practice does go: integrating research within programme development, *Groupwork*, 10, 2, 107-125.

Howard, M.; McMillen, C.; Pollio, D. (2003): Teaching evidence-based practice: Toward a new paradigm for social work education, *Research on Social Work Practice*, 13, 2, 234-259.

Humphreys, C.; Berridge, D.; Butler, I.; Ruddick, R. (2003): Making Research Count: the development of 'knowledge-based practice', *Research Policy and Planning*, 21, 1, 11-19.

IASSW = International Association of Schools of Social Work (2001): International Definition of Social Work. Copenhagen: International Association of Schools of Social Work and the International Federation of Social Workers.

JUC/SWEC = The Joint University Council/Social Work Education Committee (2006): A Social Work Research Strategy in Higher Education 2006-2020. London: Social Care Workforce Research Unit, Kings College.

Kolbo, J.; Horn, K.; Randall, E. (1997/98): Implementing a novel groupwork model: application of an innovation – developmental process, *Groupwork*, 10, 1, 41-51.

Longress, J.; Scanlon, E. (2001): Social justice and the research curriculum, *Journal of Social Work Education*, 37, 447-464.

Macgowan, M. (2006): Evidence-based group work: a framework for advancing best practice, *Journal of Evidence-Based Practice*, 3, 1, 1-21.

McNeece, C.; Thyer, B. (2004): Evidence-based practice and social work, *Journal of Evidence-Based Social Work*, 1, 7-25.

NASW = National Association of Social Workers (1996): Code of Ethics. Revised and adopted by the Delegate Assembly of the National Association of Social Workers. Washington, DC: NASW Press.

NASW = National Association of Social Workers (2003): Policy statement on peace and social justice. Social Work Speaks: The National Association of Social Workers Policy Statements 2003-2006 (6th ed.). Washington, DC: NASW Press.

Newman, T.; McNeish, D. (2002): Promoting evidence-based practice in a child care charity: the Barnardo's experience, *Social Work and Social Sciences Review*, 10, 1, 51- 62.

Nutley, S. (2002): Evidence-informed professional practice: overview and rationale, Seminar Paper, 7th November. Reported in Solesbury (2003): Integrating Evidence-Based Practice with Continuing Professional Development: A Seminar Report. London: ESRC UK Centre for Evidence-Based Policy and Practice, Working Paper 15.

Nutley, S.; Davies, H.; Walter, I. (2002): Evidence Based Policy and Practice. Cross Sector Lessons from the UK. Working Paper 9. London: ESRC UK Centre for Evidence Based Policy and Practice.

Pawson, R.; Boaz, A.; Grayson, L.; Long, A.; Barnes, C. (2003): Types and Quality of Knowledge in Social Care. London: Social Care Institute for Excellence.

Pelton, L. (2001): Social justice and social work, *Journal of Social Work Education*, 37, 433-440.

Pollio, D. (2002): The evidence-based group worker, *Social Work with Groups*, 25, 4, 57-70.

Preston-Shoot, M. (2004): Evidence: the final frontier? Star Trek, groupwork and the mission of change, *Groupwork*, 14, 3, 18-43.

QAA = Quality Assurance Agency (2000): Subject Benchmark Statements: Social Policy and Administration and Social Work. Gloucester: The Quality Assurance Agency for Higher Education.

Randall, J. (2002): The practice-research relationship: a case of ambivalent attachment? *Journal of Social Work*, 2, 1, 105-22.

Reamer, F. (1995): Malpractice claims against social workers: First facts, *Social Work*, 40, 595-601.

Reid, W. (1994): The empirical practice movement, *Social Service Review*, 68, 165-184.

Reilly, B.; Hart, A.; Evans, A. (1998): Part II. Evidence-based medicine: A passing fancy or the future of primary care? *Dis.Mon*, 44, 8, 370-399.

Rosen, A.; Proctor, E.; Staudt, M. (2003): Targets of change and intervention in social work: An empirically based prototype for developing practice guidelines, *Research on Social Work Practice,* 13, 2, 208-233.

Sackett, D.; Richardson, W.; Rosenberg, W.; Haynes, R. (1997): Evidence-Based Medicine: How to Practice and Teach EBM. New York: Churchill Livingstone.

Schneewind, E. (1996): Support groups for families of confused elders: issues surrounding open peer-led groups, *Groupwork*, 9, 3, 303-319.

Shaw, I. (forthcoming, 2007): What makes social work research distinctive? *Social Work Education*, 26, 5.

Sheldon, B.; Chilvers, R. (2002): An empirical study of the obstacles to evidence-based practice, *Social Work and Social Sciences Review*, 10, 1, 6-26.

Smith, D. (2002): The limits of positivism revisited, *Social Work and Social Sciences Review*, 10, 1, 27-37.

Steiner, J.; Briggs, T.; Gross, G. (1984): Emerging social work traditions, profession and curriculum policy statements, *Journal of Education for Social Work*, 20, 23-31.

Tew, J.; Gell, C.; Foster, S. (2004): Learning from Experience. Involving Service Users and Carers in Mental Health Education and Training. Nottingham: Mental Health in Higher Education.

Thyer, B. (2003): Evidence based practice in the United States. In Thyer, Kazi (eds.): International Perspectives on Evidence-Based Practice in Social Work (pp. 29-44). Birmingham, UK: Venture Press.

Thyer, B.; Wodarski, J. (1998): Principles of empirical social work practice. In Thyer, Wodarski (eds.): Handbook of Empirical Social Work Practice (pp. 1-21). New York: Wiley.

TOPSS = Training Organisation for the Personal Social Services (2002): The National Occupational Standards for Social Work. Leeds: Training Organisation for the Personal Social Services.

Wallace, A.; Croucher, K.; Quilgars, D.; Baldwin, S. (2004): Meeting the challenge: developing systematic reviewing in social policy, *Policy and Politics*, 32, 4, 455-470.

Walter, I.; Nutley, S.; Percy-Smith, J.; McNeish, D.; Frost, S. (2004): Improving the Use of Research in Social Care Practice. Knowledge Review 7. London: Social Care Institute for Excellence.

Manoj Pardansani

Reconstruction and Redevelopment. The Role of Social Work in Fostering Inter-disciplinary Collaboration, Community Participation and Social Action

1. Introduction

The Indian subcontinent is among the world's most disaster prone areas with a population of more than 1 billion Geological data show that almost 54 percent of the land is vulnerable to earthquakes, 21 percent of the land is vulnerable to drought, 8 percent of the land is vulnerable to cyclones and 5 percent of the land is vulnerable to floods (Sinha, 2001). Gujarat, one of 25 states in India, came into existence in 1960. It is bounded by the Arabian Sea in the West, Pakistan in the north-west, and other Indian states in the east and to the south. The state's territory extends over 122,500 square miles and comprises 18,618 villages and 242 towns. The population of Gujarat is approximately 56 million and nearly two-thirds of its residents live in rural areas. In addition to a relatively high literacy rate (69.9 percent), it is one of the most prosperous states of the country, having a per-capita GDP significantly above the national average (CMIE, 2004; GoG, 2005). Agriculture, dairy-farming, diamond trading, textiles and oil refineries contribute significantly to this rapidly growing economy. However, as is the case with the rest of India, development has not been even. Rural areas in Gujarat suffer from low economic development, lack of opportunities, lower rates of literacy, higher concentrations of poverty, and lack of developmental infrastructure (Cheenath, Solanki, 2001; Prasai, 2002; Sandhu, 2001).

On the western edge of the state, lies an arid, sparsely populated region called the Rann of Kutch. This area is a sensitive border district and has a high defense presence. It is a disaster prone area and has a history of recurrent long-drawn droughts (3 in 5 years), cyclones (2 in last 5 years), and earthquakes (2 in last 50 years). There are negligible industries in the area with few mineral-exploitation-based entities and its approximately 1,26 million residents subsist mainly on farming, sea-salt harvesting and the selling of handicrafts. The last great earthquake in this region was recorded in 1819 and left tremendous devastation and loss in its wake. Since then, there have been minor quakes that have resulted in limited destruction of property and loss of life (Bhargava, 2001; Cheenath, Solanki, 2001; GoG, 2001; Prasai, 2002; Sandhu, 2001; Sinha, 2001). Even though this region has experienced earthquakes in the past and is reportedly in a high-risk region, no measures were taken to create a disaster mitigation or risk management plan for the region.

2. The Earthquake of 2001

On January 26, 2001, an earthquake measuring 7.7 on the Richter scale hit the Kutch region in Gujarat. Nearly 14,000 lives were lost and 167,000 were injured (GoG, 2001; Sandhu, 2001; Singh, 2001). Mansingh (2005) and Relief Web (2005) offer the following estimates:

- Over 10 million residents affected
- 7,633 villages adversely affected while 450 villages were flattened totally
- 4 major towns were devastated
- 400 miles of national highways destroyed
- Nearly 147 telephone exchanges and 82,000 telecommunication lines damages
- 50 percent of the power capacity destroyed
- Water supply to 18 towns and 1,340 villages disrupted
- More than 1,500 schools destroyed
- 215,000 homes were destroyed while another 920,680 were severely damaged
- Over 300 hospitals and community centers were destroyed

Langenbach (2001) and Prasai (2002) report that the quake left most of the social and economic infrastructure of the region destroyed or disrupted. Langenbach (2001: 33) was struck by the immense scale of destruction in cities and villages and the overwhelming prospect for reconstruction and rebuilding. Access conditions to earthquake disaster areas hindered initial relief and rescue operations (Langenbach, 2001). Several first-response centers such as health clinics, hospitals, fire and police stations and community centers had also been badly damaged or destroyed (Prasai, 2002). The local and federal governments, the civil administration and citizens were faced with the prospect of confronting a wide variety of issues ranging from physical reconstruction to livelihood concerns. Planners, relief experts and government officials recognized the need for a comprehensive plan of action that encompassed both short-term and long-term goals. The disaster needed to be seen in the light of specific social, cultural and historical relations that generate every aspect of life in this region. Economic, social and political inequities contributed to the complexity of planning efforts. In the absence of any organizational capacity or infrastructure to deal with a disaster of this magnitude, there was tremendous debate and confusion initially (Bhargava, 2001; Cheenath, Solanki, 2001; GoG, 2001; Prasai, 2002; Sandhu, 2001; Sinha, 2001).

Despite the initial confusion, the response to this disaster occurred simultaneously at several levels with varying degrees of coordination and cooperation. To summarize the relief and rehabilitation efforts, the responses by the governmental agencies and non governmental organizations (NGOs) are categorized separately.

2.1 The Governmental response

The state and federal governments created a Central Relief and Rehabilitation Center in Bhuj, the largest city in the affected region. A Chief Coordinator was appointed to guide and coordinate the relief efforts. The Center established a temporary communications network to organize the rescue operations. Additionally, the following steps were taken:

- The armed forces that were stationed nearest to the earthquake-hit region and had the capacity to respond were pressed into duty. 23,500 army troops and 3000 paramilitary forces along with 48 aircraft and 3 ships were assigned to this operation.
- Crisis Management Control Rooms were established at the state and federal level.
- Teams of government and civil service officials were air-lifted to Bhuj.
- A team of doctors and health professionals were dispatched from public hospitals nationwide to assist in the rescue and relief efforts.
- Emergency supplies such as food, blankets and water-purification kits were assembled for distribution.
- Earth-moving and other life-saving equipment was deployed to the region.
- International agencies, relief organizations and NGOs (non-governmental organizations and agencies) were asked to coordinate their work with the Central Relief and Rehabilitation Center (Bhargava, 2001; Cheenath, Solanki, 2001; GoG, 2001; Mansingh, 2005; Prasai, 2002; Sandhu, 2001; Sinha, 2001).

Recognizing the need for manpower, equipment, skilled and experienced relief/rescue workers, and financial aid, the government requested the assistance of several international relief agencies, as well as the World Bank, United Nations (UN) and the Asian Development Bank (ADB). The process for obtaining visas and work permits for foreign workers was simplified and expedited. In conjunction with the administrative officials on the ground, the World Bank and the Asian Development Bank developed a joint damage and needs assessment. The report estimated that the total asset loss due to the quake amounted to $2.1 billion, while the disruption in economic activity and losses in productivity would cost the government another $2.3 billion in lost revenue. Recognizing the inability of the Indian administration to finance the relief and reconstruction efforts on its own, the ADB and World Bank made available loans amounting to $1.2 billion. The state and federal government covered the rest of the costs themselves with some material assistance from NGOs and international relief agencies, and charitable contributions from individuals and organizations (World Bank, 2002).

The response to the disaster involved a multitude or agencies, departments, organizations, agencies and individuals representing diverse professional disciplines that were required to work in coordination with one another. The relief, reconstruction and rehabilitation efforts were divided into three distinct phases:

Phase I:

The initial focus was on the rescue and recovery efforts. Teams of workers and volunteers were dispatched to the affected towns and villages to assist local community members search for their loved ones. The teams also assisted in the recovery of the deceased and helped bury/cremate their remains immediately in order to prevent any health-related outbreaks. Emergency medical services were provided by mobile crisis teams (GSDMA, 2005; GoG, 2001; Langenbach, 2001; Mansingh, 2005; World Bank, 2002).

Phase II:

The next stage was focused on restoring living conditions and basic infrastructure. These efforts addressed the immediate psycho-social and physical needs of the affected communities. In addition to restoring housing, repairing infrastructure and providing essential needs, this phase needed to concentrate on the issues of sustainable livelihoods and income generation for the affected communities:

- Sustenance: Immediate monetary relief for those affected was approved by the state and federal governments. Plans were made to distribute cash assistance based on family size.
- Livelihoods: Repaired irrigation systems; restored farming and salt-manufacturing processes; re-established handicrafts industry; increased access to credit.
- Housing: Temporary shelters were constructed; debris and rubble removed; damaged homes demolished; housing reconstruction plans using earthquake-resistant construction developed; plans encouraged utiliza-

tion of traditional building materials and modern disaster-related technology.

- Health: Food packets distributed; blankets provided; temporary clinics established to treat the injured; mobile medical teams and counseling centers set up; medicines and health supplies distributed.
- Safety: Damaged dams and irrigation systems repaired; water supply restored; roads, bridges and railways lines repaired; mobile and satellite communications established; temporary power provided by generators.
- Public Facilities: Plans for schools, colleges, universities, hospitals, community centers, power plants, oil refineries, port facilities and businesses to be repaired or rebuilt (GSDMA, 2005; GoG, 2001; Mansingh, 2005; Prasai, 2002; World Bank, 2002).

Phase III:

This phase was the most ambitious and focused on capacity building, community development, risk mitigation and disaster management. Hazard mitigation, community knowledge management and risk transfer were the long-range goals of this phase.

- Risk Mitigation: Risk assessment; mapping, modeling and scientific analyses of geological data; regulatory land-use planning; earthquake-resistant construction manuals and community-based disaster management plans.
- Community Knowledge Management: Facilitate participation of all stakeholders in the planning and management process; increase the technical and knowledge capacity of NGOs, citizens councils, local, state and federal governments; establish a Disaster Management Institute; initiate research on disaster reconstruction and rehabilitation; develop and maintain a web-based, interactive, knowledge management site.
- Risk Transfer: Create a pilot project to provide disaster insurance to those living in the region (GSDMA, 2005; GoG, 2001; Mansingh, 2005; World Bank, 2002).

This phase of the redevelopment and reconstruction plan involved the coordinated and cooperative efforts of the various agencies, organizations, elected representatives, governmental departments, aid officials, social workers, and community leaders in order to create and implement a multi-faceted plan of action for the future. Reconstruction can never erase the loss of natural disasters but it should enable people to restore the life and meaning of their communities. Villages and towns in this region and their unique infra-structure embodied centuries of complex social, spatial and architectural thought. Such places represented a cultural treasure that could not be replaced with simple reconstruction of new homes and buildings. While immediate attention was be paid to restoring basic living conditions and re-establishing local infrastructure, long-term efforts focused on capacity building, disaster management and community empowerment in order to achieve transformation that was long-lasting and meaningful.

2.2 The Non Governmental Organizational Response

As the initial news of the devastation and losses filtered out to the world, several countries such as Mexico, France, Spain, Poland, Switzerland, UK, Russia and Turkey sent "Search and Rescue" teams to aid in recovery efforts. International relief agencies such as the Red Cross, USAID, CARE Canada and Norway, Catholic Relief Services, American India Foundation, OXFAM, and several constituent units of the United Nations (UNDP, UN Disaster Management Program, WHO, UNICEF, WFP, UNFPA, ILO, and FAO) provided relief supplies and assistance. Many Indian expatriates from the USA, Europe, Australia and South Africa established relief funds, organized fund-raising efforts and sent medical teams to the region. Several national NGOs such as SEED, SEWA, Arya Samaj, etc., responded to the crisis as well. However, due to the initial confusion and lack of coordination, many grass-roots efforts and campaigns went unreported. Estimates of the number of NGOs involved in the relief, reconstruction and rehabilitation efforts range from 32 to 180, highlighting the then urgent need for coordination and cooperation. Since the regional NGOs had limited financial and material resources that were inadequate to meet the diverse needs of this natural disaster, they utilized the services of volunteers and social work, civil service, and public health students to operate their programs. Additionally, NGOs dispatched a cadre or peer counselors and workers with previous disaster experience to work with the affected communities. This ensured prompt needs assessments and delivery of relief services in remote regions, and facilitated communication between communities and relief agencies.

One of the few locally established NGOs from the region, the Kutch Navnirman Abhiyan (KNA) also sprung into action. The KNN is a collaborative of 22 Kutch based NGOs who came together following the 1998 cyclone to coordinate the relief and rehabilitation work. Since then the group has stayed together to forge people-centered development of the district. The group works upon various issues spanning from women, handicraft, sustainable ecology, livelihoods, water conservation, industrialization, health and education. The KNN set up 2 key supply logistics coordination depots and 16 sub-depots to service remote and the most affected villages. It also set up a control room to coordinate efforts of 200 NGOs for effective canalization of relief materials and resources. A "NGO desk" was set up at the Central Relief and Rehabilitation Center and at the Bhuj airport. By the tenth day of the disaster, preliminary survey of 360 villages had been completed. Volunteers were drawn from diverse technical fields ranging from engineers, planners, social workers, database experts, communication designers, medical experts, rehabilitation experts and others. Their cumulative experience and expertise was assimilated, shared extensively and relayed to the policy level body of the district and the state administration. Since the disaster, several newly established NGOs have continued rehabilitative efforts in the areas of reconstruction technology (Navsarjan), promotion of local crafts (Kala Rakshan), women's empowerment (Kutch Mahila Vikas Sangathan), post-traumatic counseling (Sneh Samudaya), disaster risk management, crisis response training and economic development (Bhargava, 2001; GoG, 2001; Mansingh, 2005).

3. The Rationale for Community Participation and Involvement

Large-scale disasters, such as the Gujarat earthquake, reduce the "social capital" of a community. Social capital is a measure of the resilience of a community to withstand crises and the level of interconnectedness among members (Pardasani, 2006). It is not just the sum of institutions which underpin a society, but the "glue that holds them together" (World Bank, 1999). Trust, mutual understanding, shared values and behaviors that bind human networks and communities together are the hallmarks of social capital (Cohen, Prusak, 2001). A large-scale disaster not only destroys lives but lays waste to the delicate social fabric that binds a community. The earthquake not only destroyed physical manifestations of a community (such as homes, schools, hospitals, governing infrastructure, etc.), it also killed community members, scattered survivors and severed social relationships. Bonds that had been built through generations, traditional ways of life, and means of maintaining cultural ties were also threatened or destroyed. This hampers a community's ability to respond to a crisis and begin the process of rebuilding. On the other hand, rebuilding only physical structures without paying attention to the human relationships, community networks and social norms that have governed that community would be meaningless to the survivors. Thus, it is imperative that reconstruction and rebuilding efforts focus on rebuilding a community physically and psychologically.

Proponents of the relevance of social capital to community building emphasize the importance of including the broadest cross-section of community members in any decision-making process (Bourdieu, 1983; Coleman, 1988; Jacobs, 1961; Putnam, 1995). Civic engagement and social connectedness are vital to the overall health and well-being of communities, as well as it allows for greater attention and resources to be directed at the most pressing needs (Homan, 2005: 40). Frequently the individuals hardest hit by a disaster are those that have a limited or no access to resources. These individuals will receive emergency supplies and rations of food; however, when it comes to rebuilding sustainable communities, their voices may not be included. In many under-developed countries, the poorest communities have limited representation in governing bodies and may not have adequate supports to press their case. The involvement of all affected persons and communities is the key to the success of any sustainable, long-term rehabilitation and risk mitigation plan (Andharia, 2002; Coghlan, 1998; McCamish, 1998; Tribe, 2004). If this is not achieved, the social capital or resilience of a community to respond to future challenges is severely compromised.

The post-disaster plans envisioned a model of reconstruction that would be environmentally, socially and culturally significant for the survivors through the process of inter-disciplinary collaborations. The Government of Gujarat's espoused vision for reconstruction was "to go beyond reconstruction and make Gujarat economically vibrant, agriculturally and industrially competitive with improved standards of living and with a capacity to mitigate and manage future disasters" (Mansingh, 2005). Furthermore, the government believed that the mandate for rehabilitation went beyond the immediate priorities and embodied the pursuit of broader social and economic issues impinging on the household, community development and empowerment (Prasai, 2002). Planners envisioned a holistic reconstruction and rehabilitation plan that included capacity building and community empowerment as integral components. They believed that the initial participation and eventual leadership of community members was essential to ensuring sustainable and meaningful redevelopment and rehabilitation. Prasai (2002: 8) argues that any community development program in the aftermath of a disaster must include programs that strategically and directly create qualitative changes in the lives of the people. Evaluations of disaster relief efforts in other countries such as India and Japan (in the aftermath of earthquakes or natural disasters) have shown that inclusion of affected individuals in the planning and implementation of rebuilding efforts ensures their overall success and contributes to a higher quality of life for the residents (Mansingh, 2005; Konishi, 2005). Thus, culturally appropriate redevelopment that is rooted in local building and craft traditions is essential because these projects enable people to maintain and extend inhabitation patterns, uniting new communities with the unique history from which they've grown. Such efforts also provide unique opportunities to redress social or historical inequities and promote cultural transformation (Pardasani, 2006).

While researchers agree that participation of affected communities is imperative, there is some disagreement on the extent of the participation and the stages of their inclusion in decision making (Buckle, Marsh, 2002; Coghlan,

1998; McCamish, 1998; McDowell, 2002; Tribe, 2004). Some argue that the involvement of communities begins with the identification of pressing needs, and that they should be the driving and deciding forces in the process. Others feel that the expert role in rebuilding cannot be discounted and these efforts must not be driven by local community members alone. Some experts believe that community participation at all levels may be a hindrance, and that community voices should be included in specific endeavors only. They argue that community members may be unwilling to accept changes even if it is ultimately beneficial to them and may end up delaying the process of building sustainable communities. This author believes that local community members may have a greater insight into their own communal lives and their inherent perceptions and beliefs should be regarded as strengths and coping mechanisms evolving from environmental influences. When these inherent strengths and wisdom are harnessed through community participation, efforts at reconstruction will be meaningful and sustainable. A community development model that includes local participation in decision making promotes the recognition, acquisition, maturation and connection of community assets and produces self-reliant, self-sustaining and empowered communities (Delgado, 2000; Homan, 2005; Kramer, Specht, 1983). Thus, any process of rebuilding has to develop a framework for development and decision making with established guidelines for local participation.

In order to ensure peoples' participation in the reconstruction and rehabilitation plan, the following guidelines were established by the Relief and Rehabilitation Center:

- All decisions regarding location, relocation and construction based on formal involvement of the affected people;
- all village and town plans decided by their respective local councils;
- relocation decisions left to the affected people;
- women to receive equal ownership in reconstructed housing;
- people's awareness for participation created through planned media campaigns;
- training provided for disaster management and risk mitigation;
- formal grievance redressal mechanism set up at every operational level with the appointment of Ombudsmen (Mansingh, 2005).

Although the plan issued by the Gujarat government had committed to consultation with local communities in any long-term planning initiatives, poorer, marginalized communities have sometimes been neglected in favor of economically privileged groups (Prasai, 2002). If local communities and affected individuals are not involved in this process, there may be a disconnection between organizationally identified needs and those outlined by local communities and NGOs. Thus, it is imperative for local communities to be involved in the needs assessment process, and in the subsequent and design and implementation of the redevelopment efforts. The role of community members and local NGOs in the initial needs assessments was also limited due to the lack of coordination among various governmental and non governmental entities, thus depriving the beneficiaries of the relief and rehabilitation efforts from identifying their own perceived needs. This negatively hindered the impact of rehabilitation plans in addressing the comprehensive needs of the affected communities.

One of the challenges of increasing community involvement and participation is the lack of knowledge, awareness, capacity and experience among the affected populations. Another challenge faced by planners is the immense socio-economic and educational inequities that exist in this region. In order to seek and promote community involvement, community members and affected citizens first need to be educated, trained and empowered to participate in local planning and decision-making processes. If individuals feel powerless, have traditionally been disconnected from the electoral process or are not integrated into the social and economic fiber of the region (such as women, religious minorities, lower-castes and impoverished rural communities), the community participation process is unlikely to be fair or representative (Pardasani, 2006). Individuals and communities need to be empowered to engage in the political process and negotiate administrative systems in order to guide the transformational processes (Delgado, 2000; Kettner, Moroney, Martin, 2004; Pardasani, 2005). Empowerment is the process of by which individuals and/or groups derive power to make decisions for themselves or affect decision-making processes that impact their lives (Gutierrez, 1990). Individual empowerment leads to increased group consciousness and group empowerment in turn, enhances the functioning of its individual members (Gutierrez, 1995; Stevens, 1998). The process of community empowerment involves allowing members to identify and define their own needs, increasing the skills of its members to advocate for their needs, connecting members with needed resources (material and non material), helping members negotiate complex bureaucratic and political systems, ensuring the equal and fair participation of all members, and increasing the capacity of members to be self-reliant (Pardasani, 2006). Thus, Indian reconstruction experts needed to reach out to the vast population affected by the earthquake, convince them to participate in the planning process, train community members in community planning processes, identify and promote local leadership, navigate diverse and often competing concerns and needs, and coordinate the implementation efforts of a vast network of governmental agencies, NGOs and relief agencies. While social workers were involved in every stage of the planning and implementation to some extent, it was at this crucial stage that their role in community education, outreach, empowerment and service coordination was vital to the eventual success of any plan.

4. The Role of Social Work

Social work has played a prominent role in community development and empowerment efforts worldwide (Earles, Lynn, 2005; Gray, Fook, 2004; Mbakogu, 2004; Mok, 2005; Pardasani, 2005; Schmid, Salman, 2005). The significance of community organization and empowerment has been recognized both nationally and internationally, especially in under-developed countries in Asia and Africa (Abram, Slosar, Walls, 2005; Gray, Fook, 2004; Mbakogu, 2005; Mok, 2005; Pardasani, 2005). Social workers have adapted or developed unique strategies for promoting community involvement and participation among the disempowered and disengaged, thereby helping individuals fight for social justice and human dignity. Chief components of community social work practice models have been identified as consciousness raising, education, outreach, grassroots organizing and participatory decision making (Abram, Slosar, Walls, 2005; Gray, Wolfer, Maas, 2005; Speer, Zippay, 2005). Advocates for community organization have highlighted the utilization of community empowerment models in meeting a diverse array of practice goals such as health promotion (Kelley, 2005; Miller, Shinn, 2005), establishment of care trusts (Fawcett, South, 2005), reduction of poverty (Baker, 2005; Grobler, 2005), child and youth welfare (Mannes, Roehlkepartain, Benson, 2005; Murray, Belenko, 2005), women's empowerment (Hammer, 2005; Pardasani, 2005), self-help groups (Mok, 2005), and community development (Daugherty, 2005; Earles, Lynn, 2005; Mbakogu, 2004; Schmid, Halman, 2005).

The challenges for social workers operating in under-developed countries are several. On one hand, they are faced with community members who are unfamiliar with social or political advocacy methods and organization tactics, or are uninterested in any empowerment efforts. On the other hand, community members are frequently disenfranchised and focused on meeting their daily survival needs rather than striving for systemic change. Many organizational efforts fail due to the devaluation of indigenous practices and knowledge in change efforts (Mbakogu, 2005; Miller, Shinn, 2005), incongruence of values between programs and host communities (Miller, Shinn, 2005), conflicting needs (Fawcett, South, 2005), economic inequity between the helpers and the beneficiaries (Larrison, Hardey-Ives, 2005), lack of knowledge and information about the communities being assisted (Daugherty, 2005; Gray, Fook, 2004; Grobler, 2005), failure of previous developmental programs (Larrison, Hardey-Ives, 2005; Miller, Shinn, 2005), and inadequate communication strategies (Mbakogu, 2005). An additional impediment in disaster-affected communities is the plethora of governmental departments, relief agencies and NGOs operating simultaneously in an uncoordinated manner. Evaluators of relief and reconstruction efforts in Gujarat noted that although the Central Relief and Rehabilitation Center made valiant efforts to coordinate the work of over 84 NGOs, 32 international agencies and a host of governmental units, many resources were initially wasted due to service duplication and lack of cooperation between the entities.

The agencies and organizations operating in India represented a diverse range of practice disciplines, field experiences, values and service goals. Whiteside (2004: 381) notes that frequently individual disciplines work in silos, and fail to recognize that they have more in common than they believe. Proponents of international development and rehabilitation efforts have called for inter-disciplinary and transdisciplinary models that utilize collaboration, dialogue, community participation in decision-making, pooling of resources, comprehensive planning and coordinated implementation. Such efforts, experts believe, will ensure that scarce resources are used effectively and efficiently. Furthermore, any future disaster management or risk mitigation plan cannot be sustainable unless the changes are meaningful to the communities involved and has them convinced of its utility and relevance to their welfare. Once again, social work already has a wealth of knowledge and experience in developing collaborative models or negotiating through complex, multi-layered systems.

In the initial phases of the relief operations, social workers were instrumental in providing counseling and other direct services to those whose lives were impacted by the earthquake. They collaborated in the conduct of needs assessments, assisted the survivors in obtaining shelter, financial and material support, and provided a vital link between remote communities and relief institutions. Social workers also comprised a significant portion of the staff of many NGOs that operated in this region. But social workers have a more important role to play in the later phases of rehabilitation. As in most redevelopment efforts, the various participating entities usually depart once their initial work plan is completed. As Prasai (2002) reports, most NGOs that were involved in the initial relief and recovery efforts have departed, leaving behind few agencies and organizations that are engaged in continued community development and skills-building. Thus, community members and leaders are left with the responsibility for sustaining the redevelopment and transformation processes. Therefore, it is essential for creating an infrastructure that helps develop/increase the capacity within communities to sustain and support development. This is an arena where social workers excel. Social workers can educate, train and help build the capacity of affected communities and local NGOs to play a significant role in the implementation of the redevelopment and rehabilitation plans. Community practitioners can encourage greater participation of disenfranchised and oppressed groups in village and town councils, and highlight any issues of injustice or unfairness. They can help various organizations and governmental entities work in a coordinated manner, and function as independent watchdogs to ensure transparency and accountability at all levels. Social work has already had a significant impact on the lives of those affected by the earthquake and has gained credibility and trust among community members, government officials and international funding agencies. Their role in fostering inter-disciplinary collaboration and community empowerment has been recognized and lauded.

The inter-disciplinary process of reconstruction and rehabilitation has already witnessed major accomplishments. Infrastructure has been repaired and modernized, coordinated disaster management systems and first-response mechanisms have been established (GSDMA, 2005), risk mitigation programs such as housing insurance and geological units have been developed, income generation opportunities have been created, economic systems re-established, local involvement in planning has been codified, and the lives of those impacted have been improved significantly (Mansingh, 2005; Prasai, 2002). However, both public and private evaluations of rehabilitation efforts stress the importance of continued community development and empowerment efforts to ensure that the changes achieved so far are sustained, as well as greater benefits are realized to the people of Gujarat for years to come.

5. Implications for Social Workers and Community Development Practitioners

The recovery and rehabilitation efforts in India provide a model for transdisciplinary collaboration and coordination. Despite some initial kinks, this model can be adapted in communities worldwide that are impacted by natural or man-made disasters such as the devastating Asian Tsunami. The model emphasizes cooperation and coordination in planning and implementation efforts. Private and public entities such as relief agencies, state and federal governments, local businesses, banks, schools and universities, hospitals, city and village councils, as well as ordinary citizens worked collaboratively to ensure the success of reconstruction and rehabilitation strategies. Some of the lessons learned from this disaster management plan can be summarized as follows:

- Utilizing peers/volunteers/citizens with disaster experience to supplement professional workers and facilitate greater communication.
- Recruiting social work and public health students as counselors.
- Working with educational institutions to guide vocational education, retraining, and general education efforts.
- Working with business schools, economic professionals, banks and fiscal agencies to guide the management of fiscal aid and employment generation efforts (loans, promotion of local artisans/handicrafts, etc.).

- Respect for local skills, knowledge and culture through the recruitment, involvement and participation of local tradesmen, businesses and community leaders in the reconstruction plans. Training traditional workers in modern technologies for rebuilding.
- Community involvement and participation in planning and implementation efforts. Empowering people and communities to manage continued needs assessments, reconstruction and recovery after the various agencies, organizations and officials have completed their initial phase of work.
- Utilize social workers to educate, train, empower and enhance the capacity of communities and NGOs to play a significant role in decision-making.
- Assist/educate communities in crisis management and risk mitigation. Mandatory housing insurance for all reconstructed neighborhoods and the establishment of the GSDMA, a central coordinating agency for comprehensive and efficient national disaster response.
- Help facilitate dialogue between government, elected representatives and reconstruction agencies and affected communities.
- Recognize the opportunity for social/cultural transformation (women, discriminated groups, etc) through inter-disciplinary planning and organization. Women and some lower-caste groups have benefited from becoming property owners through reconstruction, gaining access to greater employment opportunities, as well as from increased participation in the decision making processes.

Recovery, reconstruction and rehabilitation in the aftermath of a natural disaster is a complex, multi-layered process that is aided by collaboration and participatory decision making. Large scale devastation such as the one experienced in Gujarat has significant short-term, as well as long-term repercussions. While immediate attention must be paid to restoring basic living conditions and re-establishing local infra-structure, long-term efforts must focus on capacity building, increasing community resilience, disaster management and community empowerment. This case example proves only with the participation of local communities and people in the rehabilitation and redevelopment process can a successful model of sustainable and meaningful redevelopment be realized. Most importantly this case study underscores the relevance of collaborative interdisciplinary models in community development and disaster rehabilitation efforts.

References

Abram, F. Y.; Slosar, J. A.; Walls, R. (2005). Reverse mission: A model for international social work education and transformative intra-national practice. *International Social Work*, 48, 2, 161-176.

Affolter, F. (2004). On the absence of a "socio-emotional enablement" discourse component in international socio-economic development thought. *Scandinavian Journal of Caring Sciences*, 18, 4, 424-436.

Andharia, J. (2002). Institutionalizing community participation: The challenge in disaster management. *The Indiana Journal of Social Work*, 63, 2, 236-242.

Baker Collins, S. (2005). An understanding of poverty from those who are poor. *Action Research*, 3(1), 9-31.

Bhargava, A. (2001). Experience of NGOs: Lessons learned from Gujarat Earthquake. World Health Organization: Regional Office for Southeast Asia. www.whosea.org, retrieved November 1, 2005.

Bourdieu, P. (1983). Forms of capital. In Richards (ed.), Handbook of Theory and Research for the Sociology of Education (pp. 241-258). New York: Greenwood Press.

Buckle, P.; Marsh, G. (2002). Local assessment of disaster vulnerability and resilience: Reframing risk. Conference Paper: International Sociological Association (ISA) Conference, July 7-13, 2002, Brisbane, Australia.

Center for Monitoring the Indian Economy (2004). The Economy of Gujarat, Regional Monitoring Service. www.cmie.com. retrieved December 1, 2005.

Cheenath, J.; Solanki, D. (2001). Practical experiences of post-disaster management in Gujarat: Lessons learned from Gujarat Earthquake. World Health Organization: Regional Office for Southeast Asia. www.whosea.org, retrieved November 1, 2005.

Chenoweth, L. (2004). Organizing for community controlled development: Renewing civil society. *Australian Social Work*, 57, 4, 417-419.

Coghlan, A. (1998). Post-disaster redevelopment. Conference Paper, International Sociological Association (ISA), July 26-30, 2002, Montreal, Quebec.

Cohen, D.; Prusak, L. (2001). In good company: How social capital makes organizations work. Boston, MA: Harvard Business School.

Coleman, J. C. (1988). Social capital in the creation of human capital. *American Journal of Sociology*, 94, 95-120.

Delgado, M. (2000). Community social work practice in an urban context: The potential of a capacity enhancement perspective. New York: Oxford University Press.

Daugherty, R. (2005). Rural social work: Building and sustaining community assets. *Journal of Community Practice*, 13, 2, 132-135.

Earles, W.; Lynn, R. (2005). A space in between: A case study of the Mareeba community response group. *Rural Society*, 15, 1, 77-91.

Fawcett, B.; South, J. (2005). Community involvement and primary care trusts: The case for social entrepreneurship. *Critical Public Health*, 15, 2, 191-204.

GoG = Government of Gujarat (2005). Demographics of Gujarat. www.gujarat-india.com, retrieved December 1, 2005.

GoG = Government of Gujarat (2001). Sustainable Recovery and Vulnerability Reduction: Conference Report. www.undp.org.in, retrieved November 1, 2005.
Gray, K. A.; Wolfer, T. A.; Maas, C. (2005). The decision case method: Teaching and
  training for grassroots community organizing. *Journal of Community Practice*,
  13, 1, 105-120.
Gray, M.; Fook, J. (2004). The quest for a universal social work: Some issues and
  implications. *Social Work Education*, 23, 5, 625-644.
Gray, I.; Stehlik, D.; Lawrence, G.; Bulis, H. (1998). Community, communion and
  drought in rural Australia. *Journal of the Community Development Society*, 29, 1,
  23-37.
Grobler, M. E. (2005). *Community development in a urban third world context.* Dissertation Abstracts International, *The Humanities and Social Sciences*, 6, 10,
  3991-A.
GSDMA = Gujarat State Disaster Management Authority (2005). Gujarat Emergency
  Earthquake Reconstruction Project: Summary Progress Report, Government of
  Gujarat, May, 2005.
Gutierrez, L. M. (1990). Working with women of color: An empowerment perspec-
  tive. *Social Work*, 35, 2, 149-153.
Gutierrez, L. M. (1995). Understanding the empowerment process: Does conscious-
  ness make a difference? *Social Work Research*, 19, 4, 229-237.
Hammer, D. (2005). El Salvador: An international field experience. *The New Social
  Worker*, 12, 1, 13-15.
Hardina, D. (2004). Guidelines for ethical practice in community organization. *Social
  work*, 49, 4, 595-604.
Homan, M. S. (2005). Promoting Community Change: Making it happen in the real
  World (3rd ed.). Belmont. CA: Wordsworth/Thompson Learning.
Jacobs, J. (1961). The death and life of great American cities. New York: Random
  House.
Kelley, M. A. (2005). Community-based participatory research for health. *Journal of
  Community Practice*, 13, 1, 141-145.
Kettner, P. M.; Moroney, R. M.; Martin, L. L. (2004). Designing and managing pro-
  grams: An effectiveness-based approach (2nd ed.). Thousand Oaks, CA: Sage
  Publications.
Konishi, Y. (2005). Creative reconstruction following the great Hanshin-Awaji earth-
  quake. Coordination Meeting on Rehabilitation and Reconstruction Assistance to
  Tsunami-Affected Countries", Manila, Philippines, March 18, 2005.
Kramer, R.; Specht, H. (1983). Readings in community organization practice (3rd ed.).
  Englewood Cliffs, NJ: Prentice Hall.
Langenbach, R. (2001). A rich heritage lost: The Bhuj, India, earthquake. *Cultural
  Resource Management*, 24, 8, 33-34.
Larrison, C. R.; Hadley-Ives, E. (2004). Examining the relationship between commu-
  nity residents' economic status and the outcomes of community development
  programs. *Journal of Sociology and Social Welfare*, 31, 4, 37-57.
Mannes, M.; Roehlkepartain, E. C.; Benson, P. L. (2005). Unleashing the power of
  community to strengthen the well-being of children, youth, and families: An as-
  set-building approach. *Child welfare*, 84, 2, 233-250.
Mansingh, L. (2005). Key lessons from the rehabilitation and reconstruction efforts
  following the Gujarat earthquake. Coordination Meeting on Rehabilitation and

Reconstruction Assistance to Tsunami-Affected Countries, Manila, Philippines, March 18, 2005.

Mbakogu, I. A. (2004). Forging a link between indigenous communication, effective community social work practice and national development. *Studies of Tribes and Tribals,* 2, 2, 89-95.

McCamish, E. (1998). The role of community recovery workers in development following a disaster. Conference Paper, International Sociological Association (ISA), July 26-30, 2002, Montreal, Quebec.

McDowell, C. (2002). Involuntary resettlement, impoverishment risks and sustainable livelihoods. *Australian Journal of Disaster and Trauma Studies,* 6, 2, 1174-1187.

Miller, R. L.; Shinn, M. (2005). Learning from communities: Overcoming difficulties in dissemination of prevention and promotion efforts. *American Journal of Community Psychology,* 35, 3-4, 169-183.

Mok, B. (2005). Organizing self-help groups for empowerment and social change: Findings and insights from an empirical study in Hong Kong. *Journal of Community Practice,* 13, 1, 49-67.

Murray, L. F.; Belenko, S. (2005). CASASTART: A community-based, school-centered intervention for high-risk youth. *Substance use & misuse,* 40, 7, 913-933.

Pardasani, M. P. (2005). A context-specific community practice model of women's empowerment: Lessons learned in rural India. *Journal of Community Practice,* 13, 1, 87-103.

Pardasani, M. P. (2006). Tsunami reconstruction and redevelopment in the Maldives: A case study of community participation and social action. *Disaster Prevention and Management,* 15, 1, 79-91.

Prasai, S. (2002). Gujarat Earthquake: Planning concerns in post-disaster development. Report to the Mid-America Earthquake Center, University of Illinois at Urbana-Champaign, August 2002.

Putnam, R. D. (1995). Bowling alone: America's declining social capital. *Journal of Democracy,* 6, 1, 65-78.

Sandhu, G. S. (2001). Practical problems in the management of mass casualties during the Gujarat earthquake: Lessons learned from Gujarat Earthquake. World Health Organization: Regional Office for Southeast Asia. www.whosea.org, retrieved November 1, 2005.

Schmid, H.; Salman, H. (2005). Citizens' perceptions of the neighborhood council: The case of Arab neighborhoods in east Jerusalem. *Journal of Community Practice,* 13, 2, 61-75.

Sinha, A. (2001). Earthquake in Gujarat: Lessons learned from Gujarat Earthquake. World Health Organization: Regional Office for Southeast Asia. www.whosea.org, retrieved November 1, 2005.

Stevens, J. W. (1998). A question of values in social work practice: Working with the strengths of black adolescent females. *Families in Society,* May-June 1998, 288-296.

Speer, P. W.; Zippay, A. (2005). Participatory decision-making among community coalitions: An analysis of task group meetings. *Administration in Social Work,* 29, 3, 61-77.

Tribe, R. (2004). Internally displaced Sri Lankan war widows: The women's empowerment program. In Miller, Rasco (eds.), The Mental Health of Refugees: Eco-

Manoj Pardansani

logical Approaches to Healing and Adaptation (pp. 161-186). Mahwah, NJ: Lawrence Erlbaum Associates.

Ungar, M.; Manuel, S.; Mealey, S.; Thomas, G.; Campbell, C. (2004). A study of community guides: Lessons for professionals practicing with and in communities. *Social work,* 49, 4, 550-561.

Whiteside, M. (2004). The challenge of interdisciplinary collaboration in addressing the social determinants. *Australian Social Work,* 57, 4, 381-393.

World Bank (2002). Gujarat Earthquake- One year later. World Bank/Asian Development Bank Gujarat Earthquake Assessment. www.wbln1018.worldbank.org/SAR/, retrieved November 1, 2005.

Cultural Issues in International Social Work

Even at a national level, social workers and scholars conducting research are coming into contact with different cultures that must be respected. Culture in this sense is not limited to ethnicity but also includes gender, religion, class, age, as well as differences between social work and related professions. From an international perspective, this raises questions as to whether there is a common social work base, and whether there is a risk of imposing or colonizing different ways of life. In the introductory chapter, it was mentioned that social work as a discipline encompasses broad ideological principles that are of universal application. Direct social work practice, however, varies from society to society, depending on cultural variables such as politics, the economy, culture, and religion. It is also worth repeating that social work has traditionally been seen as a local, culture-bound activity. Thus, this chapter will take a closer look at social work in terms of cultural issues.

The first contribution in this part of the book is from Joshua Miller and Susan Donner, who present a model of social identity development. They argue that social identities shape both our idea of who we are in the world as well as our sense of the other. Henry Tajfel's definition of social identity is taken as a starting point, although other models and concepts of social identity are referred to, such as racial and ethnic identity. The authors then apply these frameworks to aid understanding of inter-group dynamics, as well as teaching, counseling, and other contexts that rely on interpersonal interaction. Before presenting their model, the authors introduce six basic assumptions to give a broader idea of their approach to social identity, contending that social identity development is a process of phases not stages, that it is highly subjective, that it consists of different dimensions throughout the lifespan, and that it is influenced by environmental factors. Each of these assumptions will be discussed in detail. To illustrate the complexity of their social identity model, they provide an example of a hypothetical student coping with a classroom dynamic.

The second contribution by Otrude N. Moyo focuses on the diversity of cultural conceptions of parenting and the difficulties that African immigrants experience in their new living conditions in the United States. African immigrants are often perceived as "bad" parents because of their cultural otherness compared with the universal ideas of presumed "good" parenting. Immigrants often encounter human service providers wanting to take on the role of omnipotent experts, following dominant deficit views, and aiming to "americanize" the "newcomers" by criticizing and changing their ways of parenting by implicit or explicit comparison to the model or styles of American middle-class parenting. As Moyo points out, even the literature about the parenting styles of African migrants tends to label their parenting as both too authoritative and collectivist. In conjunction with several partners she carried out an ethnographic study of the living conditions of African immigrants in the US state of Maine. The results of her study provide interesting insights into the impact of often dire and conflicting socio-economical influences on parenting abilities, and typical difficulties in the interaction between immigrants and service providers. The different views on roles, rights and responsibilities in parenting, and the lack of culturally sensitive communication and reflection, were striking themes arising from her interviews. She points out that, despite the different views about parenting, reproducing prejudices about culturally major or minor conceptions of responsible parenting should be avoided. Given the background of increasing migration and international interdependence, human services should realize the international dimensions of their work and offer suitable programs. Human services should thereby not follow a "one size fits all" philosophy, but instead become culturally sensitive by embracing diversity without neglecting legitimate criticism, where necessary.

In the last contribution in this part of the book, Christian Spatscheck focuses on how young people create their youth cultures within an ongoing dialectic of public control and youth cultural emancipation. He is thereby dealing with a classical yet still vital and pressing topic in social work theory and practice. In his contribution, he summarizes the leading theoretical approaches to the interpretation of socio-cultural dimensions of youth cultures from a Western European perspective, from the post-war era until present times. He concludes that, when social workers are working with young people, they should be aware of the socio-cultural mechanisms that emerge within the dialectic of public control and emancipation of youth cultures.

Joshua Miller/Susan Donner

The Complexity of Multidimensional Social Identity Development

1. Introduction

Social identities profoundly shape both our idea of who we are in the world as well as our sense of the other. The way in which an individual or collective of individuals who share salient aspects of their social identity experience a common notion of self and other has implications for psychological, social, inter and intra group relations in macro and micro contexts, and thus social identities and the related politics of social identity matter. Though, of course, the phenomena of social identities is not new and have likely impacted human behavior as long as difference has existed, the study and investigation of social identity as a field is fairly recent. The work of Tajfel (1981) and Tajfel and Turner (1986) in the late 1970's and 80's provided impetus for this burgeoning field of study. This chapter aims to contribute to the growing appreciation of the complexity of social identity.

Tajfel (1981: 255) defined social identity as "that part of an individual's self concept that derives from his knowledge of membership in a social group (or groups) together with the value and emotional significance attached to that membership." This definition stresses both the sense of membership and belonging, as well as the accompanying feelings and values. Other approaches focus not on how the individual feels about his or her identity, but rather on the socio-cultural-historical contexts, as well as myths, discourses and inter-group relationships, which shape social identities (Jussim, Ashmore, Wilder, 2001). Both of these definitions are particularly concerned with a person's sense of self and affiliations in the moment and the implications of this for inter-group relations.

There are models of aspects of social identity, such as racial and ethnic identity (Cross, 1991; Helms, 1990; Hardiman, 1994; Sellers, Shelton, 2003) that attempt to inject a developmental dimension into identity formation. These models provide frameworks for understanding processes and domains relevant to social identity development. Such models have relevance for understanding inter-group dynamics but are useful as well for teaching, counseling, and other contexts that rely on interpersonal interactions. We have found in our teaching and clinical experience that many people resist looking at themselves as having a "racial identity", without being able to integrate this with other aspects of their social identity (gender, class, sexual orientation, etc.). At times the reason for wanting to consider other aspects of social identity have to do with shame, lack of awareness, or resistance to looking at one's privileged racial status. For example, white students who feel more comfortable embracing their oppression as women or by virtue of being gay, resist exploring their race privilege and how this is part of their identity. This may be in part an act of denial but may also reflect the fact that awareness of social identities is often developed in the context of one's own experience of oppression. We have also worked with students of color who objected to assumptions that their primary social identity was racial or ethnic. People like to be seen and often think of themselves as whole and complex social beings. For an interesting study which looks at the complex interplay between an individual's multiple social identities, some which carry privilege, and some which are targeted identities see Croteau, Talbot, Lance and Avano (2002).

We are also struck by the interplay between internal psychological processes and external historical and social conditions. We use the concepts of "webs of oppression" and believe that these describe not only external realities but become maps that people internalize, which become part of one's self-concept. In turn, how ones views oneself and the external world influences what actions people take to influence their social and historical conditions as does the knowledge or lack of knowledge one has about social and historical reality.

In this paper we present a model of social identity development that accounts for this interplay, while also reflecting the fluidity and complexity of social identity development. We are sketching a conceptual model based on literature about social and racial identity, relevant research in social psychology, psychodynamic theory (which deals with the development of self concept and self esteem), and symbolic interactionism which considers the constructed internalized maps we have of who we and others are. Our ideas also reflect our experiences in teaching and in practice. We also take a social constructionist approach, in that we believe that social identity is co-constructed through the interaction of individuals and groups. Thus it is neither fixed nor frozen and although there is a developmental dimension to identity formation there is a strong contextual component as well. Our model of social identity development is diagrammed in Figure 1. We have a number of assumptions that we would like to articulate, which are infused in this model.

The first is that we see social identity development as being one of phases, rather than stages. We do not view this as being a linear process, in which everyone goes step by step through all phases. We hold that such phases are constructs that we use to generalize and make sense of others and ourselves but they are not fixed or objective realities, rather they are contingent and contested frameworks and also influenced by context. A person may be in more than one phase at a time and different constructs are likely to stimulate different phases.

A second assumption is that with each aspect of social identity development, some people are in a more privileged status (objectively in society), although how people view themselves in relation to others is highly subjective. For example, even if an Italian or Jewish Caucasion in the United States does not define themselves as white, there will be many social contexts in which she/he will be treated as white. The social identity one claims may be at odds with that which is externally conferred.

Identity is mediated by social forces; where one is in the social structure differentially impacts on one's ability to influence or be influenced by the appraisals of others (Croteau, Talbot, Lance, Evans, 2002). Those in higher positions of social status are in a better position to influence how those lower in social status see themselves rather than the other way around. Put differently, those with higher status have more resources to control social verification and self esteem related to it. Though there are always mediating and mitigating factors, those on the lower ends of social hierarchy may need to expend more resources on the regulation of self esteem related to social identity issues.

A third assumption is that there are a number of dimensions for each phase of each aspect of social identity. We have identified four dimensions: social (who the person wants to affiliate with), emotional (how the person feels about their identity and the identity of others), cognitive (how a person thinks, sees themselves and others), and ego/self (how a person describes themselves).

A fourth assumption is that social identity development occurs within a lifespan context. Factors such as age, health, one's social and economic situation, and cohort status influence social identity development. For example, the demographics of the large and aging baby boom cohort in the United States may positively influence how society at large views the social identity of seniors.

A fifth assumption is that social identity is also strongly influenced by a person's environmental context. This includes the macro context (history, politics, culture, economics, nationality), mezzo context (profession, agency affiliation, schools attended), and micro context (interactions, places, bill boards, songs, relationships). We also take a social constructionist position, influenced by symbolic interactionism (Cooley, 1922; Mead, 1913) about micro-contexts, believing that social identity is co-constructed in a given moment when people or groups of people interact.

Our final assumption is that there are a number of resolutions/stances that accrue from social identity phases, some of which are conscious or intentional and others that are less intentional. These are organized, working, cognitive, and emotional schemas that direct an individuals functioning in the domain of social identity. Among the resolutions and stances that we will consider are an integrated vs. an unintegrated identity, complex vs. simple identities, flexible/adaptable vs. fixed/rigid identities, active vs. passive identities, stable vs. unstable identities, and finally identities that lead to a stance of collaboration or conflict.

We will discuss all of our assumptions and also provide a vignette to illustrate how the interaction of all of these aspects of identity influences a hypothetical student's experience in the classroom.

2. Presentation of the Model

Our model[1] of social identity development posits that we all have social identities, which can be disaggregated into distinct axes. Among the more common coordinates that are part of a person's social identity are race, ethnicity, gender, social class, economic class, sexual orientation, nationality, religion, age, health/disability status or even identity organized around athletic teams (Burdsey, Chapell, 2004). This is not an inclusive list. For example, we have worked with clients or students whose regional identity, such as coming from the southeastern United States, was very salient for them. One of us also consulted to a U.S. social service agency staffed by Asian and Asian American clinicians, where immigration status, linguistic preferences and competency were very significant social identity factors. And even with our original list of social identity coordinates, the valence and relevance of different aspects of social identity varies considerably among individuals and groups.

For each aspect of social identity however, we believe that there are corresponding social statuses. These statuses carry different levels of privilege and degrees of oppression. Although we do not subscribe to a binary, either-or way of conceptualizing the differences in these social statuses, for the purposes of illustrating this model, we have presented potential phases of social identity development using what we have called target and agent identities (Adams, Bell, Griffin, 1997). Target identities are those aspects of social identity, which correspond to social statuses that are socially marginalized, scapegoated, and where groups of people suffer social exclusion and oppression. Agent identities are those that correspond to social statuses that are privileged by society and reflect dominant norms, assumptions and are

---

1   Before presenting the potential phases of social identity development for aspects of targeted and agent identities we would like to again acknowledge our theoretical debt to those who conceptualized racial identity development (Cross, 1991; Hardiman, 1994; Helms, 1990). Our model is greatly influenced by their work and we have extrapolated some of their insights to other aspects, other than race, of social identity. We would also like to acknowledge our colleague, Anne Marie Garran, who has worked on this model with us.

afforded unearned and unequal rights by virtue of this status. The terms agent and target are problematic as they presume levels of activity and passivity that may be both inaccurate and stigmatizing and yet they are the current currency in social identity theory. We continue to look for better terms.

2.1 General comments on Targeted and Agent Identities

In order to progress to complex social identities, which do not elicit internal conflict, many individuals, whether with a targeted or agent identity have to reject an earlier assumption of their social identity (Cross, 1978). There is frequently, though not always, an undoing and a redoing of an earlier identity plateau. Some ideas from self psychology (Kohut, 1984) and symbolic inter-actionism (Mead, 1913; Goffman, 1959) are helpful here.

A key concept in the psychodynamic theory of self psychology is that of mirroring. This is the interactive process by which we internalize a sense of who we are from how external others reflect upon us. In earlier development the repetitive ways our caretakers mirror us, shapes, in not small measure, how we organize an internal view of who we are, including our social sense of self. Our caretaker's understanding of their social identity is apt to be a piece of how they mirror us. As we begin to have a sense of the larger social world, we receive reflections of how we are seen and who we are supposed to be. Caretakers may or may not provide positive and powerful mirroring for those in both targeted and agent groups. For target groups, however, the larger society in the form of the media, social interactions, school systems, and various forms of discrimination, may be a source of powerful negative mirroring. The message, represented in a myriad of ways, is that there is something about one that is problematic, less than deserving and inferior in a particular aspect of social identity (Donner, 1988). While one's family and social identity group may be a powerful antidote to societal mirroring, a degree of the negative messages may become internalized. Moving through progressive stages of social identity development involves shedding the negative internalization and replacing it with something else. Complicating this process is the phenomenon described earlier: those with higher social status and whose social identities are more positively reinforced by society are often in a better position to influence how those with a lower social status see themselves. Also relevant is the dynamic where people tend to assume that the social categories to which they belong are better than those to which they do not and as they over-evaluate their own social identity group and under-evaluate those to which they do not belong. (Leary, 2004)

Symbolic interactionism (Cooly, 1992; Goffman, 1959) stresses that all of interpersonal interactions have a symbolic meaning. This includes not only the wishes and pressures of how we want to present ourselves but how the other person expects us to present ourselves. Some of those pressures are positive. For those with a targeted status many are negative. Research on stereotypes for example, indicates that many students of color, and women, have internalized a stereotype, in particular domains, that labels them as academically less able, and will perform their ability on related standardized tests (Steel 1997).

For those with an agent identity, mirroring is likely to have been very positive in ways not always commensurate with actual achievement. It is not necessarily that those with agent identities have not deserved or earned positive mirroring but that the nature of the mirroring has led them to believe that all of their privilege has been earned.

Thus for an individual with agent identity, moving forward with social identity development means giving up aspects of identity that may have felt positive. It also means coming to grips with what has really been earned and what has been merely conferred by birth into a privileged social identity. This is a painful process as it may involve at least temporarily exchanging positive for negative feeling about one's self. Hopefully the pull of better and more expanded genuine relations, a better ability to deal with reality, the wish for social justice and less inter-group conflict propel and motivate a person to relinquish their agent identity.

2.2 Phases of Identity Development

Targeted Identity

We believe that the task for a person wrestling with a targeted aspect of their identity is to ultimately embrace their identity while externalizing and rejecting the webs of social oppression that may have become internalized in the form of low self esteem, self doubts, self alienation, or even self rejection. This reveals our clinical and political value that internalized oppression is destructive to individual and collective well-being and that a task of social identity development for those whom are targeted is to value and be at peace about one's social self.

Phase One – Awareness of Difference

At some point a person becomes aware that they are similar to and different from other people. This can happen as a child, noticing that one's skin color is darker than classmates or television actors, or as an adult, as one realizes that unlike many heterosexual friends, he/she is gay or bisexual.

What message get mirrored, how powerfully and by whom will affect what the child makes of his or her difference and becomes a factor in social identity development.

Figure 1: Social Identity Development Phases

- Targets – Members of social identity groups that are socially oppressed (Hardiman & Jackson)
- Agents – Members of social identity groups with unearned privilege (Hardiman & Jackson)
- Social identity moves through 4 dimensions: 1. Social, 2. Emotional, 3. Ego/self, 4. Cognitive
- Social Identity moves through different axes (e.g. race, gender, sexual orientation, religion, social class) at different rates although different aspects of social identity interact and become integrated into a sense of self.

TARGETED IDENTITY
1. **Awareness of difference** – awareness that not all people are the same and that there are differences in race, religion, sexual orientation.
2. **Recognition of targeted status** – not only are people different but an aspect of one's social identity is socially targeted.
3. **Emotional and cognitive reactions** – person can experience a range of explanations and emotions, which can result in different stances (e.g. withdrawal, passing, assertion of difference).
4. **a. Denial** – person seeks to deny their targeted status. May involve denial of their identity or attempts at 'passing.
   b. Seeking group support – person may seek support from people sharing some of their social identity. Can involve withdrawal from and aversion of people who are agents.
5. **Shedding internalized oppression** – feeling better about your self, pride. Embracing identity without internalized feelings of oppression.
6. **Comfort with self and others** – feeling comfortable and at peace with one's own identity while respecting and valuing the identities of other people.
7. **Social activist** – working with others for social justice.

AGENT IDENTITY
1. **Awareness of difference** – awareness that not all people are the same and that there are differences in race, religion, sexual orientation.
2. **Assumption of agent status** – internalization of assumptions about privilege and power as being normative.
3. **Encounters with targets** – interactions or encounters that challenge assumptions and worldviews. Can lead to emotional and cognitive dissonance.
4. **a. Retreat and regression** – person retreats to the familiar, retrenches with their assumptions and blames victims for their problems.
   b. Painful realizations – person experiences guilt, shame and responds with humility to their realizations. May seek support from other agents experiencing similar reactions.
5. **Aggressive distancing** – person distances him or herself from their agent status and attempts to forge a non-privileged, non-oppressive identity. May idealize people in target status and have little tolerance for agents who are perceived as being less aware of their privilege.
6. **Non-oppressive identity** – person is no longer overwhelmed by guilt and is able to accept their social identity but not the unearned privilege that accompanies it. Able to respect and appreciate people with different identities.
7. **Social activist** – working with others for social justice.

Phase Two – Recognition of targeted status

This phase can occur very soon after the first phase or can take some time. It is during this phase that a person becomes aware that this aspect of their social identity is accompanied by social isolation, or stigmatization and social oppression. The feelings evoked during this phase can be very dispiriting and painful. Recognition can happen through memorable and traumatic encounters, which we call *critical incidents*, or through more solitary experiences, such as reading or watching television. Recognition may also occur through small repetitive micro-aggressions, negative encounter that taken alone are not so powerful but in their ongoing aggregate, oppressive remind one of his or her differences (Solorzano, Ceja, Yosso, 2000).

Phase Three – Emotional and cognitive reactions

This closely follows or can overlap with the second phase, as a person begins to generate feelings and thoughts about their targeted status. This is often quite painful and can lead to attempts to withdraw, hide, or minimize this aspect of social identity, or conversely through a strong statement affirming these differences. There can also be feelings of pride during this phase if a person receives sufficient validation and social support.

Phase Four – Denial or Seeking Group Support

We have identified two possible aspects of this phase. Only one of them may occur, or a person may move through them sequentially, but it is unusual to have them happen simultaneously. They are similar to what Helms (1990) has called immersion/emersion. The first aspect involves denial. If a person is flooded with overwhelming or negative affect in association with their targeted identity, they may seek to deny their targeted status. This can be conscious, such as trying to present oneself to appear like a person with agent status, or unconscious, such as repressing one's actual social identity. Attempts at conformity with agent group members or 'passing' are common.

The second part of this phase can be to seek social support from other people who share one's targeted social identity and status. This has been referred to as "buffering" by Cross (1991). This can also be accompanied by withdrawal, as much as is possible, from contact or interactions with people with agent status. Solorazano, et al. (2000) has described this reaction occurring on college campuses when students of color experience micro-aggressions and we, the authors, have certainly seen it in our own classrooms.

Phase Five – Shedding Internalized Oppression

This is a very important phase in the person's sense of their ego/selves, how they view themselves in relation to others, who a person affiliates with, and how they feel about their identity. During this phase, a person with targeted identity takes on less responsibility for their targeted status, externalizing it as they become more aware of societal inequities and social injustice. There is recognition that he/she, as well as others like him/her have been unfairly victimized. Feelings of pride in one's identity can accompany this phase although there may still be strong negative feelings about people with agent status.

Phase Six – Comfort with self, comfort with others

In this phase, a person has internalized a sense of pride about their identity and feels as if they know who they are. The security of this can make it easier for the person to now appreciate people who are different from them. Sometimes it is easier to first appreciate people with other but different targeted statuses before feeling comfortable with some people with agent status. It may always prove challenging to trust or feel at ease with people with agent status, particularly with people who have not examined this status.

Phase Seven – Social Activist

This phase reflects our values as social workers. We believe that it is different from phase six in that a person is not satisfied to merely feel good about himself and herself and others, but has made commitments to work for social justice and the amelioration of the social conditions that maintain their targeted status. This can be generalized to other forms of oppression, even in domains where she/he has agent status, where the person with targeted status with as allies with others with different social identities.

Agent Identity

While the task for people with targeted identities is to shed internalized oppression, for people with agent identities, the charge is to recognize their agent status, which is often initially invisible to them, and to shed internalized feelings of superiority. While people with targeted identity status usually have to confront that status in the face of oppression, people with agent status can more easily ignore their privileged identity and social group membership. Thus it is also easier to *not* move through many of the later phases, as society is structured to mirror the agent identity status and there are risks and challenges to discarding agent status. Because one function of social identity is self enhancement for agent identities initial change from one phase to another is complicated by a task that initially is in conflict with a psychological function social identity usually plays.

Phase One – Awareness of Difference

Although this can occur at any age, a person with agent status is more likely to recognize their difference at a later age than a person with targeted identities. We often have heard from our students that they did not meet anyone who was not white until they went to high school, or someone who was poor or not heterosexual until college.

Phase Two – Assumption of Agent Status

Interestingly, the assumption of agent status and the sense of entitlement and privilege that accompanies this can occur even before a person becomes aware that there are many people who do not share their identities or enjoy the same privileges. This internalized sense of superiority may be unconscious because it is so socially reinforced.

Phase Three – Encounters with people with targeted Identities

These are interactions or exchanges with people with targeted social identities that challenge or confront a person's agent saturated worldviews and assumptions. Perhaps a person makes a statement in a class about "we Americans believe in fairness", only to find that there are others in the class who are not U.S. citizens or those who are citizens but who have not experienced the U.S. as a 'fair' country. Or a person may ask a friend when they plan to marry, only to find that their friend is unable to marry because same-sex marriages are not legal in their state or nation. These encounters can also be 'critical experiences' that are memorable and induce a sense of discomfort.

Phase Four – Retreat, regression and/or painful realizations

During this phase, a person may initially find the identification of their agent status to be too cognitively dissonant and emotionally charged to want to pursue this further. This can lead to denial, rationalizations, retreating back to what is more familiar, even anger towards and blaming of people with targeted status. Again, as this is reinforced by social structures, leaders and social discourses, many people with targeted status remain in this phase.

Some however, stay with their pain, guilt, and confusion and allow their agent status to become part of their ongoing, conscious awareness. This can be a painful and humbling phase to experience and it can be helpful to seek social support from other people with agent status about these reactions. It can also be a time where people with agent status seek to have more contact with people with target status, to 'learn' from them, which may or may not be welcomed by the recipients of such overtures. When the overtures are aimed at getting a person with a targeted status to expiate the guilt of one with an agent status, the interaction is unlikely to be a happy one.

Phase Five – Aggressive distancing from the privileges of Agent Status

During this phase, people with agent status can become very angry and re-sentful over unearned privileges and seek to disown them. This is a time when there can also be attacks against other people with agent status who are seen to be less enlightened or willing to interrogate their privileges. Some-times these attacks can be against family members or close friends. While the person is working on forging a non-oppressive identity, the forceful, at times antagonistic confrontations with other people with agent status can mask his/her fears, guilt or shame. During this phase, people with targeted status may become idealized.

Phase Six – Achieving a non-oppressive Identity

During this phase, a person accepts who they are while not accepting the unearned privileges that accompany this status. There is less personal guilt and more of an appreciation of the historical and social forces that bestowed the unearned privileges that are now being challenged and discarded. There is also an appreciation of people with different social identities without ideal-izing or romanticizing them.

Phase Seven – Working with others for Social Justice

During this phase, a person goes beyond their emotional and psychological realizations and resolutions and works with others, as an ally, to change the social conditions that granted one's privileges in the first place. Working as an ally implies that the person with agent social identities does not usurp leadership positions and is able to work collaboratively and respectfully with people with differing social identities.

2.3 Interactions Between Axes

Social identity development is uneven, non-linear, episodic, and unpredictable. All social identity axes combine in a person's sense of self, although the meaning and importance of each axis varies considerably. Each axis develops at its own rate and does not necessarily influence the progress of another axes. For example, a white middle class lesbian may have a complex understanding of herself as a lesbian and have moved into phases 6 or 7 with this aspect of her identity, while she has done little thinking about her racial or class identities, where she is still in phases 3 to 4. Conversely, because of her targeted status as a lesbian, she might have responded more empathically to encounters with people who are targeted due to race or class, which may have accelerated her identity development.

Figure 2: Social Identity Pie

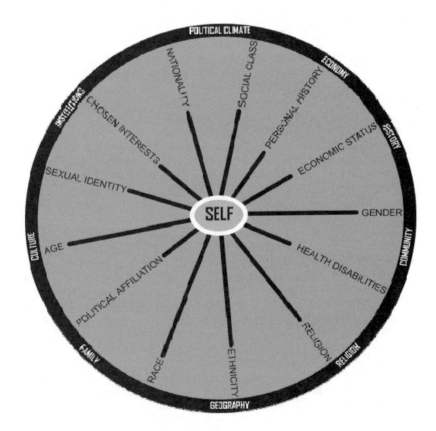

We have developed a "social identity pie", see figure 2, that we use at the beginning of any training involving social identity. We ask people to draw their own pie to make a statement about their social identity. We suggest that for some people, some aspects of the pie that we have presented in figure 2 are salient while for others they are not. For some, their gender may take up most of the pie, while for others there will be many smaller slivers of social identity pieces. After people draw their pie, we break them into pairs to discuss what they have drawn. We ask them to talk about which parts of their identity are most meaningful and why. Which parts are most/least obvious? Which give them the greatest sense of pride or cause the most ambivalence? Which aspects of their identity come to life in their work?

What we have found from this exercise is that rarely does a person have a social identity where they are equally aware of all of their identity axes and that each axis has developed at the same rate. As stated earlier, people tend to be most aware of their targeted identities and have done the most work with these axes. Sometimes, a person is so preoccupied with one aspect of their identity, often a targeted aspect, that they are resistant to investing much of themselves in reflecting on other aspects of their social identity.

3. Social Identity Variables

3.1 Social Identity Dimensions

We have identified four dimensions that operate at any phase of social identity development: social, emotional, cognitive, and ego-self. The social dimension refers to whom people identify or disidentify with and with which groups of people they spend time. This also includes what people often refer to as their community, which is more of a socially constructed sense of community and less a geographic area. The emotional dimension of identity development refers to the feelings that a person has about an aspect of their identity, which can include the full range of emotions. Pride or shame are two powerful emotions, but there are many other feelings, such as rage, sorrow, resigned acceptance, indifference, interest, etc. that people experience about different axes of their social identity and those of others.

In addition to feelings, people tend to have rich cognitive schemas in relationship to each phase of social identity development. This includes how one thinks about oneself, about others, society, and the world at large. These cognitive schemas influence perception and analysis; how one sees, what one hears, the meaning that one makes of experience. Another dimension of social identity is the about oneself, the story of identity that a person tells themselves and others.

3.2 Life-span Context

Social identity development occurs throughout the lifespan. The meaning and sense of one's gender will probably be quite different at ages 2, 5, 16, 25, 40, and 65. And the meaning is likely to differ according to each person. Some women became aware of their targeted gender status as children or adolescents, others in middle age, while yet others may never have moved beyond the phase of awareness of gender difference. However, at whatever age a person grapples with some aspect of their social identity, their lifespan development influences how they process and come to terms with their social identity. And age is in itself an axis of social identity.

Lifespan development also can influence a person's social status. For example, older couples who are still in the workforce tend to be wealthier than younger people who are just entering the workforce. Thus they will probably be confronting different issues that influence their sense of social and economic class. Health also varies considerably throughout the life course, which can have a bearing on social identity development.

3.3 Environmental Contexts

Who we are and how we see ourselves is profoundly influenced by environmental contexts, past and present. Even future contexts shape the contours of social identity, as we imagine where we want to go or who we hope to be. Environments affect who we encounter, what we see or do not see and create a gestalt, where some aspects of identity become figure and others ground. For example, a white teenager from a predominantly white suburb may not have thought much about her racial identity until she finds herself riding on a subway through a predominantly African American section of a city, where there are few other white riders on a train. Or a working class male may not have thought about his agent social status until attending a social work program that is predominantly female. Middle class women in the same program may not have paid much attention to their class status until engaged in discussions with the aforementioned working class male.

We have grouped environmental contexts into three categories: macro, mezzo and micro. Macro contexts include large historical and societal contexts. For example, if a country is at war, a person may be much more aware of their citizenship, gender, and age than during peacetime. Political environments affect social identity, as witnessed by the influence of the Civil Rights movement and Great Society on raising awareness about racial oppression and racial identity. Macro contexts also are likely to influence how much or how little others are stereotyped. For example in times of war the enemy is likely to be demonized and seen as monolithic. Mezzo contexts include professions, schools, agencies, and other organizations that we find ourselves in throughout much of our lives. Children attending highly diverse and integrated schools are likely to have a very different consciousness about their racial identities than students attending very homogenous schools. A social service agency in San Francisco is likely to have a very different discourse about sexual orientation than one in a rural town in Mississippi, which will influence how workers think about themselves and interact with one another.

Micro contexts are the small, quotidian, and ubiquitous fabric of everyone's lives. They are the streets that we walk down, the stores that we pass or shop in, the songs that we hear on the radio, the food that is available (or unavailable) in the supermarket. Micro contexts contain social and cultural markers that privilege certain social identities while marginalizing others. If Hispanic style foods in the United States are contained in an aisle marked "foreign foods", this makes a strong statement about ethnic identity and power.

3.4 Resolutions/Stances

We have identified six resolutions/stances that occur in social identity development that transcend any one axis of social identity. A resolution or stance is a position one assumes, or a set of approaches vis a vis social identity. Exploring these factors can be useful when considering interpersonal and inter-group relationships.

Integrated vs. Unintegrated

Some people have social identities that integrate most aspects of their social identity while others have very unintegrated parts of their social identity, which may include blind spots or areas of great ambivalence. For example, one person may feel very passionately about their class background and work to challenge class oppression while having done little thinking about his racial identity, gender and sexual orientation. Another person may have made many connections between the various parts of her social identity and has been able to integrate her targeted and agent axes and has a sense of how her identity reflects her privileges and areas where she is oppressed.

Complex vs. Simple Identities

Related to the above discussion is how complex or simple a person's social identity is. A person with a clear sense of one aspect of their identity but not others, may have a very clear, but simple sense of who he is in the world, while someone else might see herself as having many identity strands that cohere in intricate and multifaceted ways.

Stable vs. Unstable

Not only are some social identities integrated or unintegrated, simple or complex, but they may be stable or unstable. This can be influenced by lifespan development and environmental contexts. Some people are very clear about their social identities and comfortable with them while others are in a state of flux and transition, with more questions about who they are than answers. Though all social identities are context dependent, unstable identities are more so than stable social identities.

Flexible/Adaptable vs. Fixed/Rigid

Although this relates to stability it is not exactly the same. Some social identities, even when stable, are constructed in such a way that there is an ongoing process of taking in new information about oneself and others and having the capacity for plasticity and adaptation. In contrast to this, a person's social identity may have cohered at a certain lifespan phase and be constructed in such a way that there is little new information or critical experiences that will change or alter it. Environmental contexts also influence this stance. Complex societies are more likely to foster complex identities than are more homogenous or fundamentalist societies. Appiah (2006) makes the case that globalism is cultivating more complex, flexible, adaptable, and secure social identities than the world has previously seen.

Active vs. Passive

How stable, adaptable, and complex a person's social identity is can have implications for how empowered they feel and whether they believe that they have the capacity to work to change personal and social conditions, or are resigned to the status quo. This is also influenced by the phases of identity development that a person has moved through and how the various identity axes are integrated.

Collaborative vs. Confrontational

The final stance that has implications for interpersonal and inter-group dynamics is whether a person's social identity leads him to conclude that the best way to approach change is through collaboration with others, including people with diverse social identities, or through collaboration only with people of similar social identities, which often implies conflict with others with divergent social identities. This can be manifested in interpersonal relation-ships, small groups, and large groups, all the way up to how nations conduct their affairs with other nations. Some social psychology research on social identity implies that favoritism, bias, and antagonism are frequently an aspect of group identity (Leary, 2004).

4. Vignette

To illustrate the complexity of social identity and its interpersonal unfolding, we have constructed an example of a hypothetical student coping with a classroom dynamic, based on our actual experiences. We raise questions after the illustration which we believe educators should engage in order to help students manage and to seize teachable moments.

Jiang Li is a young Asian American female enrolled in a U.S. graduate social work program. She came to the United States at age 8 with her parents and her younger brother. Jiang Li began to think of herself as a lesbian to-ward the end of her recent undergraduate experience. She was acutely aware that this was totally unacceptable to her parents and a betrayal of the family plan for her future. As it was, her parents were not entirely happy with her choice of graduate program as they had been thinking along the lines of her studying to become a pharmacologist. Worse still the program was in the Northeast and not in the Northwest where her parents reside. Jiang Li is very attached to her parents but there has been some estrangement since they acci-dentally discovered she was a lesbian.

In her graduate program, Jiang Li finds many other gay students, a new experience for her, and she joins the gay lesbian transgendered student alli-ance. In classes she begins to bristle at any comments with homophobic un-dertones or statements with misinformation. She also meets other Asian stu-dents in the program none of whom seem to be gay.

Jiang Li's parents do not think of themselves as people of color but while in college she begins to contemplate identifying herself as such. However, she is not quite sure she wants to join the student run organization for stu-dents of color and does not quite know what to make of all of the conversa-tions about race and racism. In a class on cultural context, she expresses her confusion about whether or not she is a person of color. Another student of color, someone possibly embedded in the phase of racial identity where she seeks support from people of color and avoids contact with whites, comes down hard on her in class. Her loyalty to her own ethnic group is challenged and she is briskly asked, "Where have you been?" Another gay white student begins to defend Jiang Li essentially stating that no one could expect Jiang Li to be loyal to a family which no longer seems to accept her. At first, Jiang Li feels rescued by the fellow gay student. As the conversation becomes more heated and characterized by escalating accusations she begins to feel the other gay student is talking about her family in a way she cannot tolerate. She begins to cry, runs out of class, and does not return to the session.

One question to consider is how an instructor might anticipate conflicts that arise between students in different phases of identity development. This may be particularly germane in classes that focus on race and racism. Beverly Tatum (1992) suggests that teaching students about issues that arise in different phases of identity development helps students with an organizing explanation when conflicts occur. Even an intellectual understanding of identity development can provide some insight for students when those stuck moments happen.

There is also the question of how to help students to deconstruct the kind of dynamic that occurred with Jiang Li and her classmates. Though the strong affect that occurs at such moments needs to be acknowledged, the more complex task is to step back and be curious about what has occurred, why and how it is relevant to the learning in the course for every student, and the implications for social work practice. At the very least, students can come to appreciate that their reaction to the interaction is related in part to their own social identity. Every student and instructor will identify differently with every aspect of social identity that emerged in the incident. Jiang Li's social identity is extremely complex and in flux. Her particular struggle may not mirror anyone else's exactly but that there is a struggle and fluctuating tensions between aspects of her identity probably will mirror something for everyone else in class. How to connect students with that struggle inviting them to think about where they see themselves as agents and targets, and finally empowering them in the positive aspects of their identity are important opportunities.

5. Conclusion

Swami Prajnanpad urged people to embrace their own uniqueness, while respecting what is unique in others (Welwood, 2003). With increased globalization there are many more opportunities for cross-cultural fertilizations. This also brings greater opportunities for cultural misunderstandings as well as abuses of power and privilege.

The use of relationship is fundamental to social work practice throughout the world. Relationships involve individuals, families, groups and communities. Social identity is a construct that helps to explicate the complexities of such social interactions and integrates social phenomena with personal identity. We presented a model that attempts to map the complexities of social identity. As with all maps, our model should not be mistaken for the territory. Human identity and interaction will always present puzzles and raise questions to which no model will ever adequately respond. Yet the quest for understanding ourselves and others will continue.

References

Adams, M.; Bell, L.A.; Griffin, P. (1997) (eds.). Teaching for diversity and social justice: A sourcebook. New York: Routledge.

Appiah, Kiwame (2006). The case for contamination. *The New York Times Magazine Section, Jan. 1,* 30-37, and 52.

Burdsey, D.; Chappell, R. (2004). Soldiers, sashes and shamrocks: Football and social identity in Scotland and Northen Ireland. *Sociology of sports online,* http://physed.otago.ac.nz/sosol/v6i11.html, retrieved May 15, 2006.

Cass, V.C. (1979). Homosexual identity foundation: A theoretical model. *Journal of Homosexuality*, 413/219-235.

Cooly, C.H. (1922). Human nature and the social order. New York: Scribner.

Cross, W. (1991). Shades of black: Diversity in African-American Identity. Philadelphia: Temple University Press.

Cross, W. (1978). The Thomas and Cross models of psychological nigrescence. *Journal of Black Psychology*, 4, 13-31.

Croteau, J.; Talbot, D.; Lance, T.; Evans, T. (2002). A qualitative study of the interplay between privilege and oppression. *Journal of Multicultural Counseling and Development 3d.,* 239-258.

Donner, S. (1988). Self Psychology: Implications for social work. *Social Casework,* 69, 1, 19-22.

Goffman, L. (1959). The presentation of self in everyday life. New York: Doubleday Anchor.

Hardiman, R. (1994). White racial identity development in the United States. In Sallet, Koslow (eds.). Identity in multicultural perspective (pp. 117-140). Washington, D.C.: National Multicultural Institute.

Helms, J. (1990). Black and White racial identity: theory, research and practice. NY: Greenwood Press.

Jussim, L.; Asmore, R.; Wilder, D. (2001). Introduction: Social identity and intergroup conflict. In Ashmore, Jussim, Wilder. Social identity and intergroup conflict reduction (pp. 3-14). Oxford: Oxford University Press.

Kohut, H. (1984). How does analysis cure? Chicago: University of Chicago Press.

Leary, M. (2004). The curse of the self (pp. 107-108). New York: Oxford University Press.

Mead, G.H. (1913). The Social Self. *Journal of Philosophy, Psychology, and Scientific Methods* 10, 374-80

Sellers, R.M.; Shelton, J.N. (2003). The role of racial identity in perceived racial discrimination. *Journal of Personality and Social Psychology,* 84, 5, 1079-1092.

Solorzano, P.; Ceja, M.; Yosso, T. (2000). Critical race theory, racial micro-digressions, and campus racial climate. The experiences of African American college students. *The Journal of Negro Education,* 69, 1/2, 60-73.

Steele, C.M. (1997). A threat is in the air: How stereotypes shape intellectual identity and performance. *American Psychologist,* 52, 613-629.

Tajfel, H.; Turner, J.C. (1986). The social identity theory of intergroup behavior. In Worchel, Austin (eds.). The psychology of intergroup relations (pp. 7-24). Chicago: Nelson Hall.

Tajfel, H. (1981). Social identity and intergroup relations. London: Cambridge University Press.

Tatum, B. (1992). Talking about race, learning about racism: The application of racial identity development theory in the classroom. *The Harvard Educational Review,* 63, 1, 1-24.

Welwood, J. (2003). Double vision: Duality and nonduality in human experience. In J. Prendergast; S. Krystal; P. Fenner (eds.). The sacred mirror (pp. 138-158). St. Paul, MN: Paragon House.

Otrude N. Moyo

Broadening Constructions of Parenting: Perspectives from African Immigrants and Refugees in Northern New England

1. Introduction

Parenting is undoubtedly one of those roles that reflect cultural values (Freeman, 1998; Maiter, George, 2003; Peterson, Steinmetz, Wilson, 2005). As such, there is a societal expectation that parents, guardians and childcare providers adopt the practices of the wider society in which they live (Soriano, Weston, Violet, Kolar, 2001; Peterson, Steinmetz, Wilson, 2005). The subject of parenting, how adults take care of, guide and socialize children, remains saturated with voices of what constitutes 'good' and 'bad' parenting. The usual perception is that the parenting repertoires of immigrants are 'bad', simply because immigrants and refugees are the 'othered' in a society where the dominant groups' beliefs and conceptions, including about parenting roles and practices, are presumed to underpin universal models of behavior (Maiter, George, 2003). I see the simultaneous appearance of 'good' and 'bad' parenting as the two sides of the same cultural complex, for example, the entrenchment of ethnocentric perspectives when approaching difference, where those in the dominant groups use their own cultural standards as the baseline against which all groups are evaluated, with the result that the 'othered' cultural practices are judged as peculiar, inferior, immoral, primitive and/or unwise (Peterson, Steinmetz, Wilson, 2005). Understanding how immigrants and refugees relate to the ethnocentric, culturally specific ideas of the host environments is critical in devising, developing and resourcing programs that are relevant to support the parenting strategies of new immigrants and refugees.

Generally parents muddle through the seemingly joyous experience of parenting, often stumbling along the way on those challenging parts since there are no clear-cut formulae (Peterson, Steinmetz, Wilson, 2005). However, when parenting is combined with being uprooted it can become a trial (Nwadiora, 1996; Maiter, George, 2003; Remennick, 2005). Often, immigrants and refugees bring up families in environments that are unsupportive of difference and where a supportive infrastructure to enable parenting, among many roles, is lacking. Where resources are available, the guiding philosophies underpinning the support tend to be scripted in the dominant culture, generally disregarding the experiences and context of immigrant and refugee parenting (Freeman, 1998; Maiter and George, 2003). For the most part, the 'one size fits all' approaches to cultural retraining of immigrants are favored as ways to help integrate 'newcomers'. However, family relations studies have increasingly argued that parent-child relationships must be examined from a culturally sensitive perspective (Peterson, Steinmetz and Wilson, 2005). However, while advocating the need to understand the family through a culturally sensitive lens, Peterson, Steinmetz, and Wilson (2005: 13) understate the structural context of parenting, particularly the socioeconomic dynamics and factors at play in parenting.

As the dominant views of parenting are extended, the reality that parenting is continually constructed and reconstructed moment by moment, through the interface of varied social structures and personal factors, tends to be lost. In my efforts to understand the experience of new immigrants, particularly the experience of African immigrants and refugees in northern New England, it was important to examine their interactions with select human service providers, and specifically consider how the dominant discourses of parenting, as exemplified in their interactions with human service providers, influenced African immigrants' and refugees' self assessment of well-being.[1] I see this line of dialogue as a way of broadening the perspective of what is normalized, and affirms Freeman's (1998: 79) injunction "to quit universalizing experiences by applying a single standard for adaptive, healthy and competent behaviors."

Further, the historical care of 'newcomers' by the voluntary sector of human service providers has become an acceptable norm, which presents itself as an area of study. However, there has been surprisingly little research undertaken on the social interactions of human service providers and the 'newcomers' to help us understand the experience of these interactions. The growth in immigration of non-European peoples to the west presents an ever-increasing challenge for human service agencies to rethink their approaches to service provision (Maiter and George, 2003; Peterson, Steinmetz and Wilson, 2005).

---

1   This article draws on the author's on-going research, begun in 2003, into the experience of African immigrants and refugees in northern New England.

2. Immigrants and Refugee Parenting within a Context of Human Service Experts

So far, the experience of immigrants (and particularly refugees) who settle in western societies is that western governments have historically enlisted human service agencies as social care partners of 'newcomers'. In the United States, the Settlement House Movement galvanized concerns for the material and social well-being of immigrants in the movement towards societal reforms and slum clearances in the early 1900s. Despite these early efforts, disdain continues to be the predominant attitude towards 'newcomers'. As a result, standardised public involvement to address poverty remains limited to means-tested public assistance and a patchwork of non-profit organizations intervening at individual level to improve the morals and behaviors of the poor, the immigrants and the refugees. Pam McCollum (2005) notes that the resultant programs tend to be deficit-oriented, centering upon the premise that immigrant parents need to be changed in order to teach them how to work successfully with their own children in their new environments. However, this deficit approach tends to ignore the fact that immigrant and refugee parents may have ways of parenting their own children that differ from normalized US middleclass parenting strategies (Freeman, 1998; McCollum, 2005).

The emphasis of the human service approach on changing the immigrant has implicit connotations for immigrant parents. For instance, it sends a message that parents are not to be trusted to care for their own children, and instead human service workers as 'experts' are to be entrusted with the responsibility of helping 'new immigrants' find their way in the new environments. In the United States, the Refugee Act of 1980 (P.L. 96-212) established the Refugee Resettlement Program, which provided funds for income support, health services, job training and social services for refugees (Schmitz, Jacobus, Stakeman, Valenzuela and Sprankel, 2003). Through this Act, private non-profit human service agencies receive government funds to help refugees adjust. Human service agencies are thereby in essence contracted by governments to reform 'newcomers' through the inculcation of values, attitudes and ideas of the universalized 'American'. Social work theory and practice has also been built on the basis of these agenda. Often policy makers listen to the human service providers as a constituent but not to the 'new immigrants', for they are often perceived as a 'non constituent'. Because of their 'non constituent' status, 'new immigrants' rely on human service providers for assistance and advocacy (Sharry, Owen, 2000). The question remains, however: how favorable to 'new immigrants' is this reliance?

In their contribution to *Practicing Social Justice,* Schmitz et al. (2003) point to mixed messages regarding the favourability of this relationship to the 'new immigrant'. For example, in Portland Maine communities, the whole arena of language is frequently quoted as reflecting mixed messages. In conversations with Mainers, particularly those living within the Portland area, many are thrilled at the language diversity in their schools. Many Mainers around the Portland area are supportive of students who speak a language other than English. In all the 'progressive' people's conversations, many lament the fact that over fifty languages are spoken in the Portland school district, yet there has been no specific infrastructure created to deliver the curriculum and extra curriculum in ways that would help to retain and develop these languages. This is just one example of the mixed messages about human service support given to new 'immigrants'.

In an examination of current literature on immigrant and refugee experiences of parenting, Emma Gross's (2003) critique highlighted that texts about and practices with immigrants, like most theory on practice with people of color, contain unevaluated assumptions. Thus, it is problematic for these ideas to genuinely account for the life experiences of people of color in ways that can be meaningfully applied to the development of practice skills. The argument pursued in this article is that, like any social experience, parenting needs to be understood not as a unified and static entity but as perpetually being constructed. Parents, guardians, and adults who are taking care of children (parenting) come into this role with varied scripts (what Peterson, Steinmetz, and Wilson, 2005: 14 call ethno theories) about its meaning and practices. These scripts or strategies may be drawn from their own experience, or from normative ideas. Their parenting practices may also be drawn from resistance to the context and environment where parenting occurs (Maiter, George, 2003), or from parents' reflections on interactions with their children. However, it is problematic to universalize these ethno theories of parenting. As LeVine (1980), quoted by Maiter and George (2003: 411), cautions, "although parents everywhere share a common set of goals for parenting, there are also cultural differences in parenting roles, values, and behaviors that must be taken into consideration in understanding the meaning of 'effective parenting' in a society. Without this understanding, parenting behaviors that one group considers to be effective and functional can be easily construed as ineffective by another group."

In their edited volume *Parent-Youth Relations: Cultural and Cross Cultural Perspectives,* Peterson, Steinmetz and Wilson (2005) note the need for major growth in the research addressing differential parenting approaches cross-culturally in order to avoid misunderstanding and to provide services to families within a framework that is meaningful to them (Maiter, George,

2003). While the research on cultural differences features a great deal in the current literature on parenting approaches, the structural context and environment in which parenting occurs is often neglected. This neglect tends to de-emphasize the argument that there is no simple way of separating the cultural and structural context of parenting. For the most part, the role of parenting of 'new immigrants' and refugees tends to be complicated by the fact that immigrants are often negotiating not only a socioeconomic structure that shapes their experience, but also the parenting scripts of their host countries, regions, states, neighborhoods, and new communities, as well as an array of structural factors that complicate the parenting role.

3. A Brief Overview of Prevailing Literature on Parenting in the United States

Peterson, Steinmetz and Wilson (2005: 15) point out that the worst form of ethnocentrism underlies many examples of Western comparative parenting studies, driven by implicit 'deficit models'. In these models, European American child-rearing practices are referred to as 'normal' in comparison to the 'deficient' approaches of other cultures. In the prevailing literature on parenting, Baumrind's (1968, 1971) model of parenting practices is often used as the prototype for comparing cross-cultural parenting strategies (Maiter, George, 2003; Peterson, Steinmetz, Wilson, 2005).

Baumrind (1971) developed three models of parental management of children, which differentiated parents on the basis of their authority over their children. The parenting model classifies parenting as authoritarian, authoritative and permissive (Maiter, George, 2003). Baumrind conceptualized authoritarian parents as those who evaluate their children's behavior and attitudes from a certain set of standards and attempt to control and shape the children's behavior in accordance with these standards. Authoritarian parenting styles are seen as consisting largely of punitive, directive discipline and lack of expressive warmth. It is argued that authoritarian parents expect conformity to rules without question. Authoritative parenting consists of a constellation of parental attributes that include emotional support, clear bi-directional communications, firm limit-setting, reasoning, responsiveness and reluctance to use physical punishment. It is argued that authoritative parents encourage verbal give-and-take and direct their children's activities in a rational and issue-oriented manner. In contrast, permissive parents do not use external standards to regulate their children's behavior but allow the children to regulate their own behavior to a large extent. However, permissive parenting has been associated with youth problems. The argument is that parents' lax attitudes result in under-control of their children, the consequence of which is that they grow up to become delinquents (Davis, 1994).

Baumrind's conceptualization of parenting has been extensively studied within European American families (Baumrind, 1989, 1981) in relation to child behavior, social competence, school achievement and emotional adjustment (see Peterson, Steinmetz, Wilson, 2005). The ethnocentrism of Baumrind's model lies in its application; Baumrind's model has been extended to the study of other ethnic groups, for example, Querido, Warner and Eyberg (2002) in their research on parenting styles and child behavior among African American families. Chen, Dong and Zhou (1997) extended the prototypes to Chinese children, while Calzada and Eyberg (2002) focused on the parenting practices of Dominican and Puerto Rican mothers. Although the research about the applicability of Baumrind's prototypes has not been conclusive, for the most part, non white (non Euro-American) parenting styles have been found to be authoritarian in comparison to European American parents (Kinght, Virdin, Roosa, 1994), confirming the earlier assertions by Baumrind (1972) who argued that the socialization practices which characterize Black families are authoritarian by white standards, and as such would be regarded as problematic by many child rearing experts. However, increasingly over the years, the applicability of Baumrind's conceptualization of parenting has been challenged by studies of immigrants (see Calzada, Eyberg, Gorman, 1998; Chao, 2001; Maiter, George, 2003), who have argued for research that contextualizes the experience of parenting.

Maiter and George (2003) suggest that labeling non Euro-American's parenting as authoritarian reflects an ethnocentric concern with control, rather than contextualizing parenting in ways which would reflect the varied and distinctive ethno theories of parenting, and thereby have clear meaning to specific cultures. Maiter and George (2003) instead contextualize parenting approaches by looking at cultural orientation. They suggest that categorizing cultures as individualist and/or collectivist diminishes ethnocentrism, by decentering and acknowledging the cultural perspectives of others (Maiter, George 2003; McCollum, 2005).

However, there are limitations with the labels of individualist and collectivist. While they represent a societal organization, one would argue that even the highly individualistic United States has collective tendencies. According to Maiter and George (2003), collectivist cultures have been described as those that organize their subjective experiences, values, and behavioral mores around one or more groupings or collectives – the family, the extended family, the kinship network, the religious group, or the country.

However, what is hidden from this assertion is the ethnocentric nature of the discourses of what is 'American', which thrives on internalized group/country specific values as a foil of individual independence. As such, American identity is defined by group membership – of being 'American' – which relies on the culture of individualism (as self interest). Failure to parent can only be attributed to deficiencies in the parents and by extension their children. This individualist value draws from group (collective) identity (the American way), which is often set apart from the 'othered'. Because of the muddle in disentangling what is collective and individual parenting, exploration of people's experiences of their own parenting approaches is critical. Rudy and Grusec (2001) have pointed out that there is a difference in the meaning of authoritarianism, authoritative and permissive in collectivist and individualist cultures. But the very fact that what is collectivist and individualist is changing presents avenues for further exploration.

Other scholars suggest that an apparently restrictive parenting style among people of color may be the result of parents' responses to negative social environments, rather than the desire to subjugate their children (Denby, Alford, 1996; Jarrett, 1999 quoted by Maiter, George, 2003). Denby and Alford (1996), in their article *Understanding African American Discipline Styles: Suggestions for Effective Social Work,* suggest that what may appear to be restrictive parenting styles among African American families may emerge from the need to socialize children in two cultures: their culture and the dominant culture. They state that among the various cultural implications, paramount consideration should be given to dual socialization. Peterson, Steinmetz and Wilson (2004) suggest that aside from the need to ensure dual socialization of children, daily stressors of parenting in harsh environments may require 'no nonsense' direct discipline of children. Maiter and George affirm that the experience of living under surveillance, particularly 'state agency surveillance', for various people of color presents complex environments that influence parenting strategies.

The parenting strategies of recent African immigrants/refugees in United States may also be culturally and contextually unique and hence require a rethinking of the application of such concepts as authoritarian, permissive, individualist and collectivist. Indeed, African cultures have been identified in the literature as collectivist, defined in terms of the concept of *ubuntu*, especially in southern and east Africa (Nwadiora, 1996; Kamya, 1997). Particular parenting approaches have also been noted for the group, for example, community orientation and obligation, responsibility for the extended family members, respect and acceptance of the decisions and rules of elders, are a few of the values that have been attributed to Africanity (Nwadiora, 1996; Kamya, 1997; Dodoo, 1997). How parents experience their ethno theories about parenting and the interaction with institutions in the host country, such as schools and social service providers, is an area that demands exploration.

4. African Immigrants in the US and New England Area

According to the United States Census Bureau, as quoted by the Migration Policy Institute (2003), the foreign-born population of the US is estimated at 33 million, and includes people who were not citizens at birth, immigrants, and legal non-immigrants, such as refugees and people on student and work visas, as well as those illegally residing in the US. The African foreign-born population makes up about 3 percent of the total foreign-born: about 1 million immigrants are from the African continent. Over half of all African immigrants in the US are recent arrivals. According to the interpretation of the Census 2000 by the Immigration Policy Institute, 56 percent of all African foreign-born arrived in the US between 1990 and 2000, 26 percent entered between 1980 and 1989, and 18 percent entered before 1980. Djamba (1999) attests to a racial differentiation of African immigrants to the US; before 1990 more white Africans migrated and since the 1990s increasingly black Africans are migrating to the US. Western African countries make up the largest population of foreign-born people in the United States (Grieco, 2004). African countries with the highest numbers of immigrants obtaining legal permanent residency in 2002 were Nigeria and Ethiopians.

In the US, historically, immigration and naturalization laws reflected the racial and ethnic composition of the nation and dominance of particular groups, with federal laws restricting migration into the US on the basis of race (Lopez, 1996 quoted by Schmitz, et al.). In 2001, the 19,070 refugee arrivals from Africa (mainly from Sudan and Somalia) rekindled nativist politics in the US. As Schmitz et al. point out, the numbers of refugees permitted access are determined annually by presidential decree, and that agents from the Immigration and Naturalization Services (INS) are responsible for making the decision. The implementation of this law appears to be selective. Eastern European immigrants have been granted refugee status liberally, with as many as 65,000 admitted yearly. By contrast, the limit on admission of refugees from the African continent has historically been set low, with a maximum of 2000 annually throughout the 1960s, 1970s, and 1980s – time periods in which many countries in Africa were experiencing severe turmoil and civil wars. In 1992, during the crisis in Somalia, the numbers of Somali refugees admitted to the US remained low (3000), increasing only in the later 1990s to 7,000 annually. This number is negligible considering the millions of displaced people on the African continent. Social workers need to take cognizance of these realities.

Most refugees from the African continent remain in African countries, often in countries of first asylum within the African continent, where conditions are barely humane. Historically, western nations, despite their financial wealth and being better equipped to provide safe haven to uprooted persons, are currently lacking the moral and political will so to do. Materially poor African countries remain burdened with the care of people who are uprooted. Indeed, the few who come to the west face many challenges as governments there adhere to the nativist and essentially exclusionary sentiments of their constituents. Schmitz et al. (2003) highlight the curtailment of existing support programs that benefit 'newcomers' and the rapid institutionalization of restrictive legislation designed to satisfy the nativists in their constituencies (see Immigration Reform and Immigrant Responsibility Act (IIRIRA) (P.L. 104-193), and the Anti-Terrorism and Effective Death Penalty Act (AEDP) (P.L. 104-32). These Acts work cumulatively to restrict the benefits, freedoms and opportunity of immigrants in the U.S., particularly those immigrants whose legal status within the US is in question (Schmitz, et. al., 2003).

The national patterns of racial restrictions are reflected at various levels within federal states. The state of Maine as part of the New England area has not been an exception. In 2002, the Census Bureau estimated the population of Maine to be 1,317,250, with about 3 percent of this population being foreign-born. About 67 percent of the population is European and Canadian, 26 percent from Asia and Oceania, 4 percent Latin American, while Africa has 2.6 percent of the 38000 persons who are foreign-born in Maine. A history of European migration makes Maine one of the *whitest* states in the nation. Although Blacks and Native Americans have resided for a long time in Maine, diverse population groups only started dotting the Portland Maine area with greater visibility in the 1970s to late 1980s, with refugees from Afghanistan, Cuba, South-east Asia (Cambodia, Laos and Vietnam), and Eastern Europe (Czechoslovakia, Poland, and Russia). By the 1990s, the state of Maine and the city of Portland saw the arrival of African refugees. As a refugee resettlement site, Portland Maine has received 1,200 refugees over the most recent six fiscal years (FY 96-2001), an average of 200 refugees per year. African countries with the highest numbers include Somalia, Sudan, Ethiopia, Congo, Rwanda and Burundi. Other countries represented among asylum seekers include Togo, Liberia, and Sierra Leone. In addition, there are various immigrants from other African countries as well. Although negligible in numbers compared to immigrants and refugees from Europe and Canada, African refugees and immigrants present a physical presence that stirs the white population into fear of loss of privileges.[2]

---

2   For witness to this statement see the documentary, *The Letter*. This documentary highlights the tensions in one of the cities in Maine.

5. Research Context and Methods

The voices about parenting reported in this article are part of a broader ethnographic study entitled *Strategies of Strength*, which explores the experience of migration and 'the journey' made, livelihood strategies, and well-
being of families in southern Maine. The major purpose of the project is to
explore how African immigrants and refugees in northern New England
evaluate their experience of being 'newcomers' in the state of Maine and the
US. This researcher initially had conversations with more than fifty individuals, representing more than thirty-seven different countries from the African
continent, as a way to negotiate entry to the fifteen families that were willing
to have continued conversations. The study is continuing and conversation
with these fifteen families who are 'new arrivals' has been ongoing since
2003. The voices reported here are part of the observations and first interviews.

Participants include four Somali families, one Ethiopian woman and her
adult children, two families from Togo, three families from Sudan, three
families from the Congo, one from Burundi and another from Rwanda. To
maintain privacy and to secure anonymity for the participants, I have assigned numbers for the participants, one to fifteen. No further identifying
information is shared except the voices regarding parenting.

Of the fifteen families reported here, all had come to the United States
either as refugees, defined as those granted legal permission while outside
the US to enter the US because of harm or feared harm in the country of
origin, or asylum seekers, those granted legal status from within the U.S.
because of the fear of persecution in returning to country of origin. Interviews were carried out by the researcher with assistance from language inter-
preters and sometimes with cultural guides, who also facilitated the translation of some of the interviews. Interviews and observations took place wherever participants wished, such as in their homes, in the laundry mates, in
places of worship, at community meetings. This is characteristic of *in-depth*
interviewing where one has a prolonged presence and interacts with participants' experience. In sharing their experience, I am constantly aware of the
many roles I weave in and out of as a researcher. My roles include being a
listener, a learner, and an observer; seeking clarification, initiating dialogue,
and giving it meaning; pursuing dialogue from what has been shared. My
engagement also involves actively observing and being interpretative of
experience. The reiterative nature of observation, dialogue, and interpretation
ensures that the process is not a one-off event. Through my continued involvement, I have developed vignettes from my field notes, and selected
particularly from those that address parenting. The vignettes have been se-

lected to explore specific themes. The voices recounted here were not heard in a single sitting but became poignant over time with the sharing of experience.

The process of interviewing became more conversational, drawing on Pierre Bourdieu's 'reflexive and reflexivity' approach to social analysis, where reflexivity is about reflecting on power and situation. Thus, I chose to be 'intentionally reflexive', always keeping to the fore awareness of the proximity and distance I have in my status as a researcher who is also an African immigrant. I remain constantly conscious of my own position and vantage point. Questions would emerge about my own journey to become settled in the US and my own experiences, so that in divulging my experience I negotiated trust. One remarkable experience is that, after engaging in conversations for an extended period, one participant asked, "so which story should I tell you about me?" This shows that trust was never fully achieved in a single instance. Such questions, as posed by this participant, speak to points of trust evolving with contact. Trust enables conversations to develop; yet as more information is shared, trust is simultaneously tested and renegotiated. To give another example, I had been worked with one of the African immigrant families for more than ten contact times, each of which lasted more than an hour, to the extent that at one point this family asked me to help them move. Even as I tried to set myself apart, as a researcher exploring the experiences of African immigrants and refugees, to the adults and children in this family I continued to be one of the string of human service agency people, despite clarifying my position.

My interest as a recent immigrant, and a parent, was to learn from African immigrants and refugee families how they self assess their experience, and what kinds of strategies they adopt to pursue their new lives in the United States. Although the study did not specifically seek to understand parenting strategies of new immigrants, but well-being, parenting issues emerged as a strong theme. Two aspects of that theme stand out in the voices shared here; first, the effects of socio economic context in shaping parenting strategies, and second, the interactions of human service providers in influencing parenting approaches.

6. Broadening Constructions about Parenting: Voices of African Immigrants and Refugees in Northern New England

6.1 The socio-economic context and its effects in shaping parenting strategies

In this first vignette, we meet participant # 6, an African woman who is a lone parent. Her concerns were about working hard and getting ahead in the US, and as such, her children have had to "raise themselves." In this case, the lone mother's approach to parenting is to entrust her children as caretakers of one another, since she has to juggle earning a living. She values her children's responsibility for one another, and throughout her vignette this concern is highlighted.

"What many people don't realize is the difficulties of coming to the US and being a lone parent from Africa. In terms of parenting, back home things were easier because there were a variety of family members who could assist with care of children. Parenting in an African sense is never a one person thing. But here parenting is a solo activity. You have no one, just yourself, and those with husbands are perhaps better but I am my own husband and wife and have five children. There are good things we have as a family, each other. But I surely admit it; it has been hard for my children. They basically raise themselves. My life since I came to this country has been a mother who is chasing jobs and not directly caring for my children."

"When I came to Maine I did not want to limit myself. I tried whatever jobs I could find to make sure I landed something that could support me and my family securely. I am still looking. I want to find those opportunities that Americans talk about. I have to keep looking because I have to make a living for my five kids and help my oldest child back home. Although she is an adult she relies on me. I wanted to find ways to enhance my job opportunities here. When I came to Maine, I decided to branch away from other people from my own country. It is said that the US is the place in the world where you can remake yourself. So, I wanted to make sure I did that. But what could I remake myself with… working as a 'meat packer'? No ways. I have had to work two jobs to make ends meet. My children have had to learn fast to become independent and do things for themselves and the older ones helping the younger ones. My children look out for each other and that is what I emphasize to them. Even at school they know how to take care of each other. They stand for each other and when one gets in trouble I hear from the others. I have to rely on my children to become caretakers of each other, this means that I can go and work the abnormal hours that I have."

"By the time I come home I am always tired and the older ones have learnt to prepare meals. These are the important lessons for my children. Because I have tried not to limit myself to associating with only people from my country I have not had luck with sharing things like child care. It is a huge sacrifice not to become connected with people family. My from my country but I am trying to be more conscious of family, my children as children help themselves as I also help myself, this is what living here has taught us." (notes from interviews)

Participant # 2, a male lone parent raising three children on his own, whose children at the time of initial contact were in state custody because of allegations of physical abuse. The parent had spanked a child as a way of correcting behavior. Juggling shift work with a commitment towards mandatory parenting classes and undertaking therapies, while retaining the commitment to regain custody of his children, had shaped his approach to parenting. The difficulties in his work hours made it impossible to be fully present and available for his children. He had to rely on social services to provide support to his family. While this lone parent may have preferred 'no nonsense' parenting, so that his children realized the realities of his circumstances in terms of being a lone parent, in juggling an insecure job and having his life under surveillance for 'bad' parenting, he had to become a permissive parent. This has been to the detriment of his children, as he is aware that they are confused about the constant changes and the number of people who are experts in their lives, as the vignette below shows.

"It has been difficult to work and take care of my children. The work that I do is often shift work. It means that I have to rely on the system to help take care of the children. I am proud to have this job and I would like to hold on to it but it does get difficult meeting children's needs. I have had to rely on people around me to help with transportation, taking care of children, going to the grocery store but most important it is the job situation that means I have to intentionally juggle the children's time. For instance, by the time the children return from school three o'clock I have to leave for work. I have to rely on after school and before school programs. It has been difficult for the children, they don't know what to make of the changes. Many times the children are in trouble in school but I am unable to attend to the problems, not because I don't want to but because if I take time off the job I will likely lose it. If given a choice I would have raised my children in a strict manner so that they know their responsibilities but right now I can't lift a finger at them. I could get in trouble or lose them. They know this and they are taking advantage of it too because they are young and they don't understand the sacrifices that I as a parent am making." (notes from interviews)

Participant # 3 was a married new immigrant with five children, striving to find the American dream for himself and his children, and worried about social mobility. He talks about the loss of his middle class position when his family migrated to the US. His downward social mobility is explained through job discrimination incidents, but he has a desire to guide his children to better lives where they are not going to be dependent on wages like him but on their own ventures. The way that he has resolved the job insecurities and the problem of downward mobility is to become strict with his children. He pushes for academic success as a way to become self-sufficient. During observation, his children seemed to be accepting parental rules.

"I feel that I have lost out because of the war and being forced to leave my country and forced into becoming a refugee. I had a successful business at home. I come here, I started from the bottom again. I come here, I had to work as a cultural guide for outreach efforts to other immigrants. I used to have my own business now I can't even get the job that I am qualified to do. I am returning to school but there are no guarantees that my education would pay off because after all I am black. Jobs first go to whites, Asians and then blacks last. On the jobs as a black person I am not consulted about anything, yet they expected me to chart new programs. I have felt that I did not have a space. This is my reality and this is what my children's reality is going to become in this place. As a result of my negative job experiences here I am strict with my children. I want them to keep focused so that they can establish their own work instead of relying on jobs doled out unfairly in this society. I monitor where and what my children do here so that they can keep to themselves and focused on their life goals. This is the only way I see that they will avoid being discriminated against, establishing their own work. Right now I am going to school as a way to have a secure job and perhaps a life equivalent to what I had back home in social standing. But with the job experiences that I have had here I am not positive that my situation will likely change much but I keep working harder and this is what I encourage my children to do. Work even harder towards their goals." (notes from interviews)

6.2 African Immigrant/Refugee Families Interfacing with Human Service Providers

Participant # two's vignette is shared above. As previously mentioned, he was a lone parent raising three children who were at the time of these interviews in state custody for alleged physical abuse. Apparently, the father had spanked the child as punishment for breaking a window. This occurred when the family first arrived and were living in a shelter, and another parent had observed this spanking and perceived it as severe. For the safety and security of the child, all his children were taken away and put in state custody.

This lone parent was unhappy about the loss of his children and their care in foster homes.

This father had to earn his children back by engaging in programs that taught him how to manage his anger, and better parenting skills. One of the procedures meant home study/observation by family service workers who are ascribed as having a role in teaching the man parenting skills. I listened to a conversation as part of the interactions between the African parent and the family service workers. I have written the conversations as vignettes as constructed by the researcher from observations and interviews. In the first one, the African immigrant is addressing family service workers about their role in parenting.

"I am frustrated because you come to my house each week but each week your visits are not pleasant ones. Each week you (referring to the two service providers) are watching and waiting for me to do something wrong, then you write down what I have done wrong and this is used again and again to delay the return of my children ... for instance the other day when the children had come for a visit you rang the door bell and the children got excited. I knew it was you so I did not come right away to the door since you knew I was in the house. I was busy cooking in the kitchen but with one eye watching the children. As soon as the children heard the door bell, they got excited moved towards the door. Because I could not come to the door but I knew it was you I thought as responsible adults you would check that the children did not run outside onto the street. But instead you let them run off and then turned around and used that as a shortcoming in my parenting skills. It pains me to hear my children cursing. I don't curse and use foul language and even the three year old baby uses f---and s----words indiscriminately, that is not my way of talking. That is not the way we raise children." (notes from interviews)

Clearly the African parent quoted above sees the role of family service workers as co-parents, responsible adults who are coming to help him. As such, the least they could do is to make sure the children don't run off towards the street. But the family service workers had their own script of 'good parenting' emanating from their own culture and context. A good parent is one who is independent and sole manager of his or her children. The human service workers were not in the house as co-parents but as 'experts' with the know-how of what constitutes good parenting. Their job is to enforce the dominant scripts of parenting, not to help support the parents, even though their role is defined as supportive services for families. Secondly, the human service providers were seen by the African immigrant father as enforcers of the dominant culture, where parenting is individualized and one has to be in control of one's children all the time. The responsibility for children lies not with older children and other adults, but solely on the shoulders of parents, in line with the parenting standard of the privatized US nuclear family. In this case, if parents are unable to meet their roles, they are inadequate, and have to defer to human service providers on matters of child rearing; yet the human service providers in their expert role only act as supervisors, to check for 'bad parenting'. Clearly, in this vignette, the image of parental control as the main strategy remains securely in place, but the idea of a parent as a provider (for example, where the parent prioritized feeding the children while keeping one eye on them) may go unnoticed. The parent's role in enabling children to independently initiate play and take care of each other is ignored as a strength in this family. There is a selective focus on certain aspects of the concept of parenting, such that the parenting of the 'other' is scrutinized for 'badness'.

Participant # 3 is the same family man whose voice is shared in the above discussion about concerns with jobs. He was a new immigrant aspiring to find the American dream for himself and his children. His aspirations and conflicts are played out in a decision to remove his children from public school and to enroll them in a Christian school. Public education systems serve as a transformative ideological project that attempts to revise or realign new immigrant/refugee identities (Forman, 2001). Within the school, the student who is a 'new' immigrant is supposed to make the transition from remedial classes, which include English as a second language, and become assimilated into the mainstream.

"I watched my children who were fluent French speakers begin to be speakers of English only; this is part of being American to speak only English. It seems ironic though that the world is diverse but only a single language is emphasized. The other languages are to be learnt by osmosis from their homes. How could I let my children be subjected to this kind of learning? It is difficult because TV reinforces that one language. As a parent I am busy trying to get work and I work more than seventy hours a week to make ends meet. How can I ensure that my children embrace a multicultural world? I come home, I am tired. My wife stays home with the younger children and she tries to help raise them but there is no support for her. She is on her own. In the schools, the white people think they know everything and what is good for our children. I don't want to give them that authority, that they know everything, trust them to say they know everything, because in the long run how my child turns out as an adult becomes my responsibility not their problem."

"For a year we were hearing that the school was helping my children by putting them in remedial classes. If that is the help it is no help at all. I had to remove my children, send them to a Christian school. I wanted them to understand directly that school prepares them for jobs. My children have no luxury of getting things wrong. I don't have the money for extra tutoring; I don't have the money to bail them out of jails. They need structure now so that they can focus on what is important. My children have no luxuries for them to wait and find themselves. The design of the classroom and school environment here was difficult for me. There is always a schism, the public school wants children to be cooperators but yet competition is the order of the day. The schools test and test children, if my child does not succeed on these tests there is something wrong with the child. Yet, my young child's learning was designed in such as way to 'explore your own self' instead of direction and discipline."

"I value parenting that has direct rules and direction. I can tell my children this is right and wrong … I don't have to say let us explore this and that. I am a parent, I am the adult and I have to be responsible to guide my children on what is good. I had to take my children to a place of learning where there are expectations and clear guidelines about discipline. The design of the classroom in the public schools here is perhaps good for the 'white children' but it is likely to put my children at a second rate and that is not what I want for them." (notes from observation and conversations)

Being a good parent for the above adult meant assuming the responsibility of directing his children's education. The parent understands that success for his children means acquiring the culture of power. He wanted to direct his children's learning instead of endorsing the free-choice that is emphasized in the school. He understands the power of the dominant culture, which the schools try to mute by claiming that everyone is on an equal playing field. The parent understands that his children have no luxury to explore and innovate but must learn what needs to be learnt. As new immigrants who are outside the dominant culture and its power, explicit instructions about the expectations may mean success in acquiring power. Thus, the parent quoted above wants his children to learn to participate in the culture of power, instead of beating about the bush by attempting to be egalitarian in the classroom when everything else is not. Therefore, the removal of his children and enrolling them in a Christian school was an alternative for him to teach the 'culture of power' explicitly to his children, and perhaps help them achieve greater success in gaining access to jobs and the American dream.

Participant # fifteen was a woman who was herself a service provider. Trained as a social worker she was at the time "at home mothering", as she put it. In addition, she was interested to becoming part of the community and human service providers of the neighborhood where she lived. She eagerly sought to include her children in the events and activities that her community offered. To her, this cross-cultural learning was important for her children. She shares her experience in the local library's story hour:

"I do want my children to succeed in this society. My children are growing up in a different environment than I did. Many more cultures are intermingling, one has to prepare their children for that life. I have taken whatever opportunity that I can to extend those opportunities. I have tried to figure out ways that could enhance my children's reading and exposure to the culture here. I have been proactive wanting to expose my children to those areas that are positive about this society. This is what mothering is. I have taken my child (four year old son) to the main library for story hour. I have gone there every week. I sit there watching. The people who run never notice my interest. I sit there as a visitor, not an active participant where my child and the other children could learn from me. The story hour is structured in such a way that "them" white people who are themselves parents like me are the readers of stories. What does that say to my child – that every week we listen to a white parent read a story? It surely runs the message to my child that I am not capable to be a parent who can be an example to him and other children around him? There has never been a story hour in my language. There is no one who has ever invited me to share stories for children who come to story hour. This is the reason why many parents do not venture into such activities with their children. I have tried to follow the opportunities, as they say there are opportunities in the United States. I come to story hour with my child and I watch my bright child shrivel as he is slighted in conversation, he is quizzed as if he has a low IQ. What parent can subject their child to this?" (notes from observations and conversations)

The parent above is the ideal 'American' parent taking a keen interest in her children's education. The parent was ensuring that her son should begin school knowing the school environment by actively engaging in community events like story hour at the local library. Yet because she is an outsider she is hardly expected to be a full participant in the activities herself. She is not expected to be already supporting her own child in ways that her child and other children can learn from her. Ignoring parents from culturally diverse backgrounds excludes their experience.

Participants # 5 was a mother and adult daughter. The mother and daughter were reminiscing about the days when the daughter was young. She had arrived in the US as a nine year old.

"My mother has always been protective of me. She cares what I engaged in school even if she is not one of those mothers who goes directly to school to see how things are. I used to come home, she would quiz me about the day, I mean the whole how it all went and what I did. She would give advice about what I should have said, not said, done, etc. It used to infuriate me. But now I realize that it was her way of showing concern about my education and well-being. She comes from a background where parents believed in not interfering with the school, whether good or bad that belief, it has its frustrations."

"When you are young coming from another culture you need parental support. I had diffi-culties with peers and school teachers, I needed my mother to stand up for me, to come up to the teachers but she never did that. Instead, she would expect to coach me about how to. But instead she would quiz me about my day when I got home but never intervene in school."

"My mother has been cautious about my engagements in extra-curriculum activities and programs designed for at risk children. In my mother's home unlike some parents one does not show up with a slip to do and go wherever and it is signed. With my mother I had to explain everything and how it was beneficial to my development and how I will stay out of trouble. She is strict in these ways. I have always liked to dance but she has had her doubts about that. Often expressed negatively, but I do understand now – how could I expect my mother to see dance as a way of life when traditional work is what she knows. We know from experience that sometimes children come with slips from school that says your child is going where and is doing this but that is never fully explained to the mother. The mother interjects, but this is my child, I need to have full knowledge about her whereabouts. I guess when it comes to our children as refugees, explanations do not matter as long as someone is trying to do good for them. There is not an expectation that I could be doing something good for my children. But instead, their (programs) are the ones that are doing something good for our children. Sometimes this creates confusions for our children. That is why you find some parents washing their hands of raising children. Parents are already working hard to provide and then the pressures of protecting and disciplining their children is confused by all the other helpers. It becomes too much. Some parents are just not there anymore. What happens when parents wash their hands of their roles? Those are the chil-dren who end up in trouble. These are the parents who end up labeled as uncaring for their children but the question is: who has created the disastrous situation in the first place, is never raised. We know that as new immigrants we are perceived as 'at risk' just for being us. We are seen in a different light. Sometimes this seeing in a different light keeps us in a different place. A place where we are the target for change, we as adults are supposed to be taught how to raise our children. It is good to learn. I welcome tips about parenting but when one is presumed not good enough to support one's children it gets difficult."

"My mother quizzes me about everything except sexuality stuff. That is 'no go area' with African parents. I remember one time when us new immigrant students organized our-selves and advocated for changes in remedial classes, where we were placed. My mother was skeptical about my engagement in confronting the school. She spoke about us interfer-ing with the teachers who were expert in our education; she wanted me to be cautious. But

I see my mother's caution as too trusting of the education system here. She perceives school as good here and always in my best interest. But having been through the system I don't believe that schools have our interests most of the time." (notes from observations and conversations)

The child and parent conversation above refers poignantly to the conflicting expectations about parental role, and school and child interactions in education. The immigrant parent comes from a background that places high value on education but believes in non-interference in school, even though the daughter would have liked the parent to be physically there in school with her, 'to stand up' for her. The mother sees her parental role as coaching her daughter to face the difficulties by offering ways to address the situations she comes up against. But the child who is experiencing school thinks otherwise. Although the mother seems to understand the child's experience, her cautiousness about her daughter's involvement in her own advocacy is a way of protecting her. The mother was adamant that exercising caution was important because the teachers were the ones in charge and at the end of it all they are the ones who are going to make her life positive or negative. The mother understood the unequal power in the education system and still wanted to protect her daughter from any likely negative repercussions from children's advocacy, in a system where the voice of children is not usually heard.

Here we see the task of parenting as weaving in and out of the day to day experience of parent and child. Parenting is constructed and reconstructed with past and present scripts. The mother stands aside for the child to learn to handle situations herself, but she is never far away from quizzing her and coaching her on how to do things. From this vantage point, it is important to see how parents from culturally diverse backgrounds are supporting their children before the helpers instill their own patterns of parenting.

6.3 Being locked into the refugee status explicitly

"They like us here when we are helpless. We come from the war torn ravaged countries on the African continent. There is nothing that could be good from that continent we are made to feel. The desire to help 'poor people from Africa' gets to be excessive when your story of atrocities is told. Their help comes pouring like rain and in return we are supposed to be graciously grateful for being rescued. But when does the helping become detrimental to us? When I began to raise my own voice and demand that I and others like me be provided the services in a way that is respectful of us I became trouble. Then, I was no good, I was perceived as ungrateful for what this country has given. They never quite say it to my face but I would hear it in subtle remarks. Like look who is talking now!"

"How do I teach my own children to become who they want to become when the environment surrounding me says you are perpetually a 'refugee'? I tried to help as a volunteer in one of the organizations here. Although they did not say it in my face, in their forms and at intake I had to be a 'Christian' to volunteer, never mind that I am a Christian, but being Christian in the eyes of this organization means being white and middle class. Since white is helping black, my status as a refugee is to receive. Not to help one another as we know how from Africa. We as refugees are not counted among the helpers because our status here is to receive. I began to look for ways outside the helpers, that I could join with others like me for support to help teach my children that they should strive to get out the box that they have locked us 'as refugees'. I had to break away from the helpers and learn to help myself understand the two worlds my children and I live in. I am still trying to figure out how my children could strive in a place that sees them as less than human. I know I come out as tough on my children but there are pressures to move yourself out of the box that you are locked into. But when I started to make demands about appropriate service for me and the likes of me I became no good."

The above participant tries to parent with full awareness of the external environment in which he lives, where help is only given to the 'deserving', and the degradation of humanness that comes from being helped because the society you are in believes that there is something wrong with you. The participant talks about breaking away from the helping in order to find ways to cope with the two worlds. In an attempt to help his children cope with the two worlds, he is aware that his children perceive him as too strict.

7. What Can We Conclude about Parenting Approaches from the Voices of African Immigrants and Refugees?

Parenting as a socially constructed idea is highly subjective. Through the voices of parents shared here, we see that parents use a multitude of repertoires to draw from to guide, care and socialize their children. Parents whose voices are shared here use examples of their own personal experience as scripts to help them parent, but this does not provide quite enough encounters and interactions with their children, and therefore human service workers shape the parenting approaches. The reality of parenting for 'new immigrants' is that their lives tend to interface with multiple scripts: their 'own', the availability of a community infrastructure that supports parenting, internal factors related to the child and family personality and status, the normative ideas and practices of the host country as channeled through various media (particularly human service agencies, schools and the communication media), and structural factors.

In this paper, I have highlighted the socioeconomic context of new arrivals, particularly the concern for jobs as a shaper of parenting. The worries about job insecurity demands that African immigrants and refugee parents approach their parenting in a direct way, where roles are clearer, and children learn to become responsible for themselves and their siblings. This is important as it enables parents to make ends meet from multiple and often low paid jobs, where they have to work long hours away from their children. The socioeconomic context is also critical to understand as a shaper of parenting strategies for, as working class, African immigrants and refugees want their children to succeed. As part of their role as teachers to their children, parents seek clearer paths that can enhance their children's participation in the mainstream, sometimes defying unrestricted ways where children are encouraged to explore and initiate, opting instead for directed and structured learning. In this context, African parents whose experience is shared here report that they assume repertoires of success as embedded in the host country's environment, e.g. stay in school, work hard and harder, and then you will succeed. However, parents share that, in the realization that success is elusive, even with hard work, they become strict disciplinarians with their children, wanting them to work for themselves and not rely on wages.

Since refugees' lives interact with human service providers, this is another factor highlighted through the voices of African immigrants and refugees as a shaper of parenting strategies. For example, the general response of human service agencies to address the needs of African immigrants and refugees has been within the universalized western framework of 'normal' parenting of Euro-Americans, versus the 'deficient' parenting of persons of color. When parents perceive themselves within the deficit model, and where human service workers become inspectors of how this newcomer is faring as a parent, varied parenting responses emerge within this new reality. As we see in the vignettes above, some parents become protective of their children, not wanting their families to become part of the 'helpless'. Those parents who have no choice but to use social service providers may end up employing resistance strategies that attempt to educate the social service providers about what their needs actually are. As we saw in one of the vignettes above, the 'newcomer' expects co-parenting with human service providers but instead the worker sees her role as to instruct about parenting. Coming from an individualist background, the worker sees deficiencies in the parenting of the immigrant through his failure to control his children. He must, then, be taught how to control his children. The worker saw her job as an instructor, as knowing what good parenting means, in this exchange. The resistance by the newcomer developed into silent acceptance of the human service provider as the 'knower', instead of the interactions being a space of learning to co-parent. We see that parents become protective of their children when their lives are in constant contact with helpers, as exemplified by the parents' experience here with human service providers, the school and libraries.

Adopting 'deficient mode' leads to protectiveness, on the one hand, while on the other it may lead to self-exclusion, resulting in deepened alienation. The deficit model of engagement may also lead to disempowerment to the point of "washing their hands of" the ownership of their children's care because of conflicting agendas.

Through a selection of voices shared in this article, we hear that African immigrant and refugee parents may relinquish their parenting responsibilities because of both conflicting expectations and being inundated with day by day activities to make ends meet. If parents are relinquishing their responsibilities to parent because they have no choice, who is assuming the parenting role? Given the role of human service providers as instructors in care, are they ready to take up the role of co-parents? If so, what are these approaches to parenting going to be like, given the tendencies to evaluate social experience through individualist and ethnocentric perspectives?

Overall, I found African immigrant and refugee parents to be so preoccupied with the realities of their lives, jobs, making a living, their children, that stopping to have conversations about being parents brought an intense desire from them to want to understand how they were as parents. However, the reality of their busy lives often makes it unrealistic for them consciously to evaluate their parenting approaches, despite their circumstances as new arrivals and the ever changing environments demanding that they constantly reconstruct parenting approaches. As reflected in the select voices shared here, parents and children were interested just to talk about their experience. It is important here to understand how parents support their children. Often, immigrants and refugees bring up families within environments that are unsupportive of difference and disregard the contextualizing experience of immigrants and refugees. Instead, 'one size fits all' approaches to cultural retraining are favored as ways to help integrate 'newcomers'. The voices shared here challenge the use of prototypes and stereotypes in understanding parenting approaches. Let us, as researchers and human service providers, take time to explore how people of cultural diverse backgrounds are actually helping their children.

References

Baumrind, D. (1972). An exploratory study of socialization effects on Black children: some Black-White Comparisons. *Child Development*, 43, 1, 261-267.

Baumrind, D. (1971). Current patterns of parental authority. *Developmental Psychology Monographs*, 4 (Part 2), 1-103.

Baumrind, D. (1968). Authoritarian versus authoritative parental control. *Adolescence*, 3, 255-272.

Calzada, E.J.; Eyberg, S.M. (2002). Self reported parenting practices in Dominican and Puerto Rican mothers of young children. *Journal of Clinical Child Adolescent Psychology*, 31, 3, 354-364.

Chao, R.K. (2001). Extending research on the consequences of parenting style for Chinese Americans and European Americans. *Child Development*, 72, 1832-1843.

Chen, X.; Dong, Q.; Zhou, H. (1997). Authoritative and Authoritarian practices and social and school performance in Chinese children. *International Journal of Behavioral Development*, 21, 855-873.

Davis, P.W. (1994). The changing meanings of spanking. In Joel Best (eds.) Troubling Children: Studies of Children: Studies of Children and Social Problems (pp. 133-149). New York:: Walter de Gruyter, Inc.

Denby, R.,; Alford, K. (1996). Understanding African American discipline styles: Suggestions for effective social work intervention. *Journal of Multicultural Social Work*, 4, 3, 81-98.

Djamba, Y.K. (1999). African immigrants in the United States: A socio-demographic profile in comparison to native blacks. *Journal of Asian and African Studies* (Brill), 34, 2, 210-216.

Dodoo, F. Nii-Amoo. (1997). Assimilation differences among Africans in America. *Social Forces* 76, 2, 527-546.

Fooks, S. (2001). Parenting in different contexts. *Family Matters*, 59, 84-88.

Forman, Murray. (2001). 'Straight outta Mogadishu': Prescribed identities and performative practices among Somali youth in North American high schools. *Topia*, 5, 1-21.

Freeman, N. K. (1998). Look at the east to gain a new perspective, understand cultural differences, and appreciate cultural diversity. *Early Childhood Education Journal*, 26, 2, 79-82.

Gorman, J.C. (1998). Parenting attitudes and practices of immigrant Chinese mothers of adolescents. *Family Relations*, 47, 73-80.

Gross, E. (2003). Native American family continuity as resistance: The Indian Child Welfare Act as legitimation for effective social work practice. *Journal of Social Work*, 3, 1, 31-44.

Kamya, H. A. (1997). African immigrants in the United States: The challenge for Research and Practice. *Social Work*, 42, 2, 154-166.

Knight, G.P.; Virdin, L.M.; Roosa, M. (1994). Socialization and family correlates of mental health outcomes among Hispanic and Anglo American children: Consideration of cross ethnic scalar equivalence. *Child Development*, 65, 212-224.

LeVine, R. (1980). A cross-cultural perspective on parenting. In M.D. Fantini, R. Cardenes (eds.), *Parenting in a multicultural society* (pp.17-26). New York: Longman.

Lim, S.-L.; Lim, B.K. (2005). Parenting style and child outcomes in Chinese and immigrant Chinese families-Current findings and cross-cultural considerations in conceptualization and research in Peterson, Steinmetz, Wilson (eds.) Parenting-Youth Relations: Cultural and Cross-Cultural Perspectives (pp.21-42). New York: The Haworth Press.

Maiter, S.; George, U. (2003). Understanding context and culture in parenting approaches of immigrant south Asian mothers. *AFFILIA*, 18, 4, 411-428.

McCollum, P. (1996). Immigrant education: Obstacles to immigrant parent participation in schools. *IDRA Newsletter* Nov/Dec 1996. http://www.idra.org/ newslttr/ 1996/Pam.htm, retrieved May 24, 2006.

Nwadiora, E. (1996). Therapy with African families. *Western Journal of Black Studies*, 20, 3, 117-125.

Peterson, G.W.; Steinmetz, S.K.; Wilson, S.M. (2005). Parent-youth relations: Cultural and cross-cultural perspectives. New York: The Haworth Press.

Remennick, L. (2005). Immigration, gender and psychosocial adjustment: A study of 150 immigrant couples in Israel. *Sex Roles*, 53, 11/12, 847-863.

Querido, J.G.; Warner, T.D.; Eyberg, S.M. (2002). Parenting styles and child behavior in African American families of preschool children. *Journal of Clinical Child and Adolescent Psychology*, 31, 21, 272-278.

Rudy, D.; Grusec, J.E. (2001). Correlates of authoritarian parenting in individualist and collectivist cultures and implications for understanding the transmission of values. *Journal of Cross-Cultural Psychology*, 32, 202-212.

Schmitz, C.L.; Jacobus, M.V.; Stakeman, C.; Valenzuela, G.A.; Sprankel, J. (2003). Immigrant and Refugee Communities: Resiliency, Trauma, Policy, and Practice. In Stretch, Burkemper, Hutchison, Wilson (eds.). *Practicing Social Justice* (pp. 135-158), Haworth Press: New York.

Sharry, J.; Owens, C. (2000). The rules of engagement: A case study of a group with angry adolescents. *Clinical Child Psychology and Psychiatry*, 5, 1, 53-63.

Soriano, G.; Weston, R.; Violet, V.; Kolar, K. (2001). Meeting the challenges of parenting. *Family Matter,* Academic Search Premier Database, retrieved May 20, 2006.

Valdes, G. (1996). Con Respeto: Bridging the Distance Between Culturally Diverse Families and Schools: An Ethnographic Portrait. New York: Teachers College Press.

Zajacova, A. (2002). Constructing the reality of the immigrant life. *Journal of Social Distress and the Homeless*, 11, 1, 69-79.

Christian Spatscheck

Youth Cultures between Control and Emancipation – Interpretations from a Western European Perspective

1. Introduction

Young people create and develop youth cultures within an ongoing struggle between public control and youth cultural emancipation. Most of the youth cultures in Western Europe are following influences from international backgrounds that put them in contact with local traditions. Since the first known youth cultures deriving from the German bourgeois and proletarian youth movements around the First World War, public interactions with youth cultures follow an ongoing dialectic of control and attempts of (re-)liberation (Giesecke, 1975). Starting from the postwar era until present times, this essay summarizes the leading theoretical approaches to the analysis of sociocultural dimensions of youth cultures from a Western European perspective. In the following sections I provide basic information about the sociocultural mechanisms of youth cultures in society, and aim to help social workers clarify their own roles within the emerging conflicts.

2. Early Approaches: Theories about Youth and Subcultures

The first attempt to develop a theoretical description of youth cultures came at the end of the 1920s in the works of Frederic Thrasher and his colleagues at the sociological Chicago School (Moser, 2000: 15). In his research about youth gangs from the poorer areas of Chicago, Thrasher was the first to formulate the idea of a special *way of life* of the youth gangs, which reject the dominant forms of mainstream culture through the development of different rituals, symbols, and codes. The term *youth culture* was first used by the German reform pedagogue Gustav Wyneken around the time of the First World War (Spatscheck, 2006: 125). As one of the leaders of the German youth movement, he used this term to describe his hopes for a new cultural revolution through liberated young people who began to gather in peer groups without the controlling influences of adults. By 1942, Talcot Parsons had introduced the term *youth culture* into sociology (Moser 2000: 17). He regarded the passage of youth as a relatively independent social status with specific values, norms, ideas, and symbols. In 1947, the American sociologist Milton Gordon (1947) first used the term *subculture* in the context of youth cultures. He tried to describe special cultures of ethnic groups like Italian immigrants or the black Americans that follow rules that differ from the white U.S. middle classes, thereby challenging the assumption of all-embracing norms and values shared in a society (Farin, 2002: 58). Later, American essays from Albert Cohen (1957) and German essays from Fritz Sack (1971) referred to the concept of subculture as delinquency. This connection has dominated the sociology of youth for a long time and can still be found in today's discourses about youth cultures or at-risk youth.

In the German research about subcultures, the sociologist Rolf Schwendter (1971) separates subculture into *part cultures* und *countercultures*. He regards part cultures as middle class forms of cultures that are dominated by adults, oriented to consumerism and compensation, and embodying important functions of integration connected with little potential for challenge of the public order. Countercultures he describes as cultures of effective opposition to the existing system that aim to direct the change of norms and institutions. Within this *progressive type* of counterculture, he classifies the youth cultures of the hippies, beatniks, and rockers as *emotional progressive subcultures* that strongly favor individual freedom, while he identifies *rationalist progressive subcultures* within the German intellectual and student movements of the late sixties and early seventies.

3. British Cultural Studies: Subversion through Style

Since the middle of the 1960s, groundbreaking research about youth subcultures and their functions in society has been carried out at the Centre of Contemporary Cultural Studies (CCCS) at the University of Birmingham (Brooker, 1998: 59). Referring to the early works of Richard Hoggart (1957) and Raymond Williams (1958, 1961), the research at the CCCS sees Cultural Studies as a separate *science of culture*. The CCCS researchers took the decisive step to adopt a wider understanding of culture that comprises not only the works, expressions and artifacts of the official high culture but also the entire popular everyday culture (Brooker, 1998; Moser, 2000: 20ff.; Farin, 2002: 61ff.). While the former research about culture only regarded singular objects of high culture, the researchers at the CCCS were the first to include the relations between the cultural objects and the people using and producing them. From this perspective, the ways of everyday life became relevant to formal research for the first time. Rolf Lindner emphasizes (in Clarke, Honneth, 1979: 9) that 'culture' was introduced as a new conceptual approach to analyze how individuals, groups, and classes realize their social and material existence within their specific historical context.

The researchers from CCCS do not accept the concept of a holistic and uniform youth generation. Instead, they identify different youth subcultures as class-related phenomena (Holert, Terkessidis, 1997: 60; Moser, 2000: 24; Farin, 2002: 61). Youth subcultures are described as generational subsystems of the parents' class culture, which is differentiated in working class, middle class, and upper class culture. For the class cultures a continuing struggle about power and subordination is assumed. In this conflict only one class culture can become the dominant form of culture. To explain these mechanisms, the CCCS researcher Dick Hebdige (1998: 15) uses the term *hegemony* as defined by Antonio Gramsci. He understands hegemony as the authority of one class over other dominated classes. According to Gramsci (see Hebdige, 1998: 16), this authority is always designed to seem normal and natural, although the dominated classes would in fact have the possibility to rise up against the dominating class and its concepts of public order. Hebdige follows the arguments of Louis Althusser to explain this paradox with the concept of *ideology*. Althusser argues that through class-related ideologies the ideas of a "distorted" class consciousness are carried on unconsciously (Hebdige, 1998: 12). In the works of the CCCS, youth cultures are regarded in relation to their class backgrounds and the dominant classes in society. The dichotomy "either class or generation"[1] is thereby annulled (Clarke, Honneth, 1979: 45). Within the context of this class orientation, the authors from CCCS explore the ideas of typical working class youth cultures like the rockers, teddy boys, or punks, and typical middle class youth cultures like the mods or hippies (Farin, 2002: 62).

Young people's conflicts with their cultures of origin and with the dominant cultural hegemony are understood as a dispute with stylistic means that leads to a *subversion through style*. Authors like Hebdige and Clarke analyze how young people apply stylistic objects to communicate with their environment (Hebdige, 1998; Clarke, Honneth, 1979). They take up a concept of Roland Barthes, who explained how in everyday culture signs become enlarged to be *carriers of meaning* that embody a new meaning of symbolic or mythological origin. For example, Barthes refers to a special cover photo-

---

1   The quotes which were originally in German have been translated by the author.

graph of the French journal, Paris-Match. The title shows a picture of a black soldier wearing a French uniform and saluting the French flag. Beyond this overt meaning of the picture, Barthes recognizes a second one: this picture communicates for him that "France is a great empire, under whose flag all her sons, without regard to their colour, serve loyally, and that there is no better argument against the opponents of a supposed colonialism than the eagerness of this young negro to serve his supposed oppressors"[2] (Barthes, 1964: 95). According to Barthes, virtually every object of our everyday culture can be expanded into a sign with new symbolic and mythological meaning.

Hebdige shows how these processes can also be found in the youth cultures of punks and rastas, where signs are adorned with new mythological meanings as well. Through the process of *bricolage* (tinkering), objects are taken from their usual contexts and ascribed new meanings (Hebdige, 1998: 102; Nachtwey, 1987). Young people transfer their personal systems of representation to their newly designed youth cultural objects and thereby create new bearers of meaning. The newly created symbols embody their aberration from, and their refusal of and resistance to, the dominant culture and thereby take on a subversive character. Through the creation of new symbols, young people can distinguish themselves from adults and other youth cultures.

The major innovations arising from the CCCS youth culture studies are their new explanations of sociocultural mechanisms and the detailed analyses of the mechanisms of subversion through aesthetic and stylistic means. Two aspects of the work of the CCCS can, however, be criticized. Firstly, they use a culturalistic understanding of society that equates culture with social structures or even the whole society. Mario Bunge (1996: 56) argues from a sociophilosophical background that culture is only the sum of the properties of social systems and should not be equated or confused with social systems themselves. Secondly, according to newer studies, it seems no longer realistic to connect certain youth cultures directly to class-specific backgrounds (Vollbrecht, 1995, 1997; Holert, Terkessidis 1997: 60; Farin, 2002: 70; Ferchhoff, et al., 1995). At least since the late 1980s, youth cultures have become much more open to members of different class and milieu backgrounds. Therefore, a rigid class-specific division of youth cultures has become more and more obsolete. This should, however, not lead to the misconception that class-specific factors no longer influence the general life of young people.

---

2   The quotes which were originally from a German edition have been translated by the author.

4. German Debates about Subcultures and Lifestyles

At the end of the 1990s, the German sociologist Ralf Vollbrecht formulated criticisms of a class-related assignment of youth cultures: "Early groupings of youth culture were predominantly related to their milieu of origin, and that meant it could effectively be anticipated which grouping would be attractive to which adolescent. Today's youth cultures are largely disconnected from their milieus of social origin as they have for the most part forfeited their connecting force" (Vollbrecht, 1997: 23). Instead of milieu-related classifications of youth cultures, he proposed regarding them as *leisure scenes* (Freizeitszenen) that, as open formations, can freely be joined and left again. Lifestyles are regarded as aesthetic options that are not merely superficial habits of consumption and leisure. Furthermore, they mediate the affiliation to collective systems of values around a good way of life (Vollbrecht, 1995: 24). According to Vollbrecht's model, individuals choose and combine their lifestyles very freely from different cultural offers. He emphasizes that the development of lifestyles means to conduct active and ongoing debates with a flow of cultural, social, and media messages. In terms of the free choice of lifestyles, young people have the opportunity to assess for themselves different youth cultures and choose different intensities of identification with youth cultures. Vollbrecht (1997: 23) would not deny the existing influence of class and milieu origins, but his approach emphasizes the meaning derived from the subjective construction of expressive and aesthetic lifestyles.

With his basic focus on lifestyles, Vollbrecht (1995: 32) is parting from the concept of youth cultures as countercultural subcultures. Facing a general depoliticization, dehierarchisation, deconstruction, and commercialization of youth cultures, Baacke and Ferchhoff follow Vollbrecht's assessment that the concepts of subcultures and countercultures are no longer adequate models (Baacke, Ferchhoff, 1995). Schwendter still opposes this verdict. Twenty-five years after his first analysis of oppositional youth cultures he still sees countercultural potential in youth cultures (Schwendter in Ferchhoff, et al., 1995: 11).

5. A French View: Stratification and Emancipation through Cultural Capital

The French sociologist Pierre Bourdieu developed a concept of social stratification that is based on the degree of access to economic, social, and cultural capital (Bourdieu, 2003). In particular, the form of cultural capital offers strong references for an analysis of youth cultures. Through symbolic acts of design like the preference for a certain kind of music, fashion, literature, film, sport, car brand, or room design, every individual sets his or her *distinctions* (Bourdieu, 2003: 278). The hierarchic stratification of a society is built on collective valuations of aesthetic elements as low, crude, vulgar, cheap, or slavish, while others are attributed as sublime, elaborated, illustrious, or distinguished (Bourdieu, 2003: 27). Social stratification is established through shared acknowledgment of higher and lower forms of culture. The social position of a person and his or her lifestyle are, therefore, mutually and inextricably connected (Bourdieu, 2003: 11). A certain social status leads to the development of certain cultural preferences. In return, certain forms of cultural capital are necessary to gain access to certain social positions and roles. Bourdieu developed *habitus* as an analytical term to connect these two fields. The habitus is an incorporated pattern that leads to the development of "appropriate" thoughts and actions. It leads to the realization of a lifestyle that seems appropriate for the objective (resources) and subjective (class-specific perception and valuation) conditions of life. In this sense, the habitus is a set of mental structures that influences our thoughts and actions and, therefore, leads to the connection between the individual and the social structure.

Youth cultures offer many possibilities to gain cultural and social capital that otherwise would not be accessible to young people. Through membership of youth cultures and active fandom, young people can open up new forms of cultural capital (Fiske in SPoKK, 1997: 54ff.). Moreover, young people can develop new knowledge and abilities, especially when their fandom enters active or producing dimensions, whether as a break-dancer, skater, member of a band, or a DJ. With these new forms of cultural capital, they can enhance their habitus and find a new potential for acknowledgement. Likewise, young people can acquire new social capital in their peer groups. Through active communication with peers and the environment, processes of mutual social learning are very likely to occur. The cultural and social capital gained in youth cultures can be used by young people in other life contexts, offering new possibilities for upward social mobility. The development of new social possibilities out of youth cultures can help emancipate young people from the difficult life conditions that result from marginal or low social positions in society.

6. Glocalization: Youth Cultures within Postmodern and Internationalized Contexts

Through the increase of media communication and the possibilities of nearly unlimited data streams, youth cultures have become phenomena that are *globally* spread, but are reaching young people in their *local* living contexts (Roth, 2002; Neumann-Braun, 2003: 77ff. and 246ff.). However, young people do not remain passive recipients. In the sense of Roland Robertson's term *glocalization*, most of the global impulses of youth cultures are actively redeveloped as local variations and new creations (Neumann-Braun 2003: 82). Within electronic dance music there are clear conceptions about the typical sound of Detroit, Chicago, Berlin, Bristol, Cologne, Miami, or Vienna. In the Hip Hop culture the rappers interpret different local contexts in their texts, whether American, African, European, Asian, or Australian. Within most regions there are further developments; for example, the differences between the Hip Hop sound of the U.S. East and West Coasts or the stylistic battles between the German Hip Hop enclaves of Berlin, Hamburg, Frankfurt, or Stuttgart show the existing range of variations.

Research about youth cultures in the late 1990s and the early 2000s describes an increasing acceleration and diversification of youth cultural innovation and societal control (McRobbie, 1999; Eshun, 1998; Neumann-Braun 2003; Kleiner, Szepanski 2003; Holert, Terkessidis 1997; Bonz 2002; Roth, Rucht 2000; Moser 2000; Spatscheck, et al., 1997). In terms of the enormous financial interests of international corporations and the great spending potential of young people, many youth cultural elements like fashion or music have become commercial goods of global culture capitalism. Brands have become products themselves. The current objects are not relevant, but their brand names, like Nike, Adidas, The Gap, Levis, Replay, or Diesel, are products that embody a certain image of lifestyle and can be sold at much higher profit margins than their actual cost of production would imply (Klein 2001).

Holert and Terkessidis (1997) describe a current trend towards a *mainstream of minorities*. Since the middle of the 1990s, former minority youth cultures like Grunge, Brit Pop, Riot Grrls, Nu Metal, Neo-Punk, and certain branches of Hip Hop and Techno, have become dominant currents in the youth cultural mainstream, though they embody controversial and counter-cultural messages. Many protagonists emanating from these scenes became popular in the dominant cultural mainstream, though in former times they would have been highly subversive figures. All these different styles exist next to each other in a remarkable unity without one dominant style leaving the others behind. This stable, pluralized coexistence of styles leads to a cultural mainstream formation built of very different but coexisting minorities. Although what is now a postmodern formation of plural minority cultures would previously have embodied emancipatory potential in the context of Fordist industrial systems, it seems no longer able to fulfil this potential within the current contexts of globalized hypercapitalism. In the end postmodern capitalism needs exactly the flexible, dynamic, and youthful egotacticians that, like the members of the minority youth cultures, can flexibly reinvent themselves according the rapid demands of change in a global culture of competition. Likewise, globalized capitalism is highly capable of controlling minority youth cultural positions commercially and politically. While protesting against the inclusive forces of the Fordist society of their parents, postmodern youngsters are in fact creating the societal and cultural foundations for post-Fordist production, communication, and consumption (Hardt, Negri 2001: 156). From this perspective, postmodern youth has become the avant garde of their own abolition (Holert, Terkessidis 1997: 15).

From a meta-theoretical view, the aestheticization of life conditions in youth cultures can only reach liberation at the aesthetic level. This does not lead to liberation at an ontological level: the current power relations remain the same. Aestheticizations, therefore, tend to confuse ontology and epistemology. By mistaking being with design, this even veils the conditions of power in society. A change in the relations of power would only be possible by aesthetic means if aesthetic provocations and distortions refer to persons or institutions in power and thereby lead to questioning and critique of the relations (and structures) of power. Some youth cultural groups do work in this sense and try to form a *communication guerilla* to distort the power-related *cultural grammar* through their symbolic actions (Autonome a.f.r.i.k.a. Gruppe, 1998).

Within the postmodern plurality it became possible to misuse youth cultures for rather unemancipatory means. The U.S. Army tried to use the alternative pop group Blur's track "Song 2" for a commercial campaign to launch a new stealth jet, but Blur finally stopped that attempt. The French electropop act Daft Punk had to go to court to fight Jacques Chirac's attempt to use their chart hit "One More Time" for his election campaign. Terkessidis and Holert (2002) show how pop music and troop concerts are used for the moral support of the U.S. troops or even to torture imprisoned "enemies" of the U.S. As youth cultural symbols become more and more arbitrary, they can easily be adopted to new contexts. With reference to right-wing skinheads, Schröder (2000) points out: "Being a Nazi can mean a lot today: Techno haircut, skinhead music, Ballermann on holiday in Mallorca, to vote for the socialist PDS, 'with the Jews we always had a problem'. Or: Front-short-neck-long haircut, the rock group Böhse Onkelz, adventure holidays on

Ruegen, Opel Manta, 'voting is crap'. Or: Bald head, music from Nazi bard Rennicke, esoteric holidays in Stonehenge, Bolko Hoffmann and the Deutschmark. Or: Long hair with pony tail, death metal, churches."

Beyond the characterized mainstream of minorities emerge other youth cultural currents that reach beyond the average intentions of subversion and control. There are still explicitly political youth cultures like anti-fascists, anti-neoliberalism groups like Attac, ad busters, squatters, environmentalists, party-related youth groups, and other alternative scenes. Young people still care about their rights. When changes to the Criminal Justice Bill in England in 1994 led to the prohibition of public dancing to "repetitive music," thereby also criminalizing the open-air raves and parties in the old factory halls of the cities, a big protest movement of ravers and protest groups like "Reclaim the Streets" was built up very quickly (Plant, 1995; Hebdige, 1997: 16). Still, a number of explicitly political rock bands exist, like Chumbawamba, the International Noise Conspiracy, the Asian Dub Foundation, or German bands like Goldene Zitronen, Stella, Die Sterne, Superpunk, and the Boxhamsters. Also, there are political electronic dance music groups like Mouse on Mars, Carsten Jost, or DAT Politics and political Hip Hop acts like Saul Wiliams, Jan Delay, die Beginner, or Curse (Karnik, 2003: 103ff). With bands like Chicks on Speed, Le Tigre, Peaches, or Kevin Blechdom, there is an astonishing revival of feminist and gender-sensible pop and electropunk music that addresses gender conditions beyond heterosexual conditions of normality. Electronic dance music begins to rediscover the concept of performativity and thereby focuses more strongly on discourses about body and gender politics (Club Transmediale, Jansen, 2005). Since the days of the first independent record labels in the punk era, a multitude of independent labels still exist and offer exotic electro, punk, and hip hop bands a haven beyond the financial interests of the big multinational record companies (Graffé, Schubert, 2003; Savage, 2002; Teipel, 2001). Adjoining the rather uninspiring graffiti tags, city streets also show subversive creations of street artists or ad busters that aim to reclaim the public sphere from commercialization with their works of symbolic and provocative meaning (see Banksy, 2002).

7. Youth Cultures between Control and Emancipation: A Summary

Finally, the question remains whether young people can find relative independence through youth cultures or whether they are held within an ongoing process of control. This question is reminiscent of an old debate within Cultural Studies that moves traditionally between the theses of Horkheimer and Adorno on one side and Walter Benjamin on the other (see Holert, Terkessidis, 1997: 22). While Horkheimer and Adorno (1997), in their chapter about the culture industry in the *Dialectics of Enlightenment*, adopt a sceptical view that assumes constant political and cultural control of popular culture through the culture industry, Benjamin (1999), in his text *The Work of Art in the Age of Mechanical Reproduction,* puts forward the thesis that because of their technical reproducibility, works of art exist in a context of de-auratization that brings them nearer to the masses and offers opportunities for cultural redevelopment and self creation.

   The question of which position between public control and emancipatory self-production the youth cultures are or were located within the Western European postwar era can certainly not be answered in a deterministic and final way. Rather, we find here a dialectical process that oscillates between the poles of control and emancipation, and that will continue as long as the phenomenon of power exists in our societies (Kappeler, 1999). Many youth cultures were and are strongly influenced by society, state, and the culture industry and move within a strong, regulated framework. At the same time, one can discover ever new innovative movements at the fringes of youth cultures that have emancipatory impacts on the cultural and political systems. Altogether, there emerges a highly complex situation full of contradictions with a virtually unforeseeable variety of intensities of opposition and control. In the end it seems only possible to identify individually and locally which young person with which sociostructural background from which peer group gets into which constellation of emancipation or control and can use his or her youth cultural background to cope with the controlling influences. Schäfers (1994: 179) describes the tribalization of youth cultures. This concept, also common in the techno culture, seems to describe current youth cultures well. Within a whole range of controlling and emancipating currents, the classification of youth cultures within a simple polarity of countercultures and part cultures cannot fully be achieved. Many scenes and peer groups relate to the more controlled part-cultural milieus, while some scenes still offer countercultural potential that is actively used. In summary, the motto of Roth and Rucht (2000: 283ff.) seems to be apposite: "Neither rebellion nor assimilation."

   As the value of youthfulness is shared by all age groups, the creation of aesthetic difference has become much more difficult for young people. Nick Hornby (2003) remarks that it is a great challenge to listen to music that cannot be used in the next Body Shop outlet or the next TV commercial. In this sense, young people have their youthfulness dispossessed by the adults and the marketing departments of the global companies and have to find ever new strategies to maintain their separateness.

Beyond aesthetics and style, the categories of race, class, and gender are still central categories for an adequate assessment of youth cultures. It makes a profound difference whether a Hip Hop fan in Western Europe is, for example, a young man with an Arabian or Turkish ethnic background and perhaps poor educational qualifications; or a young woman from a white local family of academics. To be able to assess such situations adequately, we should keep Nancy Fraser's (2003) demand in mind: justice means to recognize cultural differences as well as to allow a redistribution of resources to all members of society.

Only in very rare cases do youth cultures explicitly follow political and revolutionary aims. The early 20th-century utopian vision of Gustav Wyneken of the first German youth movement to form a youth culture that would improve the world through its own power of new ideas, based on deeper insights, has not been fulfilled. In recent decades in particular, it seems to have broken up through the disillusionment of the youth cultures of the 1970s. Even under the authoritarian conditions of the Nazi dictatorship or the East German communist regime of the FDR, it became clear that most young people did not form youth cultures for revolutionary intentions but to obtain their personal and self-determined spaces of personal freedom (Spatscheck, 2006: 151ff.). In these systems youth cultures embodied special challenges for the governments. Youth cultures enabled young people to escape the dictatorial ideologies and the public attempts to form a "state youth" (Möding, v. Plato, 1986; Klönne 1986; Guse, 2001; Poiger, 2000; Rauhut, 2002; Wicke, Müller 1996). Within both of these dictatorships the mere attempt to form a youth culture, therefore, was itself an act of highly political relevance. In the context of postmodern Western capitalist societies, youth cultures seem to have lost this revolutionary potential to a very great extent.

Nonetheless, in youth cultures we can still find emancipatory potential directed against the disciplinary technologies of society, as Michel Foucault (1978, 1991) views it. Innovative youth cultures offer alternatives to the dominant discourses – in Foucault's sense, complexes of knowledge and power – that influence the actions of individuals in society through disciplining and normalizing functions. Here youth cultures can fulfil important functions. They support mental and real spaces of freedom that enable young people to meet needs that otherwise would not be met in the public mainstream culture. The desire to create spaces of freedom still seems to be a central motivation for the creation and existence of youth cultures. Our history shows that young people follow this desire within dire conditions of dictatorships as much as within the more open Western capitalist societies, and they tend to create ever new variations of the utopia of *all tomorrow's parties*. In this respect, they follow a culturalistic variation of Kraftwerk's futuristic musical motto, "It will always go on, music as carrier of ideas."

References

Autonome a.f.r.i.k.a. Gruppe (1998): Handbuch der Kommunikationsguerilla. Libertäre Assoziation: Hamburg.

Baacke, D.; Ferchhoff, W. (1995): Von den Jugendsubkulturen zu den Jugendkulturen. *Forschungsjournal Neue Soziale Bewegungen*, 8, 33-46.

Banksy, R. (2002): Existencillism. Banksy Press: London.

Benjamin, W. (1999): Illuminations. Pimlico: London.

Bonz, J. (2002): Popkulturtheorie. Ventil: Mainz.

Bourdieu, P. (2003): Die feinen Unterschiede. Zur Kritik der gesellschaftlichen Urteilskraft. Suhrkamp: Frankfurt/Main.

Brooker, W. (1998): Cultural Studies. Hodder & Stoughton: London.

Bucher, W.; Pohl, K. (1986): Schock und Schöpfung. Jugendästhetik im 20. Jahrhundert. Luchterhand: Neuwied.

Bunge, M. (1996): Finding Philosophy in Social Science. Yale University Press: New Haven

Clarke, J.; Honneth, A. (1979): Jugendkulturen als Widerstand. Syndikat: Frankfurt/Main.

Club Transmediale; Jansen, M. (2005): Gendertronics. Der Körper in der elektronischen Musik. Suhrkamp: Frankfurt/Main.

Cohen, Albert (1957): Kriminelle Subkulturen. *Kölner Zeitschrift für Soziologie und Sozialpsychologie*, 2, 103-117.

Eshun, K. (1998): More Brilliant than the Sun. Adventures in Sonic Fiction. Quartet Books: London.

Farin, K. (2002): Generation-kick.de. Jugendsubkulturen heute. Beck: München.

Ferchhoff, W.; Sander, U.; Vollbrecht, R. (1995): Jugendkulturen – Faszination und Ambivalenz. Juventa: Weinheim.

Foucault, M (1978): Dispositive der Macht. Merve: Berlin.

Foucault, M. (1991): Discipline and Punish: The Birth of the Prison. Penguin: London.

Fraser, N.; Honneth, A. (2003): Umverteilung oder Anerkennung? Suhrkamp: Frankfurt/Main.

Gelder, Ken (1997): The Subcultures Reader. Routledge, London.

Giesecke, H. (1975): Die Jugendarbeit. Juventa: München.

Gordon, M. (1947): The Concept of the Sub-Culture and its Application. In Gelder: The Subcultures Reader (pp. 40-43). Routledge, London.

Graffé, R.; Schubert, G. (2003): Underground Matters. In Neumann-Braun, Schmidt, Mai (eds.): Popvisionen. Links in die Zukunft (pp. 199-211). Suhrkamp: Frankfurt/Main.

Guse, M. (2001): "Wir hatten noch gar nicht angefangen zu leben". Lagergemeinschaft und Gedenkstätte KZ Moringen e.V.: Moringen/Liebenau.

Hardt, M.; Negri, A. (2001): Empire. Harvard University Press: Cambridge, Massachusetts.

Hebdige, D. (1997): Ein kleiner Planet der Gleichzeitigkeit. In SPoKK (eds.): Kursbuch Jugendkultur (pp. 14-21). Bollmann: Mannheim.

Hebdige, D. (1998): Subculture. The Meaning of Style. Routledge: London.

Hoggart, R. (1957): The Uses of Literacy. Chatto, London.

Holert, T.; Terkessidis, M. (1997): Mainstream der Minderheiten. Edition ID-Archiv: Berlin.

Horkheimer, M.; Adorno, T. W. (1997): Dialectic of Enlightenment. Verso Books: London.

Hornby, N. (2003): 31 Songs. Penguin: London.

Kappeler, M. (1999): Rückblicke auf ein sozialpädagogisches Jahrhundert. Essays zur Dialektik von Herrschaft und Emanzipation im sozialpädagogischen Handeln. IKO: Frankfurt/Main.

Karnik, O. (2003): Polit-Pop und Sound-Politk in der Popgesellschaft. In: Neumann-Braun, Schmidt, Mai (eds.): Popvisionen. Links in die Zukunft (pp. 103-120). Suhrkamp: Frankfurt/Main.

Klein, N. (2001): No Logo. Flamingo: London.

Kleiner, M.; Szepanski, A. (2003): Soundcultures. Über elektronische und digitale Musik. Suhrkamp: Frankfurt/Main.

Klönne, A. (1986): Jugendliche Subkulturen im Dritten Reich. In: Bucher, Pohl (eds.): Schock und Schöpfung. Jugendästhetik im 20. Jahrhundert (pp. 308-319). Luchterhand: Neuwied.

McRobbie, A. (1999): In the Culture Society. Art, Fashion and Popular Music. Routledge: London.

Möding, N./ v. Plato, A. (1986): Siegernadeln. Jugendkarrieren in BDM und HJ. In: Bucher, Pohl (eds.): Schock und Schöpfung. Jugendästhetik im 20. Jahrhundert (pp. 292-301). Luchterhand: Neuwied.

Moser, J. (2000): Jugendkulturen. Institut für Kulturanthropologie und Europäische Ethnologie: Frankfurt/Main.

Nachtwey, R. (1987): Pflege-Wildwuchs-Bricolage. Ästhetisch-Kulturelle Jugendarbeit. Leske und Budrich: Opladen.

Neumann-Braun, K.; Schmidt, A.; Mai, M. (2003): Popvisionen. Links in die Zukunft. Suhrkamp: Frankfurt/Main.

Plant, S. (1995): Intelligence Is No Longer on the Side of Power. http://www.altx.com/int2/sadie.plant.html, retrieved July 16, 2004.

Poiger, U. (2000): Jazz, Rock and Rebels. Cold War Politics and American Culture in a Divided Germany. University of California Press: Berkeley.

Rauhut, M. (2002): Rock in der DDR. 1964-1989. Bundeszentrale für politische Bildung: Bonn.

Roth, R.; Rucht, D. (2000): Jugendkulturen, Politik und Protest. Leske und Budrich: Opladen.

Sack, Fritz (1971): Die Idee der Subkultur. Kölner Zeitschrift für Soziologie und Sozialpsychologie, 2, 261-282.

Savage, J. (2002): England's Dreaming. Anarchy, Sex Pistols, Punk Rock and beyond. Faber and Faber: New York.

Schäfers, B. (1994): Soziologie des Jugendalters. Leske und Budrich: Opladen.

Schröder, B. (2000): Nazis sind Pop. Espresso: Berlin.

Schwendter, R. (1971): Theorie der Subkultur. Kiepenheuer und Witsch: Köln.

Spatscheck, C.; et al. (1997): Happy Nation?!? Jugendmusikkulturen und Jugendarbeit in den 90er Jahren. LIT: Münster.

Spatscheck, C. (2006): Soziale Arbeit und Jugendkulturen. Tectum: Marburg.

SPoKK (1997): Kursbuch Jugendkultur. Bollmann: Mannheim.

Teipel, J. (2001): Verschwende Deine Jugend. Suhrkamp: Frankfurt/Main.

Terkessidis, M.; Holert, T. (2002): Entsichert. Krieg als Massenkultur im 21. Jahrhundert. Kiepenheuer und Witsch: Köln.

Vollbrecht, R. (1995): Die Bedeutung von Stil. In Ferchhoff, Sander, Vollbrecht (eds.): Jugendkulturen – Faszination und Ambivalenz (pp. 23-37). Juventa: Weinheim.

Vollbrecht, R. (1997): Von Subkulturen zu Lebensstilen. In SPoKK (eds.): Kursbuch Jugendkultur (pp. 22-31). Bollmann: Mannheim.

Wicke, P.; Müller, L. (1996): Rockmusik und Politik. Analysen, Interviews und Dokumente. Ch. Links: Berlin.

Williams, R. (1958): Culture and Society. Chatto, London.

Williams, R. (1961): The Long Revolution. Chatto, London.

International Perspectives in Social Work Education

The last part of the book addresses aspects of social work teaching in international settings, including not only issues of scholars teaching abroad, but also aspects of the cooperation between universities from different countries.

The first contributor, Yasmin Dean, deals with the question of whether the teaching of social work can transcend cultural and geographical borders. In spite of the rapid globalization of higher education, she finds a paucity of available literature regarding self-selected academic expatriates in social work. Additionally, the teaching of social work in international settings is significantly affected by cultural considerations, including world view, degree of the expatriate's acculturation, and expectations of the host university. Dean tries to narrow the gap through a review of the existing literature from allied disciplines, and discuss the reasons and conditions for academic migration. Having taught in different countries herself, she describes the unique challenges inherent in teaching social work internationally. She highlights that teaching social work in an international environment must be undertaken with a philosophy of mutuality. The educator's personal practice model, in combination with the cultural norms and practices of the host culture, can collide if significant attention is not given to examining the challenges of teaching social work in today's global community.

In the second chapter of part three, Kathleen J. Tunney explores the integration of cultural and professional identity, and presents a three-culture model of international social work education, suggesting that professional norms and values be considered alongside the cultures of visiting educators and host nations. Based on her own experience in teaching abroad, the author explores dimensions of professional culture for effective teaching in host countries, and makes recommendations for social work education in order to help the social workers integrate culture and profession for an enhanced new professional identity.

In the very last contribution, Ramshi Gupta and Vijayan Pillai present an international social work curriculum in aging, and concretely illustrate how the internationalization of social work can actually work. After stating that 2006 has been the "Year of Study Abroad" in the United States, and summarizing the major points of a senate resolution, they give a short introduction into the field of global aging. They then present international curriculum, including demographic data on global aging and introduce basic concepts such as culturally competent care of elders, and gerontological social work practices including concepts, values, skills, and theories. The theoretical base for social work practice is provided by Bronfenner's ecological model from an international perspective.

Yasmin Dean

Finding Common Ground. Can the Teaching of Social Work Transcend Cultural and Geographic Borders?

1. Introduction

Anthony Welch (1997) has observed that as schools actively attempt to increase their foreign student enrolment, there is a need to maintain momentum with an internationalized faculty. Critically though, we have to ask what this means. As Haug (2001) has unflinchingly stated, this mobility really means only one of two possibilities. The first is western migration to other countries for a defined period of time and the second is 'brain drain' (Healy, 2004; Zhao, 2001) from other countries, usually in the Global South[1], for permanent positioning in the Global North[2]. It is my contention that the majority of scholars who become expatriates represent a privileged class which for the most part, refers to scholars from the Global North who possess the advantage of position and nationality to cross borders at will:

"We as Northerners so tend to take for granted our ability to travel just about anywhere we choose – for our currency work in our favor, and our citizenship open doors for us – that we forget that for the majority of the world's population, international travel – especially to a Northern country is prohibitive; politically, economically and pragmatically" (Haug, 2001: 84).

This notion of migratory privilege is echoed by Lyons (2006: 368):

"Rapid mass transport has increased the opportunities for more people (though admittedly predominantly from the affluent West) to be exposed to different cultures and to participate in international events."

In the international social work literature, there is considerable discourse regarding a one-way exportation of ideas from the Global North to the Global South and much debate over what if anything is universal in social work (Gray, Fook, 2004). To date, there has been little discussion regarding the crucial intersection between social work education from the Global North

---

1   Global South refers to countries in Asia, Africa, Central and South America, and Eastern Europe. These countries tend to be less industrialized than countries in the Global North and most have had a history of Western colonialism.

2   Global North refers to those countries that are considered to be in the Northern hemisphere such as: Australia, Britain, Canada, the United States and Western Europe.

and the experience of those expatriate academics that migrate to provide social work education in the Global South. The concept of the growing international mobility of faculty (Kaulish, Enders, 2005) and the 'boundaryless careers' (Arthur, Rosseau, 1996) of academics is repeated through much of the current literature regarding expatriate academics (Richardson, 2000). What is missing in much of this recent discourse is information on what these experiences are actually like for academics and their implications for social work education. The broader issue here is the spread or export of social work from the west to the rest of the world and the ethics of this within contexts where a more indigenous and therefore culturally relevant framework is needed (Gray, Fook, 2004). However, these generalized issues cannot be explored or understood without also examining the experiences of social work expatriate academics when teaching in host countries. Understanding these experiences is an ethical imperative for social work because unlike the experiences of many multinational organization expatriates, the academic has intense interaction with the host culture by way of teaching local students and responding to the community's educational needs (Richardson, 2000). Although in the ensuing pages, I am critical of some of our history (in which I am complicit) I raise these issues not to argue against internationalization of academia but rather to offer some strategies for mutual learning. For, as educational institutions seek competitive advantage through strategic international alliances, collaboration in teaching and research between institutions in different countries will also increase (Richardson, McKenna, 2000; Scott, 1994).

This chapter has three specific goals: the first is to provide an overview of the factors affecting migration of Global North academics. The second is to initiate a discussion regarding some of the issues facing delivery of social work education across borders. Finally, the third goal is to explore these intersections of academic migration and exportation of social work education with some of the roles and responsibilities of visiting social work educators. The chapter will conclude with some recommendations for ways in which international social work education can transcend geographical borders in a way that will facilitate the west beginning to learn from the rest of the world.

2. Factors Affecting Migration of Global North Academics

"There is no way to know what life is like in another culture until it is actually experienced" (Schultz, 1944).

The migratory patterns of Global North expatriate academics are affected by a variety of factors. The most unique attribute affecting at least some academics, is the fact they may have sought this opportunity and are therefore, self-selected. Reasons for the migration may be attributed to lack of positions in their home country, desire for escape from problems at home or work (Osland, 1995), or for notions of career enhancement. Academics also may serendipitously find the opportunity to work overseas presented to them as a result of research interests or a partnership between educational institutions.

There are hindering and facilitating factors that influence the academic's decision to work overseas. Migration expert Castles (2000) refers to a 'push and pull' which influences international mobility. Some of the pull factors refer to a labor shortage of social workers in certain parts of the world (Lyons, 2006). Other "pull" factors include financial incentive, desire for travel, adventure and opportunism. Osland (2000) identified that the majority of expatriates accept overseas positions for the adventure it offers. This research is supported by Richardson's (2000) work on expatriate academics. Richardson found that of the 30 British expatriate academics she interviewed, explanations of serendipity alongside a general call for adventure were the most compelling reason that the participants in her study accepted overseas assignments.

Financial incentive is another pull that cannot be overlooked. In Richardson's study, academics candidly admitted that the lure of better money was their initial reason for accepting the position. Further to this incentive is the many privileges that may be proffered to visiting scholars. As an expatriate in South Korea, I was frequently honored when students would greet me with low bows and offers to carry my books for me. Although this was a phenomenon that I simultaneously experienced discomfort with, it was also a unique and enticing difference from my experience in the Global North.

A significant reason for scholars to gain international experience is based in how much we can learn from our colleagues in the Global South. Social work in the South has extensive experience in fighting poverty, forming consciousness, responding to natural disasters, and engaging in community development and capacity building (Graham, 2006; Ife, 2000; Midgley, 1990; Nagy, Falk, 2000; Taylor, 1999). However, to date there is still debate over how much visiting academics absorb these lessons. According to scholars such as Ife (2000), Healy, Asamoah and Hokenstad (2003) or Gray and Fook (2004), we may still be mired in the pattern noted by Midgley in 1990 wherein the transfer of knowledge is mistakenly seen as a one way street from North to South.

Reasons for academic migration are countless. Some academics choose to work overseas for reasons of adventure and travel. Another reality is that North American colleges and universities are expanding into new frontiers. And finally, there is also a growing recognition that international experience is an expected competency for academics. Opportunities to provide higher education in regions hitherto unexplored offer ways for institutions to expand

and also to meet the internationalization mandates of their organizations. However, there is an understandable backlash to this practice. Critical review of the reasons for migration reveals that most factors tend to serve the interests of the Global North far more than they meet the needs of the Global South. In parts of Africa, Pakistan and the Caribbean for example, educators and practitioners alike are becoming increasingly critical of the carte blanche approach of applying western social work models which are not always relevant to the needs of other populations (Graham, 2006; Gray, Fook, 2004). Altbach and Teichler (2001) note that inevitable increase of students from diverse backgrounds forces academics to re-evaluate the overall design and delivery of education for students. They state, "perhaps academic staff will need to be more mobile so that they can better transmit international knowledge and understanding to students" (ibid.: 20). Thus, if we are to successfully avoid Atal's (1981) indictment of "academic colonization", academics need to work overseas with an aim to learning from the community and students how we may "restructure social work education to increase its relevance in the host country as defined by that country" (Healy, Asamoah, Hokenstad, 2003: 7).

Lyons (2006) also refers to 'push' factors which can include low pay positions or challenges in countries that may be experiencing political turmoil. This therefore, may push social workers into relocating to places that offer better incentives for their work. Other push factors can include the value of international experience by the home institution. Arthur, Giancarlo and Patton (2004) observed that although international experience was viewed as personally transformative for the women academics in their study, international work was not really supported by their institutions. The women in this study identified that while overseas experience was seen as career enhancing, it was not viewed as a career builder. In fact, by many the overseas experience was viewed as something one should only do early in their career or at the very end of the career trajectory (Arthur, Giancarlo, Patton, 2004). Despite the rhetoric of the importance of internationalization by many tertiary institutions in the Global North, this mandate is compromised by Altbach and Lewis' (1998) 14-country-study which found: "the American professoriate is the least committed to internationalism" (ibid.: 1). Without full commitment from their home universities, academics may be therefore reluctant to pursue international interests.

3. Unique Characteristics of Expatriate Academics

The majority of management expatriates are sent by their parent organization rather than self-selected. This is in sharp contrast to the usual experience of academics that actively, independently and voluntarily choose to pursue overseas assignments (Richardson, McKenna, 2000). This suggests that academic expatriates might be more adventurous than their counterparts in the management world. It also raises the question whether self-selected expatriates have a different experience when adjusting to the host culture (Richardson, McKenna, 2002).

A significant factor affecting the academic's overseas experience in comparison to the more traditional expatriate is job security. Thus, while there are serious repercussions when missions are unsuccessful, the employee has some 'protection' by virtue of their pre-assignment job at the home office. Failure to adjust to the culture in its entirety (country, job, people etc.) can lead to termination of the job itself. This has implications for the self-selected expatriate who is usually reliant upon the host country employer for their job, visa, housing, shipping, children's school and many other necessary needs (Richardson, 2000). Having worked in three international educational settings, I was witness to seemingly random contract terminations by employers. Expatriate humor often included the cautionary phrase, "don't buy green bananas". The logic was that the worker might be inexplicably fired before their bananas could be eaten. It is therefore clear that the expatriate academic is vulnerable to feelings and realities of job insecurity. (Richardson, McKenna, 2000) This issue of heightened vulnerability is something that expatriate academics need to be prepared for so as to ensure their successful acculturation to the host culture.

Academic freedom holds strong value for scholars. Yet, as Altbach (2001: 205-207) has observed, "academic freedom is rarely discussed in the context of changes taking place in higher education ... there is no universally accepted understanding of academic freedom." This possibility for different meaning to be attributed to the term 'academic freedom' has significant implications for social work. As a profession, social work holds dear the ethical value of non-discrimination. However this ethical value may not share common ground. For example, there are some countries and regions within countries which still actively discriminate against homosexuality. Such discrimination has implications for how social work faculty can teach and insist that the profession's values be applied to social work education (Healy, 2004). In my experiences of working in the Middle East, I knew of several faculty members that had to keep their sexual orientation a secret from their employer. Furthermore, I was aware of students who were struggling with issues regarding sexual orientation. However, the consequences of discussing these feelings can be dangerous for both the students and their faculty members. Healy (2004: 591) notes, "freedom to insist on social work values may be compromised by larger political, legal and social forces when professional values conflict with religious values and the law." Thus, the ethical values of social work as defined by the International Federation of Social Workers become fragile when applied to diverse contexts. And, again expatriate social work academics need to be prepared for these uncertainties prior to departure.

4. Delivering Social Work Education Across Borders

Rotabi, Gammonley and Gamble (2006) in their provocatively titled: "Ethical Guidelines for Study Abroad: Can we transform ugly Americans into engaged citizens", caution that social work students sometimes pursue study abroad opportunities for reasons of 'doing good in the world'. This motivating factor of altruism can become exploitative forms of imperialistic interventions. Zachariah, 1996 as cited by Haug (2001: 126) calls this "the third wave of imperialism – this time by intellectual and cultural colonization and global homogenization." Such warnings are reminiscent of Midgley's (1990) concerns regarding the one way street of simply exporting social work to other countries out of undeniable desire to do good but with an arrogance that prevents asking whether the intervention is needed or wanted by the host culture. I am reminded here of the lesson learned by one of my colleagues who was working briefly for an international charity in Arsi, Ethiopia. The women of the village had to travel a long way in order to get water from the river. Once they reached the river, the women had to carry heavy loads of water back to their village. The humanitarian agency determined that providing a well in the village would be advantageous for the women of Arsi. This decision was reached with little or possibly no consultation of the so-called stakeholders. After the well was dug, agency workers returned six months later to see how the well was working. However, the well was not being used and the women were still walking long distances in large groups to the river. When asked why, the explanation was that gathering water was the only time these women had to discuss personal matters and news without being overheard by the men in their community (Both, personal correspondence, June 14, 2006). This powerful example reinforces how susceptible the Global North can be to operating only from one world view. Quite obviously, to successfully teach across borders, academics need to be able to operate from other world views:

"At worst, your presence is harmful. Because people like you have come to this country, we are losing our traditional way of doing things, and people are losing confidence in our own traditional systems. Your projects are dis-empowering insofar as only your language and 'values' and expertise are recognized. You speak of empowerment but by the very structures of your systems you are saying that we are not able to manage affairs on our own, but must be supervised and taught by you" (Haug, 2001: 104).

As academic migration across all disciplines seems to be increasing, social work scholars have some important responsibilities to pay heed to. As institutions from the Global North increasingly establish themselves overseas, there will be even more pull factors encouraging Global North academics to teach in the Global South. Academics who say 'yes' to this adventure must acknowledge the power and privilege their positions cast. Having been recruited for their knowledge, expatriate social work academics have a responsibility to work with their local colleagues and students so as to help shape the South in the likeness of the South and to forcefully resist historical and colonial traditional tendencies to "shape the South in the likeness of the North, with the help and expertise of Northerners" (Haug, 2001: 4). As revealed through worthy studies by Caragata and Sanchez (2002), Graham (2006), Healy (1987) and Ife (2004); the delivery of social work education in the Global South has been based almost solely on a Western model. Tunney (2001: 435) points out, "more and more social work educators are becoming involved in teaching abroad." However most of the instructors teaching western constructs such as social work, family science, education and psychology tend to come from and were educated in the Global North. This has, disappointingly, contributed to the often single direction of teaching from North to South without encouragement for an exchange of ideas.

This history of a one way street of exportation obligates social work educators to encourage a new dialogue. However, as multiple scholars have pointed out, "much of social work's written, English-language knowledge base continues to be produced in the Global North, particularly its English language countries, but is consumed in the Global North and South" (Graham, 2006: 4). Consequently, it is not enough to talk about the desire for respectful dialogue (Haug, 2001), we need to foster opportunities for the exchange of ideas to be conducted in non-colonial languages. This means then that expatriate academics do have a responsibility to learn the language of their host culture. After all, if this is a reasonable expectation imposed upon expatriates who migrate to the Global North, why can't the same be demanded of those who migrate to the Global South?

The allure of adventure and promise of travel in exotic places can make it challenging to be mindful that textbooks originally written in English cannot simply be translated and taught in other cultural contexts. And, "for the most part, it is social workers who have been educated in the west that are involved in the development of social work education programs in so-called third world countries. More recently, this involvement has spread to Eastern Europe and the Baltic states" (Taylor, 1999: 309). Many scholars have argued that the paradigm of western social work education has been inevitably framed by values and ideals which are the product of an epistemological framework that is not universal and even with modifications, can never be truly 'sensitive' to the needs of other cultures (Al-Krenawi, Graham, 2001;

Healy, 1987; Yan, Lam, 2000). Review of the literature (Al-Krenawi, Graham, 2001; Goldberg, 2000; Healy, 1987; Leiby, 1985; Midgley, 1997) reveals the often acrimonious exchanges that occur as scholars and practitioners debate two issues. The first is whether the basic social work curriculum has attended adequately to the issue of cultural competence. The second is the question of what, exactly, is needed in practice and the curriculum to attend to this issue. Stein (1990) suggests that this educational exportation failed to account for differences in culture, economic conditions, social structures and most importantly, community values. This perspective of a European or western world view forms an untenable foundation from which to attempt cultural competence (Yan, Lam, 2000). This same viewpoint is shared by Bateson (1989: 71): "Most higher education is devoted to affirming the traditions and origins of an existing elite and transmitting them to new members." While I believe this allegation of domination to be true, I don't think our recognition of it has to be mired in hopelessness. By recognizing that whether intentionally or inadvertently, our desire for respect and mutuality has been compromised by the reality that the Global North has been so privileged, our models of practice need some dismantling and critical thought so as to avoid further exportation of academic imperialism. Like Healy (2004) and others, I argue that this recognition represents the first step in making the changes we wish to see in international social work education.

Calls for social work to 'disengage from the colonial web' (Graham, 2006) are starting to surface in the global literature. While students and educators recognize the contributions of social work from the Global North, there is now an increased demand for indigenization, reciprocal dialogue and a stronger human rights agenda in social work education (Healy, 2003; Ife, 2001; Graham, 2006). This putative demand for a reciprocal and mutual agenda is fueled by at least four critical trends. First, there is increasing need for diversity in higher education in the Global North so as to meet the academy's goals of attracting international and minority students (Canda, Phaobtong, 1992). Second, faculty shortages in Canada and other countries are resulting in international recruitment and mobility along with significant international competition for this 'brain power' (see for example: Altbach, 2004; Welch, 1997; Zhao, 2000). Third, the under-representation of visible minority faculty members in Canada may be attributed to the entrenchment of a Euro-centric world view (Graham, 2000) which fosters lack of diversity in the academy. Fourth, effective social work practice in Canada (and beyond) depends upon the development of a culturally sensitive curriculum that encourages multiple world views (Asamoah, Healy, 1997; Gray, Fook, 2004; Taylor, 1999; Yan, Lam, 2000).

Research by Gray and Fook (2004) highlights the importance for social work practice to become contextually oriented. This has important implications for both practitioners and educators to start where the client is by creating indigenous social work models that are more appropriate for the actual needs of the population. The International Association of Schools of Social Work (IASSW, 2004: 15) states: "… the claim to what constitutes good social work education in Western Europe and the USA may be based on ill-founded premises". By exploring the expatriate academic's reasons for migration and by critically examining social work's tradition of exportation, there is opportunity to enrich the emerging dialogue over how a philosophical international orientation (Gray, Fook, 2004) in social work education will be possible thereby, disengaging the profession from its colonial web. However, to successfully do this, attention must be also paid to the roles and responsibilities for expatriate social work educators.

5. Roles and Responsibilities of Social Work Educators

"Social work education should focus on training for social development: more concretely, one in which community development, self-help and mutual aid activities are central" (Taylor, 1999: 316).

Lynn Healy (2002: 180) observed that a "seamless, globalized curriculum depends largely on social work educators around the world." Healy goes on state that "many faculty members have not traveled widely or done research in international issues …" (ibid.: 187) This criticism highlights the importance for social work scholars from both the Global South and North to work overseas and therefore explore different world views. Not only will these efforts assist internationalization but, by extension, the opportunity for increased cultural understandings and learning are likely. Thus, while we must be cognizant of the many ways that expatriate academics from the Global North may unintentionally do harm where they had hoped only to do good, this does not mean we should advocate staying home. What it does mean is that we have an ethical obligation to encourage and support Healy's call for faculty with international experience while simultaneously recognizing the persistence of a Western hegemony in our social work education and practice that has been accepted as reality by many scholars (Ife, 2000; Healy, 2004; Payne, 2001).

Although some Global South countries might be desirous of social work education, the government infrastructure in the host country may not be able to offer living wages to those students who obtain a social work education. Social workers teaching in these environments need to critically reflect on how they can reconcile conflicting feelings about this. As Taylor (1999) has identified, social work education needs to "provide students with a vision of social work which emphasizes social change and teaches the necessary skills and strategies to bring about change at community, organizational and policy levels" (ibid.: 313). Numerous scholars (Gray, Fook, 2004; Graham, 2006; Healy, 2004; Taylor, 1999) have argued that international social work requires suitable, locally relevant and culturally appropriate practice models. This provokes the question of whether it is social work that is needed in the Global South or as Taylor (1999) has asserted, it is a social or community development focus that is required. It is this framework that lends itself toward social change and sustainability. Thus, it is the responsibility of those charged with teaching social work to imbue their curriculum with such questions.

6. Recommendations for Mutuality

"In an age when communications are able to bring an increased understanding of other countries and enlarge perceptions beyond the parochial, when our attention has been drawn to the inter-connectedness of economic systems, then a model which lifts social work beyond regional perspectives is needed" (Elliot, 1993: 28).

As Lynn Healy has stated, there is a need for social work educators to gain international experience. Indeed, "letting go of one world view and taking on another is one of the most frequently heard themes in expatriate stories" (Richardson, McKenna, 2002: 75). Through working overseas, academics have tremendous opportunity to begin seeing and understanding through a new lens or paradigm. Al-Krenawi and Graham (2001) identified that knowledge of cultural and community traditions alongside collaborative work with cultural mediators can help promote social work's role in society's that have has limited understanding of the profession. However, expatriate assignment alone is not enough. As Tunney (2002: 444) notes, "the visiting social work professor's role must include an increasing emphasis on indigenization…" This same recommendation is echoed by Nimmagadda and Cowger (1999: 263) who found that Indian "social workers routinely indigenize their practice … relying on culturally grounded tacit knowledge." This finding takes away the notion that western knowledge has an all encompassing power and gives credit to the local culture's ability to adjust and adapt western social work knowledge to better suit the culture of the host country. Thus, expatriate academics need to be humble enough to recognize that the models they import must be adapted to meet local needs. This humility lends itself to recent calls in international social work literature for a social development or community development focus. Taylor (1999: 312) argues that "Empowerment can, in fact, function as a unifying principle … rooted in a radical respect for the clients themselves as 'experts in their own life situations."

Finally, expatriate social work academics need to be very mindful that although they may accept an overseas assignment for altruistic reasons, each individual educator needs to consider the less than benign impact colonialism has had on much of the Global South. Furthermore, indigenization of practice with recognition of the importance of culturally grounded tacit knowledge (Nimmagadda, Cowger, 1999) is needed if social work is to transcend its geographical borders. To do this successfully, I argue that not only is a commitment to social development an ethical imperative but so too, is it ethical for expatriate academics to commit themselves to learning the culture and language of their host country. As Haug (2001: 83) has noted, "the use of English as the dominant medium for discourse regarding international social work is far from 'neutral' or 'natural'." In his dynamic speech on social work and human rights, Ife (2000: 10) reminds us, "… the people whom social workers claim to represent – the disadvantaged and the marginalized – have little voice … and the debate remains dominated by the powerful." Since most of the text books used in social work tend to be written by scholars from the Global North and in fact, since many of those teaching social work tend to also be Caucasian scholars born and raised in the Global North, one has to critically question how much of social work truly reflects other world views? Without commitment from expatriate academics to learn language and custom, I fear that social work will remain steeped in its misguided western hegemony.

7. Conclusion

"Americans went to foreign countries to teach … but not always to learn" (Stein as cited in Caragata, Sanchez, 2002).

Can the teaching of social work transcend geographical boundaries? Is common ground possible? As the preceding pages have revealed, these are complex questions which by design are intended to plague and provoke more than to provide a single answer. But, there is and there should be some cause for hope. With humility and a commitment to mutual learning, expatriate social work academics can be part of the solution toward finding common ground not just abroad but, in their home environments as well. And, the most important strategy needed to achieve these aims is one of structural change. Whether we're discussing students, academics or practitioners, social workers have an ethical responsibility to maintain a social justice focus by recognizing first, the privilege that each of us has by having the opportunity to travel to and learn from colleagues in the Global South.

Teaching social work in an international environment must be undertaken with a philosophy of unwavering commitment to mutuality of learning. The educator's personal practice model in combination with the cultural norms and practices of the host culture will collide if significant attention is not given to examining the challenges of teaching social work in today's global community. Common ground when teaching social work internationally is only possible when we make constant effort to learn from one another. We cannot merely assume that having had a professional education in a so-called developed country makes us the expert in someone else's country:

"Many students and teachers unquestioningly accept the voice of the White "expert" as speaking the truth about Africans, Aboriginals and others. White people who know a very limited amount often see themselves as 'experts' because they know more than their colleagues, who know little beyond the recorded version and current media representations" (Graveline, 1998: 119).

Some of the factors influencing migration include financial incentive, a desire to do good in the world, labor shortages, political turmoil, opportunity for adventure, serendipity and the opportunity to learn from colleagues in the Global South. These reasons people have for choosing to work overseas need to be understood in order to also understand their adaptation to the host culture.

There has been a traditional focus on experiential learning and international field placements but little has been done to date on the experiences of social work academics teaching overseas. What is not yet located in the literature are the individualized experiences of academics charged with the responsibility and privilege of teaching social work in non-western communities. There is an intersectionality of these topics that are constantly skirted around yet never focused upon. Attempts toward mutual learning and indigenization will be much less oppressive by following the lead of Tunney (2002) and locating the nexus of such activity within the experiences of individual social work instructors. For, unlike the experiences of many multinational organization internationals, the academic has direct and influential interaction with the host culture by way of teaching local students and responding to the community's educational needs (Richardson, 2000). By learning more about the experiences of social work academics teaching in the Global South, there emerges a vital opportunity to understand more about the local knowledge of social work practice in the Global South. With this opportunity comes the chance for Global North social workers to finally embrace the mutuality of learning and therefore social justice that community activists and more radical scholars have been tirelessly calling for (Al-Krenawi, Graham, 2001; Ahmadi, 2003; Asamoah, Healy, 1997; Dean, 2001; Freire, 2001; Midgley, 1981). It is time now for those of us from the Global North to go to foreign countries in order to learn.

References

Al-Krenawi, A.; Graham, J. R. (2001). The cultural mediator: Bridging the gap between a non-Western community and professional social work practice. British Journal of Social Work, 31, 4, 665-686.

Altbach, P.; Lewis, L. (1998). Internationalism and insularity. Change, 30, 1, 54-56.

Altbach, P. (2001). Academic freedom: International realities and challenges. Higher education, 41, 205-219.

Altbach, P. (2004). Globalisation and the university: Myths and realities in an unequal world. Tertiary Education and Management, 10, 3-25.

Arthur, N.; Giancarlo, C.; Patton, C. (2004). International project competencies of women academics. Paper presented at the Congress of Humanities and Social Sciences 2004. Winnipeg.

Atal, Y, (1981). Building a nation: Essays on India. Delhi: Abhinav.

Bateson, M. (1989). Composing a life. New York: Plume/Penguin.

Caragata, L.; Sanchez, M. (2002). Globalization and global need. New imperatives for expanding international social work education in North America. International Social Work, 45, 2, 217-238.

Castles, S. (2000). Ethnicity and globalization. London: Sage.

Garber, R. (1997). Social work education in an international context; current trends and future directions. In Hokenstad, Midgley (eds). Issues in international social work: global challenges for a new century (pp. 159-171). Washington, DC: NASW Press.

Garber, R. (2000). IASSW World Census of Social Work Education 1998-1999, IASSW.

Graham, J. (2006). Spirituality and social work: A call for an international focus of research. Unpublished paper.

Gray, M. (2005). Dilemmas of international social work: paradoxical processes in indigenization, universalism and imperialism. International Journal of Social Welfare, 14, 231-238.

Gray, M.; Fook, J. (2004). The quest for a universal social work: Some issues and implications. Social work education. 23, 5, 625-644.

Graveline, F. (1998). Circle Works: Transforming Eurocentric Consciouness. Halifax: Fernwood Publishers.

Haug, E. (2001). Writing in the margins: Critical reflections on the emerging discourse of International Social Work. Unpublished thesis. University of Calgary.

Haug, E. (2005). Critical reflections on the emerging discourse of international social work. International social work, 48, 2, 126-135.

Healy, L. (1987). International agencies as social work settings: opportunity, capability and commitment. Social Work. 32, 5, 405-409.

Healy, L. (2004). Standards for social work education in the North American and Caribbean region: Current realities and future issues. Social work education. 23, 5, 581-595.

Healy, L. (2002). Internationalizing social work curriculum in the 21st century. In Tan, Dodds (eds.). Social Work Around the World. International Federation of Social Workers. IFSW Press: Berne.

Healy, L.; Asamoah, Y.; Hokenstad, M. (eds.)(2003). "Models of international collaboration in social work education". Council on social work education publications.

IAASW (2004). Global Qualifying Standards for Social Work Education and Training. www.iassw-aiets.org, retrieved September 12, 2006.

Ife, J. (2001). Local and global practice: relocating social work as a human rights professions in the new global order. European Journal of Social Work, 4, 5-15.

Ife, J. (2000). Local and global practice: relocating social work as a human rights professions in the new global order. Eileen Younghusband Memorial Lecture. IFSW/IASSW. Biennial Conference, Montreal, July 31 2000.

Lyons, K. (2006). Globalization and social work: International and local implications. British Journal of social work, 36, 365-380.

Midgley, J. (1990). International social work: Learning from the third world. Social Work, 5, 295-301.

Midgley, J. (1981). Professional imperialism: Social work in the Third World. London: Heinemann.

Nagy, G.; Falk, D. (2000) Dilemmas in international and cross-cultural social work education. International Social Work, 43, 1, 49-61.

Napier, N.; Anh, V.; Hang, N.; Thang, N.; Tuan, V. (1997). Reflections on building a business school in Vietnam. Journal of Management Inquiry, 6, 4, 341-354.

Nimmagadda, J.; Cowger, C. (1999). Cross-cultural practice: social worker ingenuity in the indigenization of practice knowledge. International social work, 43, 3, 261-276.

Osland J. (1995). The adventure of working abroad. San Francisco: Jossey-Bass.

Payne, M. (2001). Social work education:International standards. In Hessle (eds.). International standard setting of higher social work education. Stockholm University; Stockholm Studies of Social Work.

International Federation of Social Work (2004). Global Qualifying Standards for Social Work Education and Training.

Richardson, J. (2000). Some preliminary thoughts on using the literature on international managers as a framework for understanding the experiences of international academics. Management Research News, 23, 2-4, 67-69.

Richardson, J. (2002). Experiencing expatriation: A study of international academics. PhD Dissertation. New Zealand.

Richardson, J.; McKenna, S. (2000). Metaphorical "types" and human resource management: self-selecting internationals. Industrial and commercial, 32, 6, 209-218.

Richardson, J.; McKenna, S. (2002). Leaving and experiencing: Why academics international and how they experience expatriation. Career Development International, 7. 2, 67-78.

Rotabi, K.; Gammonley, D.; Gamble, D. (2006). Ethical guidelines for study abroad: Can we transform ugly Americans into engaged global citizens? British Journal of Social work. 36, 451- 465.

Stein, H. (1990). The international and the global in education for the future. In Kendall (eds.). The international in American education. New York: Proceedings of an International Symposium, Hunter College School of Social Work.

Taylor, Z. (1999). Values, theories and methods in social work education: a culturally transferable core? International social work, 42, 3, 309-318.

Tunney, K. (2002). Learning to teach abroad: Reflections on the role of the visiting social work educator. International Social Work, 45, 4, 435-446.

Welch, Anthony (1997). The peripatetic professor: the internationalization of the academic profession. Higher Education, 34, 323-345.

Zhao, J.; Drew, D.; Murray, T. (2000). Brain drain and brain gain: The migration of knowledge workers from and to Canada. Education Quarterly Review, 6. 3, 8-73.

Kathleen J. Tunney

Teaching at the Intersection:
A Three-Culture Model for International Social Work Education

1. Introduction

This chapter will explore the integration of cultural identity and professional identity in global social work education. First, a brief description of the author's teaching and curriculum development experiences in Lithuania will set the stage. Second, a three-culture model of international social work education will be presented, suggesting that professional norms and values need to be considered alongside the cultures of visiting educator and host nation. Third, this chapter will explore dimensions of professional culture most important for effective teaching abroad, based on the author's experiences and lessons learned. Fourth and last, this chapter will offer recommendations for social work education which can enhance our ability to integrate culture and profession, creating new professional identities in the process.

2. Background

In the mid-1990's, I made three teaching trips to Kaunas, Lithuania, the longest of which was six months. The site of the teaching was the Centre for Social Welfare Professional Education at Vytautas Magnus University. The Centre was established in 1992 for graduate social work education, with financial support from the National Conference of Catholic Bishops (American) and located within the Lithuanian university system. The Centre also had financial and logistic support from the Lithuanian Catholic Church through the Caritas organization (Kulys, Constable, 1994). The program faculty were comprised of Western educators from the U.S., France, Germany, Australia, and the U.K. There were also local faculty members drawn from the sociology and psychology faculties of the larger university system. As the program grew and students graduated, they began to teach in the program as well as supervising students in field practice (internship) sites. The Centre, now in its second decade, has added a baccalaureate program and continuing education components.

My teaching responsibilities included classroom instruction, field seminar co-leadership, direct supervision of students in community agency placements, consultation and training for community agencies, and (with other faculty, both visiting and local) continuing design and revision of the social work curriculum as needs were identified and resources became available.

Holding these multiple roles required recognition and response to a range of challenges inherent in cross-cultural social work education. As a result of the teaching-liaison-consultation role, it became necessary to define the social work professional identity and role to a very diverse group of students and community leaders.

While I had over five years of social work teaching experience prior to my teaching trips to Lithuania, I was unprepared for the cultural challenges in classroom and field consultation settings. While the differences in the national cultures (U.S. versus Lithuanian) of course needed to be acknowledged and respected, I found that the culture of the social work *profession* was also a relevant, yet at times invisible, dimension of the cultural context.

This was especially true because prior to the break-up of the Soviet Union there had been no profession of social work in Lithuania, and hence no social work professional culture. Because of the rapid and chaotic pace of political and economic change the nation was experiencing, demands for social and professional development were acute. The educational program in Kaunas was established in 1992 to respond to those imperatives (Tunney, 2002; Tunney, Kulys, 2004).

3. The Three-culture Model

An often-overlooked aspect of international social work education is that there is a culture of the profession which has many of the same elements as the cultures of the visitor and the host nations. In other words, nations have values, rules, rewards, punishments, hopes, and goals. These elements have been derived from conflict, collaboration, and a shared history.

In general, culture can be defined as "the ideas, customs, skills, and arts of a group of people that have been cultivated and passed on from generation to generation" (Lum, 1996: 216). In addition, culture could be seen as an organized system of norms, standards, values, and mechanisms for negotiating conflicts between members of the culture (subcultures), and between the culture and other cultures, with these mechanisms representing a shared history which evolves over time. A shared language is often characteristic of a culture – at the very least, there are shared meanings for words that may mean something different outside of a specific cultural context. Applying these definitions to the social work profession would include examples such as the professional associations which promulgate standards, values, and sanctions for social work education and practice – National Association of Social Workers; International Federation of Social Workers; Council on Social Work Education; International Association of Schools of Social Work, and many more. Other examples include the state licensure boards in most countries. Social work also has a special language–our jargon and professional vocabulary includes such items as "bio-psycho-social framework"; "empowerment;" and "social justice." While other groups in society use these terms, each professional culture has a different sense of what these words mean, and how they should be acted upon.

Three overarching models of culture can be identified within which both nations and professions may be found. These models are summarized by Midgley (1993: 5) as individualist, collectivist, and populist. The individualist orientation is characterized by an emphasis on self-actualization, self-determination, and self-improvement as "conditions for the enhancement of social welfare." This individualist world view is also represented in the American/Western economic system of capitalism which "exalts individual effort, responsibility, choice, and pursuit of self-interest" (ibid.). The social work value of self-determination seems grounded in this world view. The collectivist orientation is characterized by an emphasis on the State as a primary agent in creating and maintaining social welfare systems. Collectivist models recognize "the prime importance of the State in the economic and political life, and the satisfaction of social needs" (ibid.: 7). The social work professional emphasis on the importance of human relationships seems grounded here. The populist model is defined by Midgley (ibid.: 8) as one which emphasizes "small-scale local community-based development strategies", as the best means of insuring social well-being through maintaining close linkages between perceived needs and solutions, without the entities of self-interest or State interest as intervening variables. Social justice and social action are inherently valued by social workers who emphasize this model.

Midgley and other writers have expressed caution and concern about the American tendency to export our model of culture – largely individualist – when teaching and consulting in other nations. And since social work values can be seen as a subset of larger Western cultural values (self-determination, privacy, confidentiality, rights to choice, for example), social work educators must be clear about how we apply our definition of "social work" in other places. For example, Bogo and Herington (1988: 306) note: "Recent social work literature has been critical of exportation of social work education and practice models developed in Western countries ... these writers argue that Western educators have assumed that knowledge and expertise originating in their countries are universally applicable. They have not sufficiently taken into account the impact of specific cultural, political, and economic realities on all aspects of human functioning." This is the phenomenon which Midg-ley (1981) terms "cultural imperialism". Midgley (1993: 2) also reminds us of the ideological roots of social development strategies, and urges awareness of how much "policy prescriptions are infused with ideologies which need to be clarified and accommodated." Bogo and Herington (1988: 312) further note that in order to minimize the tendency toward cultural imperialism and to maximize collaboration, both host and visitor need to "remind themselves that they are colleagues through sharing a common professional identity including some core values and knowledge ... common interests also become a basis for goal setting and work contracting." It could also be said that social workers in the West are divided on how we should conceptualize and execute our purposes: Are we agents of social control, or social change? How does our struggle to define ourselves help or hinder our international social work education initiatives?

Social work curriculums are designed to familiarize students with a range of cultural backgrounds, sometimes using the frameworks above – seeing culture as representative of a people's shared history, language, val-ues, norms and standards, and mechanisms for maintaining communications and resolving conflicts both within and outside the culture. Raising these issues allows students to locate themselves in the inter-cultural world, which contributes to them becoming more sensitive practitioners. So it is with this background on culture that social work educators approach the cross-cultural encounter, whether it is within the U.S. context, or whether it involves cross-national activities. U.S. social work educators are familiar with thinking critically and pro-actively about culture when considering racial, ethnic, or religious issues. We are less familiar with thinking about social work as a culture. Thinking about the knowledge base of the profession as an "intellec-tual export" is increasingly seen as both strategically and ethically necessary (Haug, 2005; Mohan, 2005; Morelli, 1998; Taylor, 1999; Witkin, 1999).

Can we assume that U.S. and Lithuanian social workers share a common professional identity? What might be the differences and similarities in core values and knowledge, given the differences in larger cultures from which these two groups of professionals have derived? Looking at these questions through a "three culture" framework may help in clarifying the issues.

Benefits of a "three-culture" approach include the recognition that social work values and norms are socially constructed, and therefore can be socially de-constructed, which can allow for more dialogue and new forms of social work to emerge as a result. It also may decrease the tendency toward profes-sional imperialism by recognizing that professional culture has grown up in response to the needs and conditions in a particular time and place, and should not be seen as a "one size fits all" approach to social problems. This may allow for greater empowerment of local leaders. Dangers of ignoring social work as a separate culture include the tendency to make unfounded assumptions that different nations do share a common definition of values and goals of social development, and that the traditions of Western social work only need to be slightly "tweaked" to fit the local context. This may not be the case, especially in nations such as Lithuania which represent a more collectivist culture with no history of the social work profession, wherein self-determination and personal choice must at some point conflict with other priorities such as allegiance to tradition, family, and society.

As a part of an international faculty, I was called upon to define the social work profession – its knowledge, skills, and values – but particularly its values. This is what led me to see more clearly the role of professional culture as another dimension of cross-cultural practice and education. This is "teaching in the intersection." Opening up this conversation about professional culture can lead to creation of new forms adapted to local conditions and values while still emphasizing tradition and continuity, establishing a strong "hybrid" professional identity. After all, hybrid plants are almost always stronger and more resilient than other varieties!

Figure 1: A three-culture model for social work education

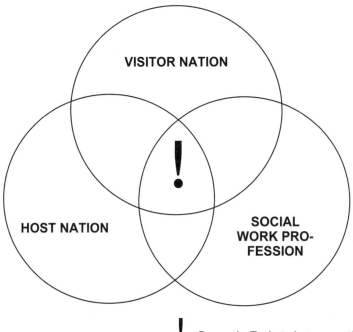

! Growth Point: Intersection

4. Relevant Dimensions of Professional Culture

4.1 Identity

Who are we? What is our purpose and function? These are difficult questions. The new definition of "international social work" was finalized in 2000 after many years of collaborative efforts, and agreement on such a document was a necessary step toward a more unified professional voice, a success at the end of a long road of conversation and compromise (IFSW, 2000).

The emphasis in this definition and supporting statement of values, theory, and practice foundations illustrates that "... the holistic focus of social work is universal, but the priorities of social work practice will vary from country to country and from time to time depending on cultural, historical, and socio-economic conditions." (IFSW, 2000).

This was particularly true in the development of the Lithuania program. The definition of professional identity and role became very important because social work as a profession did not exist during the Soviet era. Services were provided in large institutions under the auspices of the Ministries of Health, Education, and Social Welfare for pensioners, the ill, the disabled, and dependent children. The institutions took a primarily custodial approach, contrasted with the Western notion of institutions as therapeutic and remedial. Staff relations in these institutions were rigid and hierarchical, with the lowest positions have the least power and respect. The residents (patients) were on the lowest rung of the status ladder, in part due to cultural attitudes toward persons with "defects" of character, such as mentally ill persons or alcoholics. One of the biggest challenges in both classroom and field was to demonstrate how the professional role of advocate worked – and to address the implications of this role for "upsetting the apple cart" of those well-defined power hierarchies. One of the mechanisms for addressing professional identity and role issues were the weekly field seminars. There were three weekly seminars, one for first year students, one for second year, and one for field instructors. Substantive issues across the three groups included: 1) Boundary-setting: students and field instructors alike needed to communicate to the agencies the role, functions, and realistic expectations for social work interventions and outcomes; 2) Resource-finding: this centered around the need to identify, and in many instances create, resources to help with legal, accommodation (housing), and substance abuse problems; 3) Decision-making: this had to do with developing frameworks for assessment and communication with clients, and ways of evaluating and choosing among intervention options, however limited the choices might be; and, 4) Agency communication: this involved helping students and new graduates who were doing field supervision to address the attitudes of other staff toward social work clients, and to some extent toward the social workers themselves. These attitudes were punitive at worst and paternalistic at best. Seminars served as both a social support mechanism to deal with the above issues, and a way of building capacity for the future.

This social support was also offered in the classroom, as students struggled to come to grips with the severe distress of clients, and to apply some of the conceptual models that the Western educators brought with them. Students were encouraged to be selective and creative in their application of models – the attempt was made to support their development of strategies that worked for them in their context, whether or not these fit within what we might in the West consider to be professional norms and practice models. This approach seems consistent with the dialogue approach as described by Schatz, Furman and Jenkins (2003). As local cases became more available, students were encouraged to see intervention targets in clients and families – things that could be done to improve their circumstances. But students were also encouraged to see the social environment as a target for intervention – the institutions and communities within which the clients and families functioned. In other words, the "cases" were at all levels. This teaching strategy was facilitated by the fact that, in this two-year graduate program, the first year field placements focused on direct practice with individuals, families, and groups, while the second year emphasized social development (community) and program development. Students were expected, in the second year, to take what they had learned in the first year about the individual/family level needs, and turn those needs into goals for new and improved human services programs. Because of the overall lack of programs, and because of the new infusion of social development money from the West, students were successful – often spectacularly so – in the creation of new programs and even whole new agencies! They were motivated and determined and indeed tenacious in their desire to be effective on a larger scale.

However, for those first year students struggling with massive needs and massive expectations (their own and everybody else's), the seminars helped to identify realistic professional role expectations which they could be communicated to the institutions and new community agencies of which they were a part. Students in their field internship sites were essentially treated as workers – expected to "do it all," or at least to do what no one else knew how to do, or wanted to do. While this phenomenon is not unknown in the West, the problem became more acute, because the concept of "field education" was new to many, and because there was so much to do. It was difficult to fight for the educational purpose as primary, and for the institutions and agencies to see our students as students – another role challenge, in addition to the development of a professional identity. In the seminars, we emphasized the importance of collaboration in their field sites – one person could never address all the needs. Indeed, the seminars themselves were an example of collaborative work, as students problem-solved each other's cases, with the help of the seminar leaders. These students wanted to be "doers" – to respond effectively and efficiently to the needs around them. Yet they struggled with the notion that it would take time. The seminars helped to recognize the multiple challenges – establishment of professional role identity, while still offering direct services and developing programs.

4.2 Values

What do we stand for? What do we stand against? This has implications for how we use our voice, entering into debates over the role of individuals, families, communities, and governments in social welfare and social change. As we know in 2006, speaking about values from a Western perspective looks different else where in the world.

A primary issue of social work and Western cultural values related to the importance and use of social power and influence. This value principle also linked with expectations in regard to what it meant to be an "expert" on something. It was at times very difficult to present oneself with competence and authority, while recognizing the limits of outside expertise in a rapidly changing social, economic, and cultural context. In other words, we as visitors were always trying to promote our credibility in terms of the knowledge we could contribute, while at the same time remaining cautious of seeming to disregard the local expertise. This was also happening in a context where specialized knowledge was highly valued, and yet knowledge, and therefore expertise in, human services, was significantly under-developed. Another challenge was that people were not comfortable working in groups to assess problems and develop solutions. The trust level, at least initially, was not there. In the Western social work tradition, we have learned that pooling our information and working together is more likely to be successful than working alone. This belief was not shared at the outset of the Centre's development, but grew over time. Again, because the cultural value of expertise and specialized knowledge was so strong, students and community based practitioners were reluctant to speak and explore ideas, unless they felt sufficiently "expert." And, as noted above, because the human services systems were not well-understood, no one felt like an expert. There was more willingness, however, to speak about moral attitudes.

The judgmentality which was evident in the beginning in attitudes toward persons with mental illness or substance abuse problems, or those who engaged in premarital sexual behavior, is not unlike that often seen in the West, particularly in students whose life experiences and exposure to diverse social groups and conditions has been limited. Like many beginning social work students, the Lithuanian students saw personal pathology and moral defect as the explanation for "brokenness" in the clients and families. Therefore, given the rigid and judgmental attitudes of the institutions in which the students worked and did their educational internships, it was a major challenge to firmly root the social work role as advocate for human worth and dignity, along with social and economic justice for persons seen as undeserving of these things. Because the large and impersonal institutions were for a while the only surviving social service delivery system, it was necessary to work with them, using the community consultation and student placement strategies to chip away at these negative attitudes, starting with the attitudes of the students that we were teaching. In other words, if they were going to be good advocates for clients, they needed to understand the value base of such advocacy, and examine their own attitudes which might interfere with such advocacy.

We also worked with the students around the tensions between social workers as agents of social change versus agents of social control. These struggles and tensions are familiar to Western social workers, but needed to be made visible in a culture which was all about control! The notion that social workers were ethically bound to change oppressive systems would seem to be a "natural," in light of the overthrow of the oppressive Soviet system. Yet, the importance of power and control over others remained strong, even though the identity of those in control had changed. In some sense, the need for control was even stronger – without a large government bureaucracy keeping things together, other mechanisms of control (money, command of resources, prestige) became more important. Drucker (2003) challenges us to re-examine our loyalties to the poor and social development, in light of the allegiance of some to more technical-rational strategies of research and practice which responds to market-based forces and not human needs and human rights. These market-based forces are seen as tending to emphasize and reinforce privilege based on socio-economic power, not necessarily direct political power, more consistent with the populist model mentioned earlier in this chapter.

Issues of social control link with another values issue: Self-determination, respect for difference, and belief in the capacity for change. While we always tried to take a strengths-based and client-centered approach to the helping process, at that time in Lithuania there was such a dramatic lack of resources that there often were few, in any, choices for clients to make. Further, the general public was still in the process of "waking up" from the era of Soviet domination which had enervated and atrophied the decision making skills of many if not most of the population. So there were those (from the old Soviet bureaucracy) who still believed very much in the power and control motive, and there were those who were waiting for others to make decisions for them, as it had been in the Soviet era. It was in this context that we attempted to lay the groundwork for an understanding of client self-determination, conceptualizing the social worker as decision making *partner*. The notion of partnership itself, of joining together to solve problems, was unfamiliar and for some, uncomfortable. Waiting for others to decide or seizing authority seemed to be the two polarities most familiar. All social work students anywhere, while motivated to learn new ways of thinking, are still citizens of their country and culture at a particular moment in time. And this moment in time represented the confluence of social and economic forces unprecedented in the history of the country. The pressure to respond to acute needs tended to obscure the partnership principle in the urgency of the moment.

4.3 Communication

How do we exchange information about our identity and values? To what extent does the "language of the profession" (our specialized terminology and jargon) help or hinder communication? Making ourselves understandable and credible to others is a major challenge.

In my experience, communication challenges and responses were logistic, conceptual, and interactional. In regard to logistic issues, the biggest challenge was that most of the students in this graduate social work program did not speak English. So the teaching was done through a translator, present in the classroom and on field visits at all times. While some of the students could speak English, their receptive language (hearing and reading) was better than their expressive language (speaking and writing), so the translator was as much for me as for them. In other words, they could understand my English somewhat, but I could understand the Lithuanian language not at all. For the written work in the course, the students would write their papers in Lithuanian, the translator would read them to me in English, and I would make transcriptions and notes (of course in English). I would then evaluate the students' work based on these notes, and the translator would meet with me and the student for review and feedback.

Some of the strategies I found helpful in dealing with logistic challenges were to promote student presentations whenever possible. This allowed the students to address their fieldwork cases in the classroom, and I could make commentary and help them learn to apply individual/family treatment conceptual models to their own concrete situations. I also tried to promote the translation of social work materials (both didactic and case-related) into the Lithuanian language, so that students would have more direct access. This was complicated by the lack of funds to pay for written translations. I managed as best I could by using my classroom verbal translator to do occasional jobs on short informational handouts, and by using my transcriptions of student case analysis papers as an ongoing "stock" of learning materials for library reference as well as field seminar discussions.

Conceptual challenges are best illustrated by the way in which family emotional and social boundaries were defined in the social work practice courses I taught. There was no word in Lithuanian which represented the concept of "enmeshment." Through exploration between the students and the translator, they settled on a word which described the way two fluids in a beaker would join together. The resulting imagery was extremely useful, and I have used this in my "at-home" teaching of the concept. In regard to issues of family dynamics and family formation in a collectivist culture, families lived together longer than in the West, forming their own households only upon marriage, and sometimes not even then, particularly at that time when there was just not enough safe affordable housing for everyone.

The third type of communication challenge was interactional. The visiting faculty was used to a more engaged and interactive process with students (arguably, in social work education, student engagement is the norm). However, the Lithuanian students looked to the faculty member as the expert, and were reluctant to enter into discussion with the "esteemed professor," traditionally seen as the source of all knowledge. Students would be actively engaged in note-taking, but not in discussion. Paradoxically, when I insisted on discussion, they warmly and energetically complied. Further, in the fieldwork seminars and visits, an interesting communication pattern appeared to exist: when students presented cases, or when agency staff presented issues for which they were requesting consultation, it seemed that the most important information was mentioned last. This resulted in misunderstandings and "off-base" recommendations on my part until I learned to wait until the end of the presentation to ask for clarification and make my suggestions.

Another factor in cross-cultural communication could be seen as an outgrowth of the above. Eastern European people and their community and educational leaders were and are eager to receive the Western visitors, and benefit from the resources of this consultation, both in terms of expertise, and of money and materials for re-development and re-training to accelerate the pace of change and professional development (Templeman, 2004). However, along with this eagerness comes an ambivalence about the value of the Western ideas and the risks attached to accepting these ideas and implementing them in a very different cultural context (Taylor, 1999). Add to this the fact that often Western development has indeed been injurious to some nations. Americans have sometimes exported our democracy and consumerism in a way which emphasizes the superiority of these forms of social and political life. In other words, we see our ideas as the best and universally most applicable. We forget that "the good life," both personally and professionally, can be defined many ways, with some of those ways yet to be found.

5. Recommendations for Social Work Educators

These recommendations can be illustrated through use of an acronym: IDEA.

I: "Identify Yourself"

We are a product of our own professional histories, acculturation, and so-cialization processes; therefore, we need to "locate ourselves" as individuals and as educators, claiming both the common and unique aspects of our de-velopment, recognizing that these may not be universally shared. As we individually and collectively begin to understand more about how we came to believe what we believe, we can use our new understandings to become more humble and collaborative, both at home and abroad, recognizing that our experience of "the good life" is only one of many (Abram, Slosar, Walls, 2005).

D: "Discuss"

Using our basic skills of empathy, we need to (in the words of Carl Rogers) "allow ourselves to understand the other person." (Rogers, 1961). We need to acknowledge disagreements on the road to creating new professional iden-tities, and invite dialogue in the classroom–dialogue which is open to discov-ery, leaving behind outgrown and narrow understandings. We also have to be aware that change is a process, not an event, and as much as we want to move forward and solve social problems, we grope toward understanding in fits and starts. Patience and listening skills are essential.

E: "Explore Experiences"

We need to make case-based and experiential instructional methods the pri-mary foundation of our pedagogy, using lecture methods as the secondary approach, flipping the balance between these two strategies as they are now used. Particularly in global social work, case-based learning promotes the development of practice models grounded in local realities, and embodies the "reflective practitioner" identity. As with social work practice, we must have a thorough understanding of what life looks like from the client's point of view (in this instance, from the learner's point of view), before moving for-ward with interventions. When case-based instruction is utilized, students become the experts, because they are the ones with the firsthand knowledge of what's going on in the field on a day to day basis. The educator, then, becomes the expert in terms of providing frameworks for understanding the cases from theoretical, analytic, and strategic standpoints, using both lecture and discussion as teaching methods. Case based instruction promotes the capacity to think conceptually and act practically – the hallmark of a professional education.

A: "Affirm Common Goals"

Recent cross-national studies of social work students' values reflect common purposes at a values level, particularly in terms of commitments to human rights and self-determination (Abbott, 1999; Knezevic, 1999). Recognizing our commonalities and working on our differences, we can reinforce our professional values – about worth and dignity; about capacity for change; and about the power of collaboration. These values unite and move us toward action and the goal of a peaceful, just, and sustainable life for all persons.

References

Abbott, A.A. (1999). Measuring social work values: A cross-cultural challenge for global practice. *International Social Work, 42,* 455-470.

Abram, F.Y.; Slosar, J.A., Walls, R. (2005). Reverse mission: A model for international social work education and transformative intra-national practice. *International Social Work, 48,* 161-176.

Bogo, M.; Herington, W. (1988). Consultation in social work education in the international context. *International Social Work, 38,* 305-316.

Drucker, D. (2003). Whither international social work? A reflection. *International Social Work, 46,* 53-81.

Haug, E. (2005). Critical reflections on the emerging discourse of international social work. *International Social Work, 48,* 126-135.

International Federation of Social Workers. (2000). Definition of Social Work. Berne, Switzerland: Author.

Knezevic, M. (1999). Social work students and social work values. *International Social Work, 42,* 419-430.

Kulys, R.; Constable, R. (1994). The emergence of social work in Lithuania. In Constable, Mehta (eds.), Education for social work in Eastern Europe: Changing horizons (pp. 81-90). Chicago: Lyceum Press.

Lum, D. (1996). Social work practice and people of color. (3rd Ed.). Pacific Grove, CA: Brooks/Cole.

Midgley, J. (1981). Professional imperialism: Social work in the third world. London: Heinemann.

Midgley, J. (1993). Ideological roots of social development strategies. *Social Development Issues, 15,* 1-13.

Mohan, B. (2005). New internationalism: Social work's dilemmas, dreams and delusion. *International Social Work, 48,* 241-250.

Morelli, P.T. (1998). Cross-cultural considerations for social work practice: A teaching module utilizing the International Pilot Study of Schizophrenia (IPSS): Five year follow-up findings. *Journal of Baccalaureate Social Work, 4*, 75-85.

Rogers, C. (1961). On becoming a person. Boston: The Free Press.

Schatz, M., Furman, R.,, Jenkins, L.E. (2003). Space to grow: Using dialogue techniques for multinational, multicultural learning. *International Social Work, 46*, 481-494.

Taylor, Z. (1999). Values, theories and methods in social work education. *International Social Work, 42*, 309-318.

Templeman, S.B. (2004). Social work in the new Russia at the start of the millennium. *International Social Work, 47*, 95-107.

Tunney, K. (2002). Learning to teach abroad: Reflections on the role of the visiting social work educator. *International Social Work, 45*, 435-436.

Tunney, K.; Kulys, R. (2004). Social work field education as social development: A Lithuanian case study. *Social Work in Mental Health, 2*, 59-75.

Witkin, S.L. (1999). Letter from Lapland. *Social Work, 44*, 413-415.

Rashmi Gupta, Vijayan K. Pillai

U.S. Study Abroad Programs: An International Social Work Curriculum in Aging

1. Introduction

There is very little global awareness among Americans. An aspect of this is amply illustrated by the fact that a National Geographic global literacy survey found that 87 percent of students in the United States between the ages of 18 and 24 could not locate Iraq on a world map, 83 percent could not find Afghanistan, 58 percent could not find Japan, and 11 percent could not even find the United States. However, a 2002 American Council on Education poll showed that 79 percent of people in the United States agreed that students should have a study abroad experience sometime during college. Currently, only 1 percent of students from the United States study abroad each year.

On November 10, 2005, the U.S. Senate passed a resolution designating 2006 as the "Year of Study Abroad." The resolution attempted to promote and support initiatives that promote and expand study abroad programs. The resolution was introduced by Senator Richard Durbin (Democrat/Illinois), together with Senators Daniel Akaka (Democrat/Hawaii), Lamar Alexander (Republican/Tennessee), Thad Cochran (Republican/Mississippi), Norm Coleman (Republican/Minnesota), Larry Craig (Republican/Idaho), and Russ Feingold (Democrat/Wisconsin). The text of Senate Resolution 308 states that

- to ensure citizens of the United States are globally literate is the responsibility of the educational system of the United States;
- to create goodwill for the United States around the world, to work toward a peaceful global society, and to increase international trade;
- to share the values of the United States;
- to be more informed about the world and to develop the cultural awareness necessary to avoid offending individuals from other countries;
- to graduate enough students with the language skills and cultural competence necessary to meet the current demands of business, government, and educational institutions;
- provide specialized training and practical experiences not available at institutions in the United States;

- empower students to better understand themselves and others through a comparison of cultural values and ways of life;
- and to enhance the core values and skills of higher education that are enhanced by participation in study abroad programs.

2. Study Abroad Programs in Social Work

The focus of social work programs on study abroad courses is much narrower. Often the focus is on helping students reduce ethnocentrism, promote multiculturalism and developing among students an understanding of international/global components of personal and public problems (Pettys, Panos, Cox, Oosthuysen, 2005; Asamoah, et al., 1997; Garland, Escobar, 1988). The Council of Social Work Education (USA) has actively supported international social work education by promoting international exchanges and international social work field education. In addition, international practicums and study abroad courses have been extensively utilized by social work programs in the United States (Boehm, 1980; Boyle, et al., 1999; Healy, 1988; Lemieux, 2003; Wilkinson, 1998). A large proportion of the study abroad courses have European destinations.

"The Mission of the International Social Work Field Instruction project is to create international Social Work Practicum opportunities for baccalaureate and graduate students, who are enrolled in accredited social work degree programs in the United States. The Council of Social Work Education, Inc. (CSWE) is used as an institutional base from which to launch the project" (ISW, 2006).

Reichert (1998) defines a study abroad course as a brief but intensive course of study offered in a foreign country. Very few American universities offer such courses on a regular basis. When these courses are offered, the setting and content of the course would depend on a host of factors such as the area of specialization of the faculty offering the course, university ties with the foreign university and research collaborations with faculty abroad. The theoretical and methodological orientations within the course are similar to a traditional U.S. based course in the area of study. However, a study abroad course will often incorporate and provide some comparative perspectives on theories and methodologies taking into consideration the country-specific cultural, and socio-economic setting. In general, the reasons for offering study abroad courses are based on broad and general goals such as preparing citizens for a global world. However, broad goals of study abroad courses such as multiculturalism are too broad to engage a student's interest. Furthermore, these goals are seldom evaluated (Fairchild, Pillai, Noble, 2006).

Some of the current debates in the field of social work have addressed issues related to values of the profession that are related to multiculturalism and the neglect of emerging international issues such as poverty and aging. Even though promoting multiculturalism appears to be one of the often stated objectives of study abroad programs, there is an apparent lack of understanding about the implications of the concept for social work education. In a debate about the issues of multiculturalism between Van Soest (1995) and Atherton and Bolland (1997), Atherton and Bolland suggest that multiculturalism is of little relevance for social work education. In addition, they argue that the concept is hardly of any relevance to the pursuit of social justice, an important value for the social work profession.

3. Global Aging

It is well known that very many so-called national issues such as poverty are also international issues. For example, institutions such as the International Monetary Fund (IMF), USAID, and the World Bank (WB) have poured enormous resources into fighting poverty. Anymore, poverty is not an issue of local interest. Poverty anywhere is poverty every where. Similarly, a large proportion of countries have seen a significant increase in their elderly population. The older population is now increasing at a much faster rate than other age groups in industrialized countries. Worldwide, the number of people aged 65 to 84 is projected to grow nearly threefold by the year 2050 and the aged population will have outnumbered children. This explosion of aging population internationally is referred to as global aging. Global aging is bound to influence nearly every sector of public life: our economies, our politics, health care, and our infrastructures. So global aging is an issue of profound significance that demands the attention of governments, academe, business, non-profits and the public (AARP, 2003). Yet in the United States, there is very little focus on offering regular and study abroad courses in the area of aging in social work schools (Walker, Pillai, 2005). Thus, while there appears to be broad agreement on the need to offer study abroad courses for achieving goals such as multiculturalism, there are very few study abroad courses on emerging social and economic issues in a globalizing world.

4. An International Social Work Curriculum in Aging

Social work education in the United States has not adequately responded to the need to internationalize the social work curriculum. In the long run, this may result in our inability to internationalize issues as social workers while limiting our ability to learn lessons from international setting for solving local problems. In this paper we attempt to develop an outline for a study abroad course on aging taking into consideration an international social work perspective. In an era of globalization social work education programs must prepare students to live and work in a world where geographic boundaries are permeable and where information flow is rapid and widespread. The preparation of students via study abroad program is considered from the perspective of internationalizing the curriculum.

The purpose of this course is to provide students with a knowledge base on the international perspective necessary for social work practice with the aged and their families. The course presents demographic data on global aging and introduces basic concepts such as culturally competent care of elders. In this course, students will learn gerontological social work practice concepts, values, skills, and theories. Emphasis is placed on the role of the social network, social exclusion and on the availability and accessibility to formal and informal care services for the aging population. The theoretical base for social work practice is provided by Bronfenner's ecological model (Bronfenner, 1979) from an international perspective. Within this framework the course imparts a broad view of assessment and intervention techniques that are designed to resolve issues related to aging and end of life care in the field of international gerontological social work. In a contextual approach that identifies systems within which individuals act, the individual with his/her bio-psycho-spiritual characteristics is at the centre of the system geriatrics (Stanford University, 2001). The system is embedded in several layers:

- the Microsystem, including any person or environment with which the person has direct day to day contacts (e.g., family, friends);
- the Mesosystem involving the interactions of multiple Microsystems, (e.g., family members' lack of agreement with diet and prescriptions);
- the Exosystem involving the larger community, especially decision-making bodies;
- the Macrosystem, the overarching cultural belief systems which influence how individuals in each context interact with one another (e.g., social service providers' attitudes about aging, ethnic elders' view of themselves);
- the Chronosystem, the dimension of time, (e.g., the historical embeddedness of aging, social services, and ethnicity.

4.1 Objectives

Toward the end of the course students should be able to:

- assess their own attitudes, values, and feelings about older persons and show how these factors, along with feelings about their own aging, may affect their social work practice with older clients.
- be able to establish how an older person's socioeconomic status, gender, or membership in social categories of exclusion may affect social work practice.
- develop the skills necessary to assist older adults and their families with health care issues.
- use culturally sensitive therapeutic treatment models to design specific intervention approaches with older adults and their caregivers.
- identify the major components of older people's social support network and show how those relationships influence their well being.
- be informed about culture and forms of elder maltreatment.
- acquire a working knowledge of advance directives and cultural issues related to death and dying.

4.2 Major Content Areas

- Gerontology as an area within International Social Work
- Growing diversity of aging population in the world
- International social workers as care providers for elders from diverse ethnic backgrounds
- Importance of international gerontology and the need for cultural competency
- Values, value clarification, and attitudes as a context for social work practice with older persons
- The broad areas of international gerontological social work: techniques of assessment and intervention, community resources, health care services, neglect and abuse of the elderly and cultural issues related to death and dying
- The informal and formal social network relationships of older persons and their implications for social work practice
- Identifying opportunities related to community-based and institutional-based social work practice with older persons and their families, and working with caregivers and caregiving systems

Required Texts

Greene, R. (2000): Social work with the aged and their families (2nd ed). Hawthorne, NY: Aldine De Gruyter.
Anna Metteri; Teppo Kroger; Anneli Pohjola (2005): Social Work Visions From Around the Globe: Citizens, Methods, And Approaches. New York: Haworth Press.

4.3 Topics by Session

Session 1: The context and framework for international social work practice with older persons and their families

- The social and demographic characteristics of aging population and their implications for social work practice
- Demographic trend and data on elders from around the world
- Sources of data and their limitations
- Demographic characteristics available include age, gender, housing, income/poverty, marital status, living arrangements, and education
- Most recent numbers and percentages of older adults
- Past trends and future projections of changes in sizes
- Heterogeneity within elderly populations

Suggested Reading

Kosberg, J.I. (1999): Opportunities for social workers in an aging world. *Journal of Sociology and Social-Welfare. 26*, 1, 7-24.
Ram, Bali (2003): Fertility Decline and Social Change: New Trends and Challenges. *Canadian Studies in Population,* 30, 2, 297-326.
Wisensale, S.K. (2003): Global aging and intergenerational equity. *Journal of Inter-generational Relationships,* 1. 1, 29-47.

Session 2: Cultural competence, values and attitudes and the context of international social work practice with older persons

- Intercultural dynamics
- Importance of cultural factors in social service settings and in encounters between social service providers and recipients
- Understanding culture of the social service organizations
- Diversity among older adults based on culture, socio-economic and class factors
- Cultural Competence in international ethno-gerontological social work

Suggested Reading

Lavizzo-Mourey, R. J.; Mackenzie, E. (1995): Cultural competence –an essential hybrid for delivering high quality care in the 1990s and beyond. *Transactions of the American Clinical and Climatological Association.* 107, 226-237.

Tripp-Reimer, T. (1999): Culturally competent care. In Wykle, Ford (eds.): Serving Minority Elders in the 21st Century. New York: Springer.

Valle, R. (1998): Caregiving Across Cultures. Washington, DC: Taylor and Francis.

Session 3: Issues in assessment and treatment

- Conducting screening tests
- Informed Consent
- Intercultural dynamics producing possible misunderstanding
- Communication of possible negative outcomes
- Dealing with family expectations that elders should be protected from bad news
- Identifying family hierarchical patterns with implications for elder care decisions
- Learning techniques to minimize confusion and misunderstanding
- Use of cultural guides to determine acceptability of talking to older patients directly
- Asking older patients if there is a preferred spokesperson
- Asking patients if they would like to consult with, or appoint someone else as decision maker
- Asking patients to explain in their own words what they understand about the procedure

Suggested Reading

Haley, W. E.; Han, B.; Henderson, J. N. (1998): Aging and ethnicity: Issues for clinical practice. Journal of Clinical Psychology in Medical Settings, 5, 3, 393-409.

Hughes, B.A. (1993): Model for the comprehensive assessment of older people and their carers. British Journal of Social Work. 23, 4, 345-641.

Okazaki, S.; Sue, S. (1995): Cultural considerations in psychological assessment of Asian Americans. In Butcher (ed.): Clinical Personality Assessment (pp. 107-119). New York: Oxford University Press

Parker, M.; Baker, P. S.; Allman, R. (2001). MTI: A life-space approach to functional assessment of mobility in the elderly. *Journal of Gerontological Social Work,* 35, 4, 35-55.

Session 4: Community and Neighborhood Assessment in the context of international social work practice

- The social networks and family relationships of older persons
- Support from neighbourhood and community members
- Assessing overall features of the community and neighbourhood such as length of time in community, proportion of elders, children, and adults in population, intergenerational relations, status of elders
- Availability and utilization of services by elders and their family

Successful models of service
- Use of indigenous networks for education and outreach such as churches, temples, places of worship; lay leaders; promoters (non professional community based advocates); beauty salons, barber shops, other gathering places
- Use of ethnic community resources for education and outreach
- Community Centers
- Health fairs
- Community Health Representatives (CHR's)
- Parish Nurses

Suggested Reading

Damron-Rodriguez, J.; Wallace, S. P.; Kington, R. (1994): Service utilization and minority elderly: Appropriateness, accessibility and acceptability. Gerontology and Geriatrics Education, 15, 1, 45-64.

Gupta, R. (2002): Support provided by the elderly in South Asian families. Journal of Social Work Research and Evaluation: An International Publication, 3, 1, 51-63.

Hyduk, C. A. (1996): The dynamic relationship between social support and health in older adults: assessment implications. Journal of Gerontological Social Work, 27, 1/2, 149-65.

Mancini, J. A; Quinn, W; Gavigan, M. A. (1980): Social network interaction among older adults: implications for life satisfaction. Human Relations, 33, 8, 543-549.

Session 5 and 6: Health care issues

Techniques to minimize misunderstanding
- Discuss patient's and provider's explanatory models for condition being treated
- Investigate meaning of condition in the culture (e.g., is it hidden? is there a word in the language for the condition?)
- Assess literacy level, then give culturally appropriate written information in appropriate reading level
- Assess different attitudes to taking prescribed amount

Medication issues
* Culturally based differences in attitudes towards herbal and Western medication
* Cultural values relating to particular medications (e.g., antihypertensive pharmaceuticals that may contribute to sexual dysfunction)
* Physiological effects of the medications
* Effect of combining pharmaceuticals with culturally based herbal medications

Social and economic issues
* Financial ability to buy medication
* In some ethnic groups it is common to "share" medications among family and friends

Surgery: Intercultural Concerns
* Cultural beliefs in sanctity of body and adaptation of new invasive medical technologies
* Coordinating Biomedical and traditional therapies
* Include all health care providers valued and used by patient and family in the therapeutic team, including healers from non biomedical traditions
* How to honor patient's needs for healing practices or ceremonies
* Meeting the need to recognize, discuss, accept, and respect differences in goals between biomedical and traditional ethnic providers

Issues in dementia and caregiving
* Issues of caste/ethnicity/race of paid caregivers
* Culturally determined behaviors of bathing, eating, and toileting
* Cultural gender taboos concerning body touching/viewing by family
* Cultural "normalizing" of dementia behaviors
* Designing culturally sensitive cognitive testing

Suggested Reading

Gupta, R.; Pillai, V. (2002): Cultural influences on perceptions of caregiver burden among Asian Indians and Pakistanis. *The Southwest Journal on Aging*, 17, 1/2, 65-74.
Kleinman, A.; Eisenberg, L.; Good, B. (1978): Culture, illness, and care. *Annals of Internal Medicine,* 88, 251-258.
Pachter, L. M. (1994): Culture and clinical care: folk illness beliefs and behaviors and their implications for health care delivery. *Journal of the American Medical Association,* 271, 690-694.
Uba, L. (1992): Cultural barriers to health care for Southeast Asian refugees. *Public Health Reports*, 187, 544-548.

Sessions 7: Abuse and neglect

- Definition of abuse and neglect – cultural perspective
- Overt and covert forms of abuse
- Forms of abuse: Financial, emotional, verbal, physical, sexual
- Neglect: Physical, psychological, and medical
- Culturally sensitive intervention techniques for neglect and abuse
- Prevention of neglect and abuse- outreach and educational strategies

Suggested Reading

Grundy, E. (2006): Ageing and Vulnerable Elderly People: European Perspectives. *Ageing & Society,* 26, 1, 105-134.
Prakash, I. J. 2001. Elder abuse: global response and Indian initiatives. *Indian Journal of Social Work*, 62, 3, 446-463.
Schroder-Butterfill, E.; Marianti, R. (2006): A Framework for Understanding Old-Age Vulnerabilities. *Ageing & Society*, 26, 1, 9-35

Session 8: Advance Directives and death and dying

Intercultural dynamics leading to misunderstanding
- Lack of acceptability of discussion of death or disability in the culture
- Cultural, social, economic, educational, and linguistic differences between provider and patient/family
- Cultural rituals and traditions at the time of death
- Biomedical model of autonomy in decision making that recognizes cultural expectations that others (e.g., family, son, clan leader) would make health care decisions for elder
- Is patient capable of identifying person(s) responsible for medical and financial decisions?
- Does the family accept the identified decision maker?

Techniques to minimize confusion and misunderstanding
- Self-assess provider's own values and culture about death
- Use cultural guides for culturally appropriate interaction
- Ask patients to describe their customs, concerns, and beliefs about death, if appropriate
- Helping older persons and their families cope with death and dying
- End of life preferences (when appropriate)
- Preparation for death including availability of advance directives
- Preference for hospital or home end of life care
- Death rituals for care of the body and mourning behaviors during and after death
- Attitudes about organ donation and autopsy

Suggested Reading

Fox, R. C. (1988): The Social Meaning of Death. *Social Casework*, 69, 9, 575-831.

Kwak, J.; Haley, W. E. (2005): Current Research Findings on End-of-Life Decision Making among Racially or Ethnically Diverse Groups. *The Gerontologist*, 45, 5, 634-641.

Miccinesi, G.; Fischer, S.; Paci, E.; Onwuteaka-Philipsen, B. D.; Cartwright, C.; van der Heide, A.; Nilstun, T.; Norup, M.; Mortier, F. (2005): Physicians' Attitudes towards End-of-Life Decisions: A Comparison between Seven Countries. *Social Science & Medicine*, 60, 9, 1961-1974.

Yick, A.; Gupta, R. (2002): Chinese Cultural Dimensions of Death, Dying, and Bereavement: Focus Group Findings. *Journal of Cultural Diversity*, 9, 2, 32-42.

2.4 Field Experience

The objective is to provide students with opportunities for experiential learning in a foreign setting with respect to international gerontological social work.

- Hospitals
- Out patient clinics
- Adult day cares
- Long term care: Assisted living, Nursing homes
- Community based care

2.5 Expectations

Class sessions will consist of lectures, video presentations, guest speakers, local community leaders, international social workers and class discussion. Students are expected to complete all assigned readings prior to each class session and to come to class prepared to participate in the discussion of session topics. The following formula will be used to determine student grades:

Activity or Task	Maximum Points
Aging agency visit	200 pts.
Practice issues paper	350 pts.
Final examination	350 pts.
Class participation	100 pts.
Total	1000 pts

5. Conclusion

In this paper we have used Bronfenners ecological model (Bronfenner, 1979) to design an international aging social work syllabus for study abroad students. The design of the syllabus attempts to place broad issues with respect to aging in the international social context. To this end we make use of both didactic and experiential learning through agency visits and contacts. Study abroad courses in schools of social work have often provided opportunities for field agency visits in foreign settings in the substantive area of the course offering. However, one limitation has been that the value of experiential learning is limited to a specific country and therefore viewed as being not generalizable to other settings that are similar. In this piece, we have attempted to develop a curriculum that is not inimical to the issues of globalization and have attempted to widen the scope of the discussion of emerging aging issues using an international social work perspective. This attempt to relate and synthesize specific topics such as aging to the international social work perspective enhances student's understanding of the subject matter both theoretically and methodologically. The model syllabus we have provided may be too generic in scope and may have to be updated with more class room and experiential material from specific international settings.

References

AARP (2003): A Paradigm Shift: From the Challenges to the Opportunities of Aging Populations, http://www.aarp.org/research/international/speeches/a2003-06-04-novelli0603.html, retrieved September 21, 2006.

Asamoah, Y.; Healy. L.; Mayadas, N. (1997): Ending the international-domestic dichotomy: New approaches to a global curriculum for the millennium. *Journal of social work education*, 33, 2, 389-401.

Atherton, C.; Boland, K. (1997): The Multiculturalism debate and social work education: A Response to Dorothy Van Soest. *Journal of Social Work Education*, 33, 1, 143-151.

Boehm, W. W. (1980): Teaching and Learning International Social Welfare. *International Social Work*, 23, 17-24.

Boyle, D. P.; Nackerud, L.; Kilpatrick, A. (1999): The Road Less Traveled: Cross-cultural, International Experiential Learning. *International Social Work*, 42, 2, 201-214.

Bronfenner, U. (1979): The Ecology of Human Development: Experiments by Nature and Design. MA: Harvard University Press.

Fairchild, S.; Pillai, V.; Noble, C. (2006): The Impact of Social Work Study Abroad Programme in Australia on Multicultural Learning; *International Social Work*, 49, 3, 391-401.

Garland, D. R.; Escobar, D. (1988): Education for Cross cultural work Practice. *Journal of Social Work Education,* 24, 3, 229-41.

Healy, L. M. (1988): Curriculum Building in International Social Work: Toward Preparing Professionals for the Global Age. *Journal of Social Work Education,* 24, 221-228.

ISW = International Social Work (2006): International Social Work Field Instructions. http://www.isw.org/NewDefault.htm, retrieved September 5, 2006.

Lemieux, C. (2003): If Today is Tuesday. Educational Methods for Cross-national Experiential Learning. *Journal of the College of Social Work of University of South Carolina,* 27, 1, 88-94.

Pettys, G.; Panos, P.; Cox, S.; Oosthuysen, K. (2005): Four models of international field education placement. *International social work,* 48, 3, 277-288.

Reichert, E. (1998): The Role of a Study Abroad Course in Undergraduate Social Work Education, *Journal of Baccalaureate Social Work,* 4, 1, 62-71.

Stanford University (2001): Curriculum in Ethnogeriatrics. Core Curriculum and Ethnic Specific Modules. http://www.stanford.edu/group/ethnoger/index.html, retrieved September 23, 2006.

Van Soest, D. (1995): Multiculturalism and Social Work Education: The Non-debate about Competing Perspectives. *Journal of Social Work Education,* 31, 1, 55-67.

Walker, J.; Pillai, V. (2005): Assessing Emphasis on International Aging in Social Work Curricula in the United States. *Educational Gerontology,* 31, 1-8.

Wilkinson, S. (1998): Study Abroad from the Participants' Perspective: A Challenge to Common Beliefs. *Foreign Language Annals,* 31, 23-39.

About the Editors

Stefan Borrmann, Ph.D., Dipl.-Paed, is currently working as assistant to the director at the German Youth Institute, which is undertaking research in the field of children, youth and families and is the largest social science research institute in Germany. He also teaches social work at the Management Center Innsbruck in Austria and is chair of the *Society for International Cooperation in Social Work (SICSW)*. During winter 2004/2005 he was an affiliated visiting scholar in the School of Social Welfare at the University of California at Berkeley, where he conducted a survey about ethical dilemmas in social work. In addition to several articles in national and international journals, he published two monographs about social work with violent youth groups and how one can use research findings to ground social work practice. One of them has been published in a 2nd edition. He was also co-editor of a book about academia and power and another one about social work research in Germany. His main research interests are theories of social work, social work ethics and professional youth work.

Michael Klassen, Ph.D., MSW, is currently professor and director of studies of the Department of Social Work at the Management Center Innsbruck, International University of Applied Sciences in Austria, where he teaches social work theory, quality assurance in social work and scientific research. He is a member of the board of directors of the *Society for International Cooperation in Social Work (SICSW)*. He received a BSW in Germany, and a MSW in the USA. He obtained his Ph.D. from the Technical University of Berlin, Germany. Michael Klassen worked as a social work practitioner in the fields of youth crime prevention, street social work and fundraising in Russia, Germany and the USA. In addition to several articles in national and international journals, he published two monographs on social work and system theories and how those can be applied to social work practice. His main research interests are system theories of social work, quality assurance in social work and macro-social work analysis.

Christian Spatscheck, Ph.D., Dipl.-Paed, Dipl.Soz.Arb. (FH), is currently a Visiting Professor (Vertretungsprofessor) for Didactics and Methods of Social Pedagogy at the Department of Social Science and Cultural Studies at

Düsseldorf University of Applied Sciences. He also teaches social work at Alice-Salomon University of Applied Sciences in Berlin and the Management Center Innsbruck in Austria, and he is a member of the board of directors of the *Society for International Cooperation in Social Work (SICSW)*. He published a monograph about social work and youth cultures and is the co-editor of another book on this topic. In addition, he has published several articles about social work, youth and community work and media education. He has nine years of practical experience in different fields of social work and youth work in Germany und the UK, and is a member of various national and international organizations for social work and media education. His main research interests are methods and theories of social work and social pedagogy, media education, youth and community work and international social work.

About the Contributors

Yasmin Dean, MSW, RSW, is currently on faculty in the department of Social Work & Disability Studies at Mount Royal College in Calgary, Canada. Yasmin predominately teaches local and international community development for Mount Royal. She is also involved in helping to promote the development of international practicum opportunities for social work students. Yasmin has worked in social work for over 15 years as a youth probation officer, community development worker, issue strategist and postsecondary lecturer. Yasmin has a passion for international work and has worked in Canada, the United Arab Emirates and South Korea. Yasmin's wide range of interests include: disaster response, cross-cultural work and strategic planning. Yasmin also volunteers for the Canadian Red Cross as an emergency (disaster) worker. Yasmin is a Doctoral Candidate at the University of Calgary. Yasmin's dissertation focuses on the experiences of female academics teaching social work in the Global South. Yasmin's interests in the international mobility of social work academics are drawn from her experiences as an expatriate in South Korea and the United Arab Emirates.

Susan Donner, Ph.D., is Associate Dean and Professor at the Smith College School for Social Work in Northampton, USA. She writes in the areas of social identity, anti-racism work, and current Psychodynamic Theories. She is also a clinician with a small clinical practice. Susan is presently working with a colleague on editing the fifth edition of Annette Garrett's classic book on interviewing. Both she and her colleague Joshua Miller work at a school for social work which has made an explicit commitment to becoming an anti-racism organization, which is part of their School's mission statement. Each of them, along with their colleagues, actively works towards this goal.

Catherine N. Dulmus, Ph.D., is Associate Professor and Director of the Buffalo Center for Social Research in the School of Social Work at the University at Buffalo, USA. She received her baccalaureate degree in Social Work from Buffalo State College in 1989, the master's degree in Social Work from the University at Buffalo in 1991 and a doctoral degree in Social Welfare from the University at Buffalo in 1999. Dr. Dulmus' research focuses on child mental health, prevention, and violence. She has authored or coauthored several journal articles and books, and has presented her research nationally and internationally. Dr. Dulmus is co-editor of "The Journal of

Evidence-Based Social Work: Advances in Practice, Programming, Research, and Policy", co-editor of "Best Practices in Mental Health: An International Journal", associate editor of "Stress, Trauma, and Crisis: An International Journal", and sits on the editorial boards of the "Journal of Human Behavior in the Social Environment, Victims and Offenders", "Journal of Evidence-Based Policies and Practices", "Journal of Health and Social Policy" and "The Clinical Supervisor". Prior to obtaining the Ph.D. her social work practice background encompassed almost a decade of experience in the fields of mental health and school social work.

Rashmi Gupta, Ph.D., is an Assistant Professor of Social Work at San Francisco State University in San Francisco, USA. She has extensive clinical experience working with nursing home residents, stroke victims and their families in a clinical setting. Her practice and research work have been on South Asian immigrants and Chinese immigrants and refugees in the U.S. Her research focuses on the effects of caregiver burden, health promotion among Asian Indians in the United States. Currently she is analyzing cross-national data on Indian caregivers of the elderly living in India and Indian caregivers in the United States. Her latest work addresses the cultural issues of death, dying and bereavement among Chinese American population in the New York City area. This work has led to producing revised and validated versions of several instruments for measuring care giver burden. Dr. Gupta has presented in over seventy national and international conferences. She teaches Research, Human behavior, Social work practice with the aging population, Group methods and advanced social casework. Her most recent project is called, "Culture and love: experiences of older adults in America" which would be on the experiences of romantic love among the older adults.

Siobhan Laird, Ph.D, worked in cross-community politics in Northern Ireland for ten years. She qualified as a social worker in 1994 with a background in mental health and child protection. She has worked in the voluntary sector in the areas of welfare rights and residential care for young people. As a qualified practitioner her work has included delivering community care services in Belfast. She moved to Ghana in 1997 where she lived for four years and was appointed as Coordinator of Social Work at the University of Ghana. Her previous research has explored African practice models and interventions with street children in Ghana. She has published on international social policy and social work. Presently she lectures on law and social work at the University of Sheffield in the United Kingdom. Her current research focuses on cultural competence in social work practice.

Joshua Miller, Ph.D., is Professor and Chair of the Social Policy Sequence, Smith College School for Social Work in Northampton, USA. He writes, teaches and practices in the areas of anti-racism and disaster mental health and has published numerous chapters and articles on those topics. Recent publications have described the social ecology of natural disasters based on his work responding to Hurricane Katrina with the American Red Cross as well as an article about meeting the psychosocial needs of Tsunami survivors, after volunteering in Sri Lanka for two months. His most recent book was "School violence and children" in crisis published by Love Publishing and his next book (co-authored with Ann Marie Garran) "Racism in the United States: Implications for the helping professions", will be published by Thompson/Wadsworth in February, 2007. Dr. Miller is currently studying culturally responsive approaches to global psychosocial work in response to disasters and plans to write a book about this.

Otrude N. Moyo, Ph.D., teaches at the University of Southern Maine in Portland, USA. Her teaching and scholarship addresses comparative social welfare policy connecting themes on families, their work, livelihoods and well being, inequality and socio-economic concerns, extending to transnational issues of African immigrants and refugees within the realm of community and international social work. Otrude completed her doctoral degree in Social Policy from Brandeis University at The Heller Graduate School for Social Policy and Management with an interdisciplinary concentration addressing work, inequality and social change. Her forthcoming book is titled: "Trampled No More: Voices from Bulawayo's Townships about Families, Life, Survival and Social Change in Zimbabwe". Otrude is currently working on an ethnographic study comparing African immigrants and refugee experiences in the host countries of the USA, UK and the Netherlands.

Manoj Pardasani, Ph.D., received a B.A. in History/Sociology from the University of Bombay, India. He received his Master of Social Work and PhD degrees from the Wurzweiler School of Social Work, Yeshiva University (New York). Dr. Pardasani has worked as a social worker and an administrator in a number of practice settings including aging, developmental disabilities, HIV/AIDS, addictions, and homelessness. His doctoral dissertation entitled "Senior Centers: Patterns of Programs and Services", explored programming issues in senior centers in New York State. This study received the 2004 Outstanding Research Award from the National Council on Aging (NCOA). Dr. Pardasani joined Indiana University Northwest, Gary, USA, in the fall of 2004. He teaches in the Mental Health/Addictions, as well as the Leadership concentrations. His current research interests are: Aging, Community-based Services for the elderly, HIV/AIDS, Homelessness, Community Organization and Practice in Under-developed Communities, and Cultural Competence in Social Work. Dr. Pardasani has published in a number of peer-reviewed journals on topics such as reconstruction in the aftermath of disasters, senior centers, community-based needs of the elderly, housing models for the chronically homeless, community practice in rural India, and HIV/AIDS prevention in India. He is affiliated with a number of community-based organizations and social service agencies in Northwest Indiana, and provides technical assistance and strategic guidance. Currently, Dr. Pardasani is conducting a Needs Assessment survey of individuals aged 60 and over living in the 7 counties of Northwest Indiana. He has recently completed a region-wide survey to identify the housing needs of chronically homeless individuals with HIV/AIDS. In 2005, he was awarded an NIA (National Institute of Aging) fellowship to develop research proposals in the area of aging. He serves on the Board of the National Institute of Senior Centers, Grants, Inc., Center for Regional Excellence and the Indiana Chapter of the National Association of Social Workers (NASW). In 2006, Dr. Pardasani was chosen as the Social Worker of the year by the Indiana Chapter of NASW.

Vijayan K. Pillai, Ph.D., Professor at the University of Texas at Arlington, USA, is a demographer with research interests in adolescent fertility, women's health and welfare issues, HIV/AIDS in Africa, women's reproductive health in developing countries, and gender issues. He obtained his PhD in Sociology from the University of Iowa, Iowa City, MSW from Indore School of Social Work, Indore, and Post Graduate Diploma in Urban Planning from the School of Planning, Ahmedabad, India. His research work has focused on the determinants of adolescent fertility in Zambia, welfare and teenage moms in the United States, and the relationship between women's rights and reproductive health at a cross national level in developing countries. He is currently engaged in investigating the impact of stigma on psychosocial health of children living with parents with HIV in Botswana. He has published several research articles. His latest book (with Thomas Crow) is "Designing Teenage Pregnancy Prevention Programs" published by Edward Mellen Press. His last book was with Professor Paul W. Achola and was titled "Challenges of Primary Education in Developing Countries: Insights from Kenya" published by Ashgate Publishers.

Michael Preston-Shoot. Ph.D., is Professor of Social Work and Dean of the Faculty of Health and Social Sciences at the University of Bedfordshire, England. He is Chair of the Joint University Council Social Work Education, which represents the perspectives of social work education in higher education institutions. He was Editor of Social Work Education: The International Journal between 1993 and 2006 and is Managing Editor of the European Journal of Social Work. He was awarded a National Teaching Fellowship by the Higher Education Academy in 2005. His research and writing has concentrated on the interface between law and social work practice, on which in

2005 he co-authored a systematic review on teaching, learning and assessment of law in social work education for the Social Care Institute for Excellence. He has also undertaken research and published in the areas of social work education, group work, and on the needs and service outcomes for young people in public care and older people requiring care in the community.

Karen M. Sowers, Ph.D., was appointed Professor and Dean of the College of Social Work at the University of Tennessee, Knoxville, USA, in August 1997. She served as Director of the School of Social Work at Florida International University from June 1994 to August 1997 and as the Undergraduate Program Director of the School of Social Work at Florida International University from 1986 to 1994. She received her baccalaureate degree in Sociology from the University of Central Florida in 1974, the Master's Degree in Social Work from Florida State University in 1977 and the Ph.D. in Social Work from Florida State University in 1986. Dr. Sowers serves on several local, national and international boards including the Council on Social Work Education Commission on Curricular Innovation and Excellence, the International Planning Committee for the International Consortium for Social Development, the American Board of Mental Health Examiners, and the International Task Force on Social Work Education of the National Association of Deans of Social Work. Dr. Sowers is nationally known for her research and scholarship in the areas of international practice, juvenile justice, child welfare, cultural diversity and culturally effective intervention strategies for social work practice, evidence-based social work practice and social work education. Her current research and community interests include evidence-based practice, mental health practice, international social work practice and juvenile justice practice. She has authored or co-authored numerous books, book chapters and refereed journal articles. She has served as a founding editorial board member of the "Journal of Research on Social Work Practice", founding co-editor of "Best Practices in Mental Health: An International Journal" and is currently serving on the editorial boards of the "Journal of Evidence-based Social Work: Advances in Practice, Programs, Research and Policy" and "Journal of Stress, Trauma and Crisis: An International Journal".

Kathleen Tunney, Ph.D, is Associate Professor in the Department of Social Work at Southern Illinois University Edwardsville, USA. She teaches in the areas of human behavior theory and counseling skills development at both graduate and undergraduate levels, as well as advanced mental health practice at the graduate level. Dr. Tunney's research and scholarship focuses on outcomes of counseling skills training; relationships between social work students' personal and professional values; and conceptual frameworks for international social work education. Service contributions include leadership in social work curriculum development as well as faculty governance and curriculum development university-wide, with a special emphasis on the liberal arts foundation. Her work internationally has focused on program development and the application of direct practice skills to community and social development through field education.

Index

Social Work & Politics

Sabine Hering
Berteke Waaldijk
Guardians of the Poor—Custodians of the Public
Hüter der Armen—Beschützer der Öffentlichkeit
Welfare history in Eastern Europe—Eine Wohlfahrtsgeschichte Osteuropas
2006. 338 pp. Pb. ISBN 978-3-938094-58-7
The bi-lingual book describes the results of case studies about the history of social work in Eastern Europe between 1900 and 1960 in eight countries: Bulgaria, Croatia, Hungary, Latvia, Poland, Romania, Russia, and Slovenia.

Target groups:

Teachers and students of social work/social politics, Researchers in social history, general interest in EU social policy

The authors:

Prof. Dr. Sabine Hering, University of Siegen, Germany

Prof. Dr. Berteke Waaldijk, University of Utrecht, The Netherlands

Linda Shepherd (ed.)
Political Psychology
The World of Political Science—The development of the discipline Book Series edited by John Trent & Michael Stein
2006. 168 pp. Pb. ISBN 978-3-86649-027-7
The book provides detailed information about the development of the field of political psychology. It describes the evolution of concepts and theories within political psychology, international influences in the field, current concepts and methodology, and trends that augur for the future of the enterprise.

www.budrich-verlag.de • www.barbara-budrich.net

Social Work in Europe

Walter Lorenz

Perspectives on European Social Work

From the Birth of the Nation State to the impact of Globalisation

2006. 200 pp. Pb.

16.90 € (D), 17.40 € (A), US$19.90, GBP 14.95

ISBN 978-3-86649-008-6

The book offers explanations and clarifications for the bewildering variety of titles and job profiles in the social professions in Europe. It presents them both as a product of specific national welfare arrangements and as a sign of a special kind of professional autonomy that so far helped to correct national welfare trends. Now this autonomy is once more called for in the light of the complete re-structuring of all European welfare states and a European model of social work could deliver impulses for real alternatives to growing exclusion and inequality.

The author:

Prof. Dr. Walter Lorenz, Free University Bozen, Italy.

Further books and journals at www.barbara-budrich.net
Order current catalogues at info@barbara-budrich.net

Verlag Barbara Budrich

Barbara Budrich Publishers

Head-office: Stauffenbergstr. 7 • D-51379 Leverkusen Opladen • Germany
Tel +49 (0)2171.344.594 • Fax +49 (0)2171.344.693 • info@budrich-verlag.de
US-office: 28347 Ridgebrook • Farmington Hills, MI 48334 • USA • info@barbara-budrich.net
North American distribution: **International Specialized Book Services**
920 NE 58th Ave., suite 300 • Portland, OR 97213-3786 • USA
phone toll-free within North America 1-800-944-6190, fax 1-503-280-8832 •orders@isbs.com
Great Britain: Central Books • 99 Wallis Rd • London E9 5LN • UK • ph +44 (0)20.8936.4854 •
Fax +44 (0)20.8533.5821 • orders@centralbooks.com

www.budrich-verlag.de • www.barbara-budrich.net

Welfare History & Eastern Europe

Kurt Schilde
Dagmar Schulte (eds.)
Need and Care
Glimpses into the Beginnings of Eastern Europe's Professional Welfare
2005. 296 pp. Pb 33.00 € (D), 34.00 € (A), 57.30 SFr, US$34.90, GBP 19.95
ISBN 978-3-938094-49-5

The book gives a collection of case studies by national researchers from the project "History of Social Work in Eastern Europe 1900–1960 (SWEEP)". This collection is directed at teaching Social Work and History of Social Work in an international context since it focuses on Latvia, Russia, Poland, Hungary, Croatia, Slovenia, Romania and Bulgaria.

Gerd Meyer (ed.)
Formal Institutions and Informal Politics in Central and Eastern Europe
Hungary, Poland, Russia and Ukraine
2006. 329 pp. Hc. 59.00 € (D), 60.70 € (A), 100,00 SFr, US$69.00, GBP 39.95. ISBN 978-3-86649-060-4

Order current catalogues at info@barbara-budrich.net

Verlag Barbara Budrich
Barbara Budrich Publishers

Head-office: Stauffenbergstr. 7 • D-51379 Leverkusen Opladen • Germany
Tel +49 (0)2171.344.594 • Fax +49 (0)2171.344.693 • info@budrich-verlag.de
US-office: 28347 Ridgebrook • Farmington Hills, MI 48334 • USA • info@barbara-budrich.net
North American distribution: **International Specialized Book Services**
920 NE 58th Ave., suite 300 • Portland, OR 97213-3786 • USA
phone toll-free within North America 1-800-944-6190, fax 1-503-280-8832 •orders@isbs.com
Great Britain: Central Books • 99 Wallis Rd • London E9 5LN • UK • ph +44 (0)20.8936.4854 •
Fax +44 (0)20.8533.5821 • orders@centralbooks.com

www.budrich-verlag.de • www.barbara-budrich.net